1937

Gift of

Longman's Grie

This book may be kept

FOURTEEN DAYS

DRAMATIC SCENES
FROM ATHENS TO BROADWAY

DRAMATIC SCENES

FROM

ATHENS TO BROADWAY

BY

JAMES B. LOWTHER

ASSISTANT PROFESSOR OF SPEECH
WEST VIRGINIA UNIVERSITY

LONGMANS, GREEN AND CO.

114 FIFTH AVENUE · NEW YORK

1937

LOWTHER
DRAMATIC SCENES FROM ATHENS TO
BROADWAY

COPYRIGHT · 1937
BY LONGMANS, GREEN AND CO.

FIRST EDITION

PRINTED IN THE UNITED STATES OF AMERICA

To
CHARLES RANN KENNEDY
WHOSE LIFE IS AN INSPIRATION
TO ALL THOSE WHO LOVE THE BEST
IN DRAMA

PREFACE

DURING the years that I have been connected with college dramatics, the outstanding problems that my students and I have encountered have been : first, the difficulty of finding available material ; and second, the inability of many beginning students to use proper discrimination in selecting scenes. To overcome both these difficulties, this volume has been prepared. It is the outgrowth of a survey of the type of scenes needed and preferred by dramatic teachers in colleges and universities throughout the country.

In using the general classification of character types I do not champion type casting. A larger and more representative field of material can be included by listing the characters portrayed in the selections under the particular captions used in this volume. This method in no way restricts either teacher or student in his interpretation of the various characters.

The index of world drama is used in the hope that it will encourage the student to acquaint himself with the best that has been written in dramatic literature. Shakespeare has been classified separately because of the universal use of his selections in the teaching of acting.

In order to allow the student greater freedom in developing his own character delineation, I have written as little introductory material as possible.

I have included dramatic situations which contain character studies from individual pantomime to group acting in an attempt to insert scenes that will answer the need of every student as these needs have been expressed to me.

The cutting of any scene has been indicated by the usual series of dots. Indulgence is asked where a play has been ruthlessly "cut." Limitations had to be observed, and it is hoped that the extensive bibliography will assist the teacher and student in locating desired selections.

Through the courtesy of the authors and their publishers I have been able to secure a wide variety of plays. This volume should be suitable for schools, colleges, universities, dramatic schools, and Little Theatres. Due to its broad scope it should also be of interest to that great number of people who, though not directly connected with the theatre, are nevertheless interested in the best that has been written in dramatic literature.

I owe a debt of gratitude to my colleagues on the West Virginia University campus, and to B. Q. Morgan of Stanford University, who so generously gave of their time and talents to translate for me the selections listed below:

To Robert Ashburn for his translation of *A Sunny Morning* by Quintero Brothers;

To A. L. Darby and Josephine Molli for their translation of *Right You Are!* (*If You Think You Are*) by Pirandello;

To John Eiesland for his translations of *Beyond Human Power* by Björnson, and *Jeppe of the Hill* by Holberg;

To Warren F. Manning for his translation of *The Bluebird* by Maeterlinck;

To Charles Mitrani for his translation of *Pelléas and Mélisande* by Maeterlinck;

To Claude C. Spiker for his translation of *Hernani* by Victor Hugo;

To B. Q. Morgan for his translation of *Magda* by Sudermann.

I wish to express my gratitude to the authors and publishers for the copyright material used in this book. I am indebted to Stephen F. Crocker, Professor of English at West Virginia University, for his helpful suggestions in selecting excerpts from World drama; to Hubert C. Howard, Professor of English at West Virginia University for invaluable assistance in preparing the introductions, and to Professor Wilbur Jones Kay and Marja Steadman Fear for reading the manuscript. I am grateful to Opal Ada Keeny for inspiration and critical help; and to Elsie G. Cresswell for her constant criticism of this volume.

CONTENTS

ANCIENT GREEK

ANCIENT ROMAN

GERMAN

FRENCH

SPANISH

SCANDINAVIAN

IRISH

ENGLISH

ENGLISH

CONTENTS

AMERICAN

SHAKESPEARE

GREEK SELECTIONS

ANTIGONE *

By SOPHOCLES

Translated by Sir Richard C. Jebb

Antigone performs funeral rites over the body of her brother, Polynices, against the command of her uncle, Creon. So enraged is the king at this disobedience, that he imprisons her in a rocky vault where she is to die. The old blind prophet, Tiresias, comes to counsel the king, warning him that his deeds will be punished by disaster in his own household.

[Enter Teiresias, led by a boy, on the spectator's right]

Teiresias	Princes of Thebes, we have come with linked steps, both served by the eyes of one; for thus, by a guide's help, the blind must walk.
Creon	And what, aged Teiresias, are thy tidings?
Teiresias	I will tell thee; and do thou hearken to the seer.
Creon	Indeed, it has not been my wont to slight thy counsel.
Teiresias	Therefore didst thou steer our city's course aright.
Creon	I have felt, and can attest, thy benefits.
Teiresias	Mark that now, once more, thou standest on fate's fine edge.
Creon	What means this? How I shudder at thy message!
Teiresias	Thou wilt learn, when thou hearest the warnings of mine art. As I took my place on mine old seat of augury, where all birds have been wont to gather within my ken, I heard a strange voice among them; they were screaming with dire, feverish rage, that drowned their language in a jargon; and I knew that they were rending each other with their talons, murderously; the whirr of wings told no doubtful tale. Forthwith, in fear, I essayed burnt-sacrifice on a duly kindled altar: but from my offerings the Fire-

* From Treasury of the Theatre, by Burns Mantle and John Gassner. By permission of the Macmillan Company, publishers.

god showed no flame ; a dank moisture, oozing from the thigh-flesh, trickled forth upon the embers, and smoked, and sputtered ; the gall was scattered to the air ; and the streaming thighs lay bared of the fat that had been wrapped around them.

Such was the failure of the rites by which I vainly asked a sign, as from this boy I learned ; for he is my guide, as I am guide to others. And 'tis thy counsel that hath brought this sickness on our State. For the altars of our city and of our hearths have been tainted, one and all, by birds and dogs, with carrion from the hapless corpse, the son of Oedipus ; and therefore the gods no more accept prayer and sacrifice at our hands, or the flame of meat-offering ; nor doth any bird give a clear sign by its shrill cry, for they have tasted the fatness of a slain man's blood.

Think, then, on these things, my son. All men are liable to err ; but when an error hath been made, that man is no longer witless or unblest who heals the ill into which he hath fallen, and remains not stubborn.

Self-will, we know, incurs the charge of folly. Nay, allow the claim of the dead ; stab not the fallen ; what prowess is it to slay the slain anew ? I have sought thy good, and for thy good I speak : and never is it sweeter to learn from a good counselor than when he counsels for thine own gain.

HIPPOLYTUS *

By EURIPIDES

Translated by Gilbert Murray

Fearful for the life of *Queen Phaedra,* the faithful old nurse tries to discern the cause of her strange illness.

Nurse   Have I not tried all ways, and all in vain?
         Yet will I cease not now, and thou shalt tell
         If in her grief I serve my mistress well!

* Hippolytus, translated by Gilbert Murray, from *Euripides,* reprinted by permission of George Allen and Unwin, Ltd.

[*She goes across to where Phaedra lies ; and presently,
   while speaking, kneels by her*]
Dear daughter mine, all that before was said
Let both of us forget ; and thou instead
Be kindlier, and unlock that prisoned brow.
And I, who followed then the wrong road, now
Will leave it and be wiser.   If thou fear
Some secret sickness, there be women here
To give thee comfort.   [*Phaedra shakes her head*]
               No ; not secret ?   Then
Is it a sickness meet for aid of men ?
Speak, that a leech may tend thee.
               Silent still ?
Nay, Child, what profits silence ?   If 'tis ill
This that I counsel, make me see the wrong :
If well, then yield to me.
               Nay, Child, I long
For one kind word, one look !
   [*Phaedra lies motionless.   The Nurse rises*]
               Oh, woe is me !
Women, we labour here all fruitlessly.
All as far off as ever from her heart !
She ever scorned me, and now hears no part
Of all my prayers !   [*Turning to Phaedra again*]
                  Nay, hear thou shalt, and be,
If so thou will, more wild than the wild sea ;
But know, thou art thy little ones' betrayer !
If thou die now, shall child of thine be heir
To Theseus' castle ?   Nay, not thine, I ween,
But hers !   That barbèd Amazonian Queen
Hath left a child to bend thy children low,
A bastard royal-hearted — sayst not so ? —
Hippolytus. . .

THE ELECTRA OF EURIPIDES *

Translated by Gilbert Murray

In order that she may marry *Aegisthus, Clytemnestra* helps assassi-
nate her husband, *King Agamemnon,* banishes her son, *Orestes,*
and marries her daughter, *Electra,* to a peasant.   After years of

* Electra of Euripides, translated by Gilbert Murray, from *The Medea of
Euripides,* reprinted by permission of George Allen and Unwin, Ltd.

exile *Orestes* comes unwittingly to the peasant home of *Electra*,
who sends for the *Old Man* that he may bring food and wine for
the stranger.

Old Man   Where is my little Princess?   Ah, not now;
But still my queen, who tended long ago
The lad that was her father. . . How steep-set
These last steps to her porch!   But faint not yet:
Onward, ye failing knees and back with pain
Bowed, till we look on that dear face again.
  [*Enter Electra*]
Ah, daughter, is it thou? — Lo, here I am,
With gifts from all my store; this suckling lamb
Fresh from the ewe, green crowns for joyfulness,
And creamy things new-curdled from the press.
And this long-storèd juice of vintages
Forgotten, cased in fragrance : scant it is,
But passing sweet to mingle nectar-wise
With feebler wine. — Go, bear them in ; mine eyes. . .
Where is my cloak? — They are all blurred with tears.

Electra   What ails thine eyes, old friend?   After these years
Doth my low plight still stir thy memories?
Or think'st thou of Orestes, where he lies
In exile, and my father?   Aye, long love
Thou gavest him, and seest the fruit thereof
Wasted, for thee and all who love thee!

Old Man   All wasted!   And yet 'tis that lost hope withal
I cannot brook.   But now I turned aside
To see my master's grave.   All, far and wide,
Was silence ; so I bent these knees of mine
And wept and poured drink-offerings from the wine
I bear the strangers, and about the stone
Laid myrtle sprays.   And, child, I saw thereon
Just at the censer slain, a fleecèd ewe,
Deep black, in sacrifice : the blood was new
About it : and a tress of bright brown hair
Shorn as in mourning, close.   Long stood I there
And wondered, of all men what man had gone
In mourning to that grave. — My child, 'tis none
In Argos.   Did there come. . . Nay, mark me now. . .
Thy brother in the dark, last night, to bow
His head before that unadorèd tomb?

O come, and mark the colour of it. Come
And lay thine own hair by that mourner's tress!
A hundred little things make likenesses
In brethren born, and show the father's blood.

ELECTRA OF EURIPIDES *

Translated by Gilbert Murray

In order that she may marry *Aegisthus, Clytemnestra* helps assassi-
nate her husband, *King Agamemnon,* banishes her son, *Orestes,*
and marries her daughter, *Electra,* to a peasant. After years of
exile *Orestes* is reunited with *Electra,* who urges him to avenge
the murder of their father by killing *Aegisthus. Orestes* performs this deed.

* * *

Electra [*She goes and stands over the body. A moment's
silence*]
Ah me, what have I? What first flood of hate
To loose upon thee? What last curse to sate
My pain, or river of wild words to flow
Bank-high between? . . . Nothing? . . . And yet I know
There hath not passed one sun, but through the long
Cold dawns, over and over, like a song,
I have said them — words held back, O, some day yet
To flash into thy face, would but the fret
Of ancient fear fall loose and let me free.
And free I am, now ; and can pay to thee
At last the weary debt.
                                   Oh, thou didst kill
My soul within. Who wrought thee any ill,
That thou shouldst make me fatherless? Aye, me
And this my brother, loveless, solitary?
'Twas thou, didst bend my mother to her shame :
Thy weak hand murdered him who led to fame
The hosts of Hellas — thou, that never crossed
O'erseas to Troy! . . . God help thee, wast thou lost
In blindness, long ago, dreaming, some-wise,
She would be true with thee, whose sin and lies
Thyself had tasted in my father's place?

*Electra of Euripides. Translated by Gilbert Murray, from *Medea of Euripides.*
Copyrighted by George Allen and Unwin, Ltd.

And then, that thou wert happy, when thy days
Were all one pain?   Thou knewest ceaselessly
Her kiss a thing unclean, and she knew thee
A lord so little true, so dearly won!
So lost ye both, being in falseness one,
What fortune else had granted; she thy curse,
Who marred thee as she loved thee, and thou hers. . .
And on thy ways thou heardst men whispering
"Lo, the Queen's husband yonder"—not "the King."
And then the lie of lies that dimmed thy brow,
Vaunting that by thy gold, thy chattels, Thou
Wert Something; which themselves are nothingness,
Shadows, to clasp a moment ere they cease.
The thing thou art, and not the things thou hast,
Abideth, yea, and bindeth to the last
Thy burden on thee: while all else, ill-won
And sin-companioned, like a flower o'erblown,
Flies on the wind away.
                              Or didst thou find
In women . . . Women? . . . Nay, peace, peace!
   The blind
Could read thee.   Cruel wast thou in thine hour,
Lord of a great king's house, and like a tower
Firm in thy beauty.
   [*Starting back with a look of loathing*]
                              Ah, that girl-like face!
God grant, not that, not that, but some plain grace
Of manhood to the man who brings me love;
A father of straight children, that shall move
Swift on the wings of War.
                              So, get thee gone!
Naught knowing how the great years, rolling on,
Have laid thee bare, and thy long debt full paid.
   O vaunt not, if one step be proudly made
In evil, that all Justice is o'ercast:
Vaunt not, ye men of sin, ere at the last
The thin-drawn marge before you glimmereth
Close, and the goal that wheels 'twixt life and death.
Leader
   Justice is mighty.   Passing dark hath been
   His sin: and dark the payment of his sin.

Electra [*With a weary sigh, turning from the body*]
    Ah me! Go some of you, bear him from sight,
    That when my mother come, her eyes may light
    On nothing, nothing, till she know the sword. . .
       [*The body is borne into the hut. Pylades goes with it*]

Orestes [*Looking along the road*]
    Stay, 'tis a new thing! We have still a word
    To speak. . .

Electra
       What? Not a rescue from the town
    Thou seëst?

Orestes
       'Tis my mother comes: my own
    Mother, that bare me. [*He takes off his crown*]

Electra [*Springing, as it were, to life again, and moving where
         she can see the road*]
     Straight into the snare!
    Aye, there she cometh.— Welcome in thy rare
    Chariot! All welcome in thy brave array!

THE FROGS *

By ARISTOPHANES

Translated by Gilbert Murray

During a journey to Hades in search of a great poet, *Bacchus* ex-
changes attire with his servant, *Xanthias*. This works to the advantage of both until *Aeacus* accuses *Bacchus* of theft. It is
agreed that *Xanthias* will be punished for the crime. To this
proposal *Bacchus*, now the servant, objects, saying that he is a god,
which identity is also claimed by *Xanthias*. In order to deter-
mine which is the god, it is proposed that both be whipped — the
god will experience no pain.

Xanthias   That's fair enough. All right; whichever of us
         You first find crying, or the least bit minding
         Your whip, you're free to say he's no true god.

Aeacus   Sir, you behave like a true gentleman;
         You come to justice of yourself! — Now then,
         Strip, both.

   * The Frogs, translated by Gilbert Murray, from *Euripides*, reprinted by permission of George Allen and Unwin, Ltd.

Xanthias   How will you test us?

Aeacus   Easily:
You'll each take whack and whack about.

Xanthias   All right.

Aeacus   [*Striking Xanthias*]   There.

Xanthias   [*Controlling himself with an effort*]   Watch now,
if you see me even wince.

Aeacus   But I've already hit you!

Xanthias   I think not.

Aeacus   Upon my word, it looks as if I hadn't.
Well, now I'll go and whack the other.
     [*Strikes Dionysus*]

Dionysus   [*Also controlling himself*]   When?

Aeacus   I've done it.

Dionysus   [*With an air of indifference*]   Odd, it didn't make
me sneeze!

Aeacus   It *is* odd!—Well, I'll try the first again.
     [*He crosses to Xanthias*]

Xanthias   All right.   Be quick.   [*The blow falls*]   Whe-ew!

Aeacus   Ah, why "whe-ew"?
It didn't hurt you?

Xanthias   [*Recovering himself*]
              No; I just was thinking
When my Diomean Feast would next be due.

Aeacus   A holy thought?—I'll step across again.
     [*Strikes Dionysus, who howls*]

Dionysus   Ow-ow!

Aeacus   What's that?

Dionysus   [*Recovering himself*]   I saw some cavalry.

Aeacus   What makes your eyes run?

Dionysus   There's a smell of onions!

Aeacus   You're sure it didn't hurt you?

Dionysus   Hurt?   Not it.

Aeacus   I'll step across again then to the first one.
     [*Strikes Xanthias, who also howls*]

Xanthias   Hi-i!

Aeacus   What is it now?

                              Take out that thorn.   [*Pointing to
                  his foot]

Aeacus   What does it mean ? — Over we go again.
                  [*Strikes Dionysus*]

Dionysus   [*Hurriedly turning his wail into a line of poetry*]
              O Lord ! . . . "of Delos or of Pytho's rock."

Xanthias   [*Triumphantly*]   It hurts.   You heard ?

Dionysus   It doesn't !   I was saying
              A verse of old Hippônax to myself.

Xanthias   You're making nothing of it.   Hit him hard
              Across the soft parts underneath the ribs.

Aeacus   [*To Xanthias*]   A good idea !   Turn over on your
                  back !   [*Strikes him*]

Xanthias   [*As before*]   O Lord !

Dionysus   It hurts !

Xanthias   [*As though continuing*]
                            "Poseidon ruler free
              Of cliffs Aegean and the grey salt sea."

Aeacus   Now, by Demeter, it's beyond my powers
              To tell which one of you's a god ! — Come in ;
              We'll ask my master.   He and Persephassa
              Will easily know you, being gods themselves.

Dionysus   Most wisely said.   Indeed I could have wished
              You'd thought of that before you had me swished.

ROMAN SELECTIONS

HEAUTONTIMORUMENOS: THE SELF-TORMENTOR *

By Terence

Translated by John Sargeaunt

Mendemus, a wealthy old land owner, labors in his field from early morning until latest night. *Chremes*, his neighbor, thinks this behavior strange since *Mendemus* owns many slaves to do his work. One day *Chremes* approaches *Mendemus* in the fields and finds him weeping.

Chremes Don't weep, tell me your trouble whatever it is; don't be reserved or afraid. Trust me, I say; you'll find I can help you either by consolation or by advice, possibly by direct assistance.

Mendemus You would like to be told?

Chremes Yes, for the reason I have given you.

Mendemus Then you shall.

Chremes Well but your mattocks, lay 'em down for the present; whatever your trouble, don't go on working.

Mendemus. No, no.

Chremes But what's your object?

Mendemus Don't prevent me giving myself no moment's holiday from work.

Chremes No really, I will prevent you. [*Takes the mattocks*]

Mendemus Ah, that's wrong of you.

Chremes What? heavy as this? My good man! [*Weighing them in his hands*]

Mendemus I have deserved it.

Chremes Now say on. [*Lays them down*]

Mendemus I have an only son, a mere lad. Ah, what do I

---

* Heautontimorumenos, quoted from the Loeb Classical Library edition of *Heautontimorumenos: The Self-Tormentor,* by Terence, by permission of the President and Fellows of Harvard College.

say? have a son? No, I had a son, Chremes; whether I have one now I can't tell.

Chremes How is that?

Mendemus I will tell you. In Athens there is a foreigner from Corinth, an old woman of small means. My son fell desperately in love with her daughter, in fact was almost as good as married to her, all this without my knowledge. When I found it out, instead of handling the matter kindly, in the way I ought to have dealt with a stripling's lovesick heart, I took the violent line that is common with parents. Day after day I nagged at him. "So, Sir," I would say, "do you think you're to be allowed such liberties any longer in your father's lifetime, and almost as good as marry a mistress? You're mistaken, if you think so, and you don't know your man, Clinia. I am ready that you should be called my son just so far as you do what befits you; if you act otherwise you will see me find the fitting way to deal with you. Ay, all this comes merely from such a want of employment. When *I* was young I didn't busy myself with love. No, Sir, I was off to Asia because of my lack of means, and there on service, active service, Sir, got both money and glory." At last matters came to this pass: the lad by having this perpetually and painfully dinned into him was overcome. He reflected that from years and experiences I must know better than he did and could look out for him better than he could for himself. Off to Asia he went, Chremes, to take service with the king.

Chremes Do you mean it?

Mendemus Yes, he started without a word to me and has been gone three months.

Chremes You are both to blame, not but what his enterprise shows respect, yes, and spirit as well.

THE CAPTIVES*

By PLAUTUS

Translated by Paul Nixon

Ergasilus, a gluttonous parasite, makes it a point to dine at the expense of others. His last attempt has failed, and he is left philosophizing on the insociability of society.

* The Captives, quoted from the Loeb Classical Library edition of *The Captives*, by Plautus, by permission of the President and Fellows of Harvard College.

Ergasilus   It's sad when a man has to spend his time looking for his food and has hard work finding it.   It's sadder, though, when he has hard work looking for it and doesn't find it.   But it's saddest of all when a man is pining to eat, and no food in range.   By gad, if I only could, I'd like to dig the eyes out of this day, it's made every living soul so damnably mean to me! A more hungriful day, a more bulged-out-with-starvation day, a more unprogressive day for every undertaking, I never did see!   Such a famine feast as my inside is having!   Devil take the parasitical profession!   How the young fellows nowadays do sheer off from impecunious wits!   Not a bit of use have they nowadays for us Spartans, us valiant benchenders, us descendants of old Takesacuff, whose capital is talk without cash and comestibles.   The guests they're after are the ones that enjoy a dinner and then like to return the compliment.   They do their marketing themselves, too,— that used to be the parasites' province — and away they go from the forum themselves to interview the pimps, just as barefaced as they are in court when they condemn guilty defendants.   They don't care a farthing for wits these days; they're egoists, every one.   Why, when I left here a little while ago, I went up to some young fellows in the forum. "Good day," says I.   "Where are we going to lunch together?" says I.   Sudden silence.   "Where do we dine?" says I.   A shaking of heads.   I told 'em a funny story — one of my best, that used to find me free board for a month.   Nobody smiled. I saw in a moment it was a put-up job; not a one of 'em was even willing to act like a cross dog and at least show their teeth, no matter if they wouldn't laugh.   I left them after I saw I was being made a fool of this way; up I went to some others, and then to others, and to others still,— same story.   They're all in a combination, just like the oil dealers in the Velabrum. So here I am back again, seeing I was trifled with there.   Some more parasites were prowling round the forum all for nothing, too.   Now I'm going to have the foreign law on those chaps and demand my full rights, I certainly am; it's conspiracy, conspiracy to deprive us of sustenance and life, and I'm going to summon 'em, fine 'em — make 'em give me ten dinners at my discretion, and that will be when food is dear.   That's how I'll catch them.   [*Turning to go*]   Well, now, for the harbour. That's where my one hope is, gastronomically speaking; if that oozes away, I'll come back here to the old man's terror of a meal. [*Exit Ergasilus, looking in all directions for a possible host*]

MEDEA *

By SENECA

Translated by Frank Justus Miller

Pelias sends his nephew, *Jason*, son of *Aeson*, in quest of the Golden Fleece in order to keep him from the throne. With the aid of *Medea*, the enchantress, *Jason* secures the Golden Fleece and brings about the death of *Pelias*. After *Jason* deserts *Medea*, whom he has married, for *Creusa*, *Medea* sends her rival a poisoned robe, fires the palace, and is now about to put her sons to death.

Medea . . . Now I am Medea; my wit has grown through suffering.

Glad am I, glad, that I tore off my brother's head, glad that I carved his limbs, that I robbed my father of his guarded treasure, glad that I armed daughters for an old man's death. Seek thou fresh fields, my grief; no untrained hand wilt thou bring to any crime.

Whither, then, wrath, art tending, or what weapons art thou aiming at the forsworn foe? A dark purpose my fierce spirit hath resolved within me, and dares not yet acknowledge to itself. Fool! fool! I have gone too fast — would that mine enemy had children by his paramour! [*She pauses and then addresses herself*] All offspring that thou hast by him are Creusa's brood. Resolved is this way of vengeance, rightly resolved; for a last deed of guilt, I see it now, must my soul make ready. Children that once were mine, do you pay penalty for your father's crimes.

Horror has smit my heart! My limbs are numb with cold and my heart with terror flutters. Wrath has given place; the mother has all come back, the wife is banished. Can I shed my children's, my own offspring's blood? Ah, mad rage, say not so! Far, even from me, be that unheard-of deed, that accursed guilt! What sin will the poor boys atone? Their sin is that Jason is their father, and, greater sin, that Medea is their mother. [*She pauses*] Let them die, they are none of mine; let them be lost — they are my own. They are without crime and guilt, yea, they are innocent — I acknowledge it; so, too, was my brother. Why, soul, dost hesitate? Why are my cheeks wet with tears? Why do anger and love now hither, now thither

---

* Medea, quoted from the Loeb Classical Library edition of *Medea*, by Seneca, by permission of the President and Fellows of Harvard College.

draw my changeful heart? A double tide tosses me, uncertain of my course; as when rushing winds wage mad warfare, and from both sides conflicting floods lash the seas and the fluctuating waters boil, even so is my heart tossed. Anger puts love to flight, and love, anger. O wrath, yield thee to love.

Hither, dear children, sole comfort of my fallen house, come hither and link your entwining limbs with mine. Let your father have you unharmed, so but your mother may have you too. But exile and flight press hard upon me; now, now will they be torn from my bosom and carried away from me, midst tears and sighs and kisses.—Let them be lost to their father; they are lost to me. My grief grows again and my hate burns hot; Erinys, as of old, claims my unwilling hand. O wrath, where thou dost lead I follow. I would that from my womb the throng of proud Niobe had sprung, and that I had been the mother of twice seven sons! Too barren have I been for vengeance—yet for my brother and my father there is enough, for I have borne two sons.

Whither hastes that headlong horde of Furies? Whom seek they? Against whom are they preparing their flaming blows? Whom does the hellish host threaten with its bloody brands? A huge snake hisses, whirled with the writhing lash. Whom does Megaera seek with her deadly torch? Whose shade comes there dimly seen, its limbs all scattered? It is my brother, and 'tis punishment he seeks. We'll pay, yes, all the debt. Plunge your brands into my eyes, tear, burn; see, my breast is open to the Furies.

O brother, bid the avenging goddesses depart from me, and go in peace to the deep-buried ghosts; to myself leave me and use this hand, brother, which has drawn the sword— [*She slays the first son.*] With this victim I appease thy ghost.— What means that sudden noise? 'Tis arms they are making ready, and they seek me for my slaying. To the lofty roof of our palace will I mount, now the bloody work hath been begun. [*To her remaining son.*] Do thou come with me. [*To her dead son.*] Thy corpse also will I take hence with me. Now to the task, O soul; not in secrecy must thy great deed be lost; to the people approve thy handiwork.

GERMAN SELECTIONS

THE SUNKEN BELL *

By GERHART HAUPTMANN

While hanging his masterpiece to toll on the mountain-side, *Heinrich*, great bell-founder, drops with the bell into the abyss below.

Hurt and broken in spirit, *Heinrich* climbs out of the abyss and falls exhausted before the mountain hut of *Rautendelein*, a beautiful, elfin creature.

Heinrich   [*After drinking and looking ecstatically and fixedly at Rautendelein*]
Speak on!   Speak on!   Thy drink was very sweet.
But sweeter still thy voice. . .
  [*Again becoming anxious*]
           She said — a man
Not fashioned like myself.   A better man —
And yet he fell! . . . Speak on, my child.

Rautendelein   Why speak?
What can my words avail!   I'll rather go
And fetch thee water from the brook, to wash
The blood and dust from off thy brow. . .

Heinrich   [*Pleading and grasping her by the wrist. Rautendelein stands undecided*]
           Ah, stay!
And look into mine eyes with thy strange eyes.
For lo, the world, within thine eyes renewed,
So sweetly bedded, draws me back to life!
Stay, child.   O stay!

Rautendelein   [*Uneasy*]
Then . . . as thou wilt.   And yet . . .

Heinrich   [*Fevered and imploring*]
  Ah, stay with me!   Thou wilt not leave me so?
Thou dost not dream how dear to me thou art.
Oh, wake me not, my child.   I'll tell thee all.
I fell. . . Yet — no. Speak thou; for thy dear voice

---

* From *The Sunken Bell*, by Gerhart Hauptmann. Copyright 1914. Published by The Viking Press, Inc.

Has Heaven's own music.   God did give it thee.
And I will listen.   Speak! . . . Wilt thou not speak?
Wilt thou not sing to me?   Why then, . . . I must . . .
I fell.   I know not how — I've told thee that —
Whether the path gave way beneath my feet;
Whether 'twas willingly I fell, or no —
God wot.   Enough.   I fell into the gulf.
 [*More fevered*]
And then I clutched at a wild cherry tree
That grew between the rocks.   It broke — and I,
Still clasping a bough tightly, felt a shower
Of pale pink blossoms riot around my head;
Then swift was hurled to the abyss — and died!
And even now I'm dead.   It must be so.
Let no one wake me!

Rautendelein   [*Uncertainly*]
 Yet thou seem'st alive!

Heinrich
I know — I know — what once I did not know:
That life is Death, and only Death is Life.
 [*Collapsing again*]
I fell.   I lived — and fell.   The bell fell, too!
We two — the bell and I.   Was I the first —
To slip, and next — the bell?   Or — the reverse?
Who seeks to know?   And who could prove the truth?
And even were it proven, what care I?
Then I was living.   Now — ah, now . . . I'm dead.
 [*Tenderly*]
Ah, go not yet!
 [*Looks at hand*]
My hand! . . . 'Tis white as milk!
My hand! . . . It hangs so heavy! . . . It seems dead.
I cannot lift it! . . . Yet —   How sweet thou art!
The touch of thy soft hair doth bring relief,
As water of Bethesda! . . . Nay, do not fear!
My hand shall never harm thee — thou art holy!
Where have we met? . . . I surely know thy face.
Somewhere, but where, or when, I cannot tell,
I wrought for thee, and strove — in one grand Bell,
To wed the silver music of thy voice
With the warm gold of a Sun-holiday.

It should have been a master-work ! . . . I failed.
Then wept I tears of blood.

Rautendelein   Wept tears of blood ?
I cannot follow thee.   What be these tears ?

Heinrich   [*Trying to raise his head*]
Thou lovely picture ! . . . help me to sit up.
   [*Rautendelein stoops and supports his head*]
Dost thou bend down to me ?   Then, with love's arms,
Do thou release me from this cruel Earth,
Whereunto the hour nails me, as to a cross.
Release me !   For thou canst.   I know thou canst !
And, with thy tender hands, pluck off the thorns
That crown my head.   No crown !   Love — only love !
   [*His head is slightly raised.   He seems exhausted*]
Thanks ! thanks !
   [*Gently and in a lost kind of way as he looks at the land-
      scape*]
Here all is beautiful !   The rustling boughs
Have such a strange, full sound.   The darkling arms
Of the great firs move so mysteriously.
How solemnly their heads sway to and fro !
The very soul of fairy fantasy
Sighs through the wood.   It murmurs low, and then,
Still gently whisp'ring, stirs the tiny leaves.
Now it goes singing through the green wood-grass.
And now, veiled all in misty white, it nears —
It stretches out its long white hand and points
At me ! . . . Now closer, it draws !   It touches my ear. . .
My tongue . . . my eyes ! . . . 'Tis gone !   Yet thou art
   here !
Thou art my fantasy ! . . . Kiss me, sweet fantasy !
   [*He faints*]

Rautendelein   [*Half to herself*]
Thy speech is strange.   I know not what it means.
   [*She suddenly resolves to go*]
Lie thou, and sleep.

Heinrich   [*Dreaming*]
Kiss me, sweet fantasy !

THE VALE OF CONTENT*

By Hermann Sudermann

Translated by Elsie G. Cresswell

Wiedemann, a guileless, undissembling school teacher, loves his
wife, *Elizabeth,* who is much younger than he. He thinks his
wife is very happy and serene, but she has always been in love
with the suave, and domineering *Roecknitz.* As the scene opens
Roecknitz has come to demand her love, or, at least, some expression of it.

Roecknitz   What I am telling you, Elizabeth, is like a cry for
help.— I am merely trying to save my life, for this is no longer
life . . . this is mere existence, an aimless, hollow, reeling about,
hither and thither. . . And how crude I've become! how
petty! . . . All greatness has gone out of my life since you are
gone . . . the fresh air seems denied me, and I have so much
room to breathe in it. . . I work from 4:00 in the morning on
into the night, but it doesn't help. . . A man must at least
know what he works for. . . Don't come to me, with the child
. . . it is a plaything, nothing more. . . A man must have at
least one person with whom he can—   Ah, if I could feel you
near me again!—   Just think, in the evenings I'd ride over to
Angershof or—to Brickyard, no matter which,—that, your
husband could decide for himself. . . Or you would come to us
and we'd sit on the terrace again as we used to and discuss what
we had been doing and what we were going to do. When one
imagines that!—   To become, through you, a living man once
more . . . to grow in peace and strength . . . day by day!
And never again shall I talk to you of love. That I'll swear to
you with the holiest oath. . . Profits me nothing anyway. . .
Would seem merely like an insult to you. . . I'll know how to
control myself, never fear. You'll see. [*Silence*] Elizabeth
—not a word?

Elizabeth   [*After continued silence, deeply moved, though out-
wardly calm*]   Dear friend, what you tell me is all very fine
and tempting, but unfortunately it will not do.

Roecknitz   Why won't it do?

Elizabeth   I see, I must give you the reason which will convince
you, or who knows how long we will torment each other.—I

* The Vale of Content, translated for the author by Elsie G. Cresswell.

still love you, Roecknitz—I have never ceased to be fond of you.—But surely you see it will not do—don't you?

Roecknitz [*Rushes up to her with out-stretched arms*] Elizabeth!

Elizabeth [*Frightened—she avoids him and flees into a corner*] Have mercy! Spare me!

Roecknitz At last! At last! [*Trying to snatch her to him*]

Elizabeth At last! [*Exultantly she flings herself upon his breast, and after his long kiss, remains—eyes closed, apparently lifeless, in his arms*]

Roecknitz Elizabeth! [*She doesn't answer—he leads her to a chair. She sinks into it with her head against the arm, he kneels before her*] Elizabeth! Come back! Or I'll have to call for help!

Elizabeth [*Her eyes fly open—she raises herself slowly upright and lays her hands on his shoulders as she looks into his eyes*] This is what he is like! So he is mine! This once! This once!

Roecknitz Woman—adored!

Elizabeth [*Laying her hand on his mouth*] Quiet! Not a word! Not a word!

Roecknitz [*Springing up*] Ah, what a life it will be! what a life it will be! One great celebration!—what say you, Elizabeth?—ha, ha, ha!

Elizabeth [*Anxiously*] What do you mean by that?

Roecknitz What do I mean by it? My goodness, is that so difficult?—Is it really so difficult?

Elizabeth For us there can be no future meetings in this world. We dare not meet again. . . Roecknitz, surely that is self-evident, if we are to have the courage to live at all.

Roecknitz No, no, no! Everything—but, Elizabeth, surely we are no longer children—we didn't just drop out of the moon. God above, woman, you, you,—how the woman can kiss! Give me no more refusals! I want no more resistance or I'll go mad. I'll raze both your house and mine to the ground, before I'll let you go again! I'll give you until this evening, and if then you say not "yes," then—

Elizabeth What—then?

Roecknitz   That you shall see.   Then I'll have to act on my own responsibility.   There is no other way —   Adieu, my dear —

MAGDA *

By HERMANN SUDERMANN

Translated by B. Q. Morgan

Rather than marry the man of her father's choice, *Magda* leaves home and goes on the stage; the shock, to the militant old Lieutenant-Colonel *Schwartze* is so great it brings on an apoplectic stroke from which he never fully recovers. Years later she returns, a famous opera singer. Although still unreconciled, the father admits her to the home. Later he discovers that twelve years ago she has had an affair with a certain *Von Keller* and is the mother of his son. Believing that the only honorable thing left for *Magda* is marriage with *Von Keller,* *Schwartze* tries to force her into the marriage.

Schwartze   There!   Now we are alone.   No one sees us but *he!*   [*Looking at the bust of Emperor William I*]   And I want him to see us. . . Don't keep walking around. . . We have things to say to each other, my child.

Magda   [*Sits down*]   Good! — I think this will clarify the issues between my home and me.

Schwartze   You will surely concede that I am quite calm now?

Magda   Certainly.

Schwartze   Quite calm, am I not? —   Not even my arm trembles.   What is done is done.   But I just now told your fiancé —

Magda   My fiancé? —   My dear father!

Schwartze   Yes, I gave your fiancé my word of honor.   And that must be kept; you see that, I hope?

Magda   Yes, but if that is not in your power, father dear?

Schwartze   Then that means my death . . . then that simply means — my death . . . for one cannot go on living, when one . . . You're an officer's daughter, after all.   Surely that is clear to you?

Magda   [*Compassionately*]   Good heavens!

Schwartze   But before my death I must put my house in order, mustn't I?   Listen, my daughter, everybody has something

---

* Magda, translated for the author by B. Q. Morgan.

that he holds sacred.   What is there in the world that is absolutely sacred to you ?

Magda   My art !

Schwartze   No, that is not enough.   It must be holier than that.

Magda   My child.

Schwartze   Good.   Your child. . . Your child . . . and you love it ?   [*Magda nods*]   And you would like to see it again ? [*Magda nods*]   And — a, a — if you were to swear by — by the life of your child [*He makes a gesture of laying his hand on a child's head*], then you would not swear falsely ?

Magda   [*Smiles her denial*]

Schwartze   Well, that is good !   [*Rising*]   Either you will now swear to me by the life of your child that you will become the honest wife of its father, or — neither of us two will leave this room alive !   [*He drops back into the chair*]

Magda   [*After a brief silence*]   My poor old papa !   Why do you torture yourself ?   And do you think that I shall quietly let you kill me behind closed doors ? . . . You can't demand that.

Schwartze   You'll see.

Magda   [*In growing agitation*]   What do all of you want of me ?   Why do you cling to me ? . . . I might almost have said : What have I to do with you ?

* * *

Schwartze   Ah, there it is !   There is the spirit of revolt that is passing through this modern world !   My child — my dear child, tell me that you weren't really in earnest just now — that you — that you — have pity — if — [*Eyeing the box of pistols*] Otherwise I don't know what may happen . . . child !   Have pity on me !

Magda   Father, father, hush, I can't bear that.

Schwartze   And I won't do it. . . And I can't do it. . . [*Looking towards the box*]   Put that away, put it away !

Magda   What, father ?

Schwartze   Nothing, nothing.— I ask you for the last time —

Magda   Then you insist !

Schwartze   My child, I warn you.   You know that I can't help it.

Magda Well, father, you leave me no choice. Very well, then. . . But do you know whether you have a *right* to saddle that man with me ? . . . [*Schwartze pricks up his ears*] Whether I am even worthy of him, according to your ideas ? [*Hesitantly, looking into space*]   I mean, whether he was the only man in my life ?

Schwartze [*Gropes for the box and draws out a pistol*]   You harlot ! [*He takes some steps toward her, trying to lift the weapon. At the same instant he suddenly falls back into the chair, where he remains sitting motionless with fixed gaze, holding the pistol in his limp hand*]

Magda [*With shrill scream*] Father ! [*And flees toward the stove in order to seek shelter from the gun, then, clapping her hands to her face, she takes a few steps back and forth*] Father ! [*And drops her knee on to a chair, hiding her face against its back*]

[*Outside, cries and noises. The door is burst in. Enter the Pastor, Max, Mrs. Schwartze, Marie*]

Mrs. Schwartze Leopold, what ails you ?—Leopold ! [*To the pastor*]   Oh God, that's the way he was then !

Marie Dear papa, say something ! [*Throws herself down to the right of him*]

Pastor Run for the Doctor, Max.

Max Is it a stroke ?

Pastor Apparently.—[*Exit Max*]

Pastor [*In a low voice to Magda*] Come to him. [*As she hesitates*] Come. It seems to be the end. [*Leads her, as she quivers with pain, to Schwartze's chair*]

Mrs. Schwartze [*Having tried to take away the pistol*] Let go, Leopold ! What do you want with it ?—Just look, there he is holding the pistol and won't let go.

Pastor [*Softly*] It is probably a convulsion. He cannot. . . My dear old friend, do you understand what I am saying to you ?

Schwartze [*Inclines his head a little*]

Magda [*Sinks down to the left of him*]

Pastor God, the All-Compassionate, has called down to you from above ; thou shalt not judge. . . Have you no token of forgiveness for her ?

Schwartze [*Slowly shakes his head*]

Marie [*Sinking down beside Magda*] Papa, give her your blessing, dear papa! [*Over Schwartze's face passes a transfiguring smile. The pistol drops out of his fingers. He lifts his hand with an effort, to lay it on Marie's head. In the midst of this movement a jerk goes through his body. . . His arm falls back. His head drops forward*]

Mrs. Schwartze [*Screams*] Leopold!

Pastor [*Grasping her hand*] He has gone home. . . [*He folds his hands. Silent prayer, punctuated by the sobbing of the women*]

Magda [*Leaping up and raising her hands in despair*] Oh, I wish I had never come!

Pastor [*Makes a defensive gesture that bids her be quiet*]

Magda [*Misunderstanding the gesture*] So you are driving me away already? . . . I brought him to his death — I hope I may be allowed to bury him?

Pastor [*Simply and peaceably*] No one will prevent you from praying by his coffin.

(*The curtain falls slowly*)

MAGDA *

By HERMANN SUDERMANN

Translated by B. Q. Morgan

Rather than marry the man of her father's choice, *Magda* leaves home and goes on the stage; the shock, to the militant old *Lieutenant-Colonel Schwartze* is so great it brings on an apoplectic stroke from which he never fully recovers. Years later she returns, a famous opera singer. Although still unreconciled, the father admits her to the home. Later he discovers that twelve years ago she has had an affair with a certain *Von Keller* and is the mother of his son. Believing that the only honorable thing left for Magda is marriage with *Von Keller, Schwartze* tries to force her into the marriage.

Magda You reproach me for having given myself in my fashion, without asking permission of you and the entire family. And why shouldn't I? Was I not without a family? Had

---

* Magda, translated for the author by B. Q. Morgan.

you not sent me out into the world to earn my bread, and then disowned me besides, because my way of earning it was not to your taste? . . . Whom did I deceive? Against whom did I sin? . . . If I had remained a mere daughter like Marie, who is nothing and can do nothing without someone's protecting roof, who is transferred straight from the hands of her father into those of her husband — who receives everything from her family: bread, ideas, character, and what not? . . . Yes, then you would be in the right. The smallest misstep would ruin everything in *her* — conscience, honor, self-esteem. . . But I? . . . Look at me. I was a homeless cat. . . I had long been one of those creatures who knock about the world as defenceless as any man, and dependent upon the labor of their hands. . . But if you give us the right to hunger — and I *have* hungered — why do you deny us the right to such love as we can have, and the right to happiness as we understand it?

Schwartze I suppose you think, my child, that because you are independent and a great artist, you are privileged to disregard the —

Magda Leave the artist out of it! I don't claim to be anything more than any seamstress or servant girl who has to turn to strangers for her bit of bread and her pittance of love. — Oh, we know well enough what the family and its morality demand of us. . . They have left us in the lurch, they give us neither protection nor pleasures, and nevertheless we are supposed to live in our solitude by the laws which only have a meaning for them. . . We are expected to perch in silence in our little corner, and wait there, nice and modest, until some worthy suitor comes along. . . Yes, *until!* And meanwhile the struggle for existence is consuming us body and soul. — Before us lies nothing but a withered body and an embittered heart, and we are not even to dare to take what we may have left of our youth and our superabundant strength and give it to the man for whom our whole being cries out? — Hobble us if you will, blunt our minds, lock us up in harems and in convents — and that might even be the best thing for us! — But if you grant us freedom, then don't be surprised if we make use of it.

VOLPONE *

By STEFAN ZWEIG

Translated by Ruth Langner

Corvino, a dishonest merchant, is competing with *Corbaccio,* an equally conniving person, for the fortune that each believes he will inherit from the crafty *Volpone. Corbaccio* has come to confer with *Mosca, Volpone's* sly, clever servant, who knows quite well the shrewd plan of these two old tottering usurers — these "legacy hunters."

Corvino Master Corbaccio, in the flesh! Ah, so you're not dead yet? They told me your legs were so lame you couldn't move and here you come dancing up the stairs; this must be a wonderful little business deal, a little hundred per cent profit to make you leave your treasure chests alone for a whole hour. I wish you luck. . . I wish you luck.

Corbaccio [*An ancient, tottering, lame old man with a bony face*] Thanks . . . I'm alive . . . thanks . . . I know your mind . . . no better than your credit . . . I wouldn't lend ten copper soldi on it.

Corvino I don't need your loans. No man you've strangled in your usurious grip has ever got off living. Grab, go on grabbing money; but take care, some day you may slip.

Corbaccio No fear . . . my money's kept well guarded — like your wife.

Corvino 'Fore God, what has my wife to do with you?

Corbaccio What has my business to do with you!

Corvino My wife . . . what are they all saying? [*To Corbaccio*] The devil break your neck! [*He rushes out*]

Corbaccio [*To Mosca*] An uncomfortable person. Much malice, little gold. What does *he* want here?

Mosca [*Wondering, innocent*] What does he want? Why, to crib a legacy, of course. Why else come to a rich dying man between the doctor and the grave-digger?

Corbaccio I . . . he, he . . . he, he . . . I like to look at dying men. I've seen so many and I enjoy each one more. I'm seventy-five. . . I've buried four brothers, sisters, friends,

* From *Volpone,* by Stefan Zweig. Copyright, 1928, by The Viking Press, Inc., New York.

12575

enemies, and I'm still alive. I'll outlive them all. I've known many of them in the cradle, and seen 'em grow up and all at once they lie there, blue, cold, dead . . . he, he . . . and old Corbaccio stands by feeling the warm breath in his mouth . . . blood in his fingers. I can work, walk, make money . . . he, he. It does me good to see it happen over and over. I'll outlive 'em all . . . and now this one, too . . . he, he . . . he lived a merry life,— young, could have been my son,— and he's come to die already. I want to take a look at it . . . he, he . . . and how are things today?

Mosca Bad, very bad.

Corbaccio Good, you mean . . . he, he . . . nearing the end. . . Pulse?

Mosca Thin as a fly's leg.

Corbaccio Good. . . Breath?

Mosca Whistles like an organ.

Corbaccio [*Rubbing his hands*] Fine, fine. . . His tongue?

Mosca Thick, yellow, hard, shoe-leather.

Corbaccio Ah, excellent! . . . Sweat: hot or cold?

Mosca Cold as a serpent's tail.

Corbaccio He, he, then it's coming soon. I know. . . Seen it often . . . it will soon be jolly. . . No air, pumps . . . pumps . . . pumps . . . can't raise any more . . . blue then, pale . . . he, he . . . coming soon now. . . Then stiff, no feeling . . . ears dulled, lids yellow . . . he, he, I know. . . 'Twill soon come to that.

Mosca Woe, he's there already, just as you described it. He lies like a log, does Messer Volpone, since this morning, just as you picture it, hears nothing, feels nothing, notices nothing. . . Look, if you don't believe me. [*Yells at Volpone*] Hey, you Levantine thief, not dead yet? Am I rid of you at last, you bawd, you miser, you rheumy braggart, you stinking billy-goat? [*To Corbaccio*] See, you could discharge a cannon in his ear, he'd hear nothing! Lay hold of him, he'd feel nothing.

Corbaccio [*Gloatingly to Volpone, prodding him with his cane*] Here, stand up, carcass, face the old man. . . You're younger, you have better legs . . . stand up . . . he, he. . . Often you've mocked poor old Corbaccio for being miserly and grudging others everything . . . he, he . . . who's mocking now, you libertine, you windbag, you glutton . . . He'll outlast you all, will old Corbaccio. He has more breath in his money than you have. He'll plunder you all and lie on your coverlets and live in your houses. . . he, he, corpse . . . he, he. . . You can't laugh any more . . . you laughed first . . . he, he . . . but I laugh last. . . [*Lets the curtain fall. To Mosca*] Keep the will here ready on the table. I want my money back at once. I invested fourteen hundred sequins, three thousand with interest . . . he, he . . . but I knew I'd outlive him. . . . He doesn't make any unsafe investments . . . old Corbaccio. . . I had good security . . . he, he. . .

Mosca [*Scratching his head*] The will . . . yes . . . but don't you know . . . Messer Volpone has invited the Notary again today. He wants some more — what did he call them? — codicils to his will.

Corbaccio [*Stammers excitedly*] A new will? Why codicils? If I hadn't seen him will me twenty thousand sequins . . . seen with my own eyes . . . never have given him the money . . . only safe investments. . . It's my guarantee, how can he change it . . . after he's dead?

Mosca Look, the Notary gave him this goblet and Master Corvino three hundred sequins; he means to remember them in his will.

Corbaccio And take it out of me, I suppose? . . . This can't be!

Mosca You see, the poor fool measures friendship by presents! If you were bright you'd quickly give him even more, so I could manage a good strong codicil for you.

Corbaccio These spendthrifts. [*Fingering the goblet*] Gold, solid gold . . . three hundred sequins. . . I have nothing more. . . I'm a poor man. . .

Mosca Perhaps this ring?

Corbaccio Ring! . . . thirty carats . . . worth a thousand sequins. . . I paid a hundred and twenty myself. . . No, no . . . too much . . . too much.

Mosca [*Flattering him softly*] It's only for a few hours. The corpse will scarce be cold when I tear it off its finger!

Corbaccio [*Starting toward Volpone*] True; he's three-quarters dead already. . . Here, take it, show it to him if he wakes again . . . and when he dies, then bring it back. Here . . . this is for you. [*Gives him money*] . . . Right back

. . . right off his finger before anybody sees it . . . here, take it . . . [*Fearfully.*] Lovely ring, lovely, brilliant fire. . . Wait, wait, I'll exchange it . . . bring another with a flaw this afternoon. . . He can't tell the difference any more. . .

Mosca He takes no more heed than a millstone. But go now, or the others will notice.

Corbaccio Better he died now . . . upsets me . . . another thousand sequins . . . lovely ring . . . bad business, bad business. [*Exit Corbaccio, murmuring*]

FRENCH SELECTIONS

TARTUFFE *

By MOLIÈRE

Translated by Curtis H. Page

The hypocritical, boastful *Tartuffe* has so completely deceived *Orgon* that he has not only given him his possessions but is trying to force his daughter, *Mariane*, to wed the culprit. *Orgon* will not believe that all the while the deceitful *Tartuffe* has been making advances toward his wife *Elmire*.

Tartuffe   The heart within my bosom is not stone.

Elmire   I well believe your sighs all tend to Heaven,
      And nothing here below can stay your thoughts.

Tartuffe   Love for the beauty of eternal things
      Cannot destroy our love for earthly beauty;
      Our mortal senses well may be entranced
      By perfect works that Heaven has fashioned here.
      Its charms reflected shine in such as you,
      And in yourself, its rarest miracles;
      It has displayed such marvels in your face,
      That eyes are dazed, and hearts are rapt away;
      I could not look on you, the perfect creature,
      Without admiring Nature's great Creator,
      And feeling all my heart inflamed with love
      For you, His fairest image of Himself.
      At first I trembled lest this secret love
      Might be the Evil Spirit's artful snare;
      I even schooled my heart to flee your beauty,
      Thinking it was a bar to my salvation.
      But soon, enlightened, O all lovely one,
      I saw how this my passion may be blameless,
      How I may make it fit with modesty,
      And thus completely yield my heart to it.
      'Tis, I must own, a great presumption in me
      To dare make you the offer of my heart;
      My love hopes all things from your perfect goodness,

* Tartuffe, reprinted by the courtesy of Curtis Hidden Page.

And nothing from my own poor weak endeavor.
You are my hope, my stay, my peace of heart ;
On you depends my torment or my bliss ;
And by your doom of judgement, I shall be
Blest, if you will ; or damned, by your decree.

Elmire   Your declaration's turned most gallantly ;
But truly, it is just a bit surprising.
You should have better armed your heart, methinks,
And taken thought somewhat on such a matter.
A pious man like you, known everywhere. . .

Tartuffe   Though pious, I am none the less a man ;
And when a man beholds your heavenly charms,
The heart surrenders, and can think no more.
I know such words seem strange, coming from me ;
But, madam, I'm no angel, after all ;
If you condemn my frankly made avowal
You only have your charming self to blame.
Soon as I saw your more than human beauty,
You were thenceforth the sovereign of my soul ;
Sweetness ineffable was in your eyes,
That took by storm my still resisting heart,
And conquered everything, fasts, prayers, and tears,
And turned my worship wholly to yourself.
My looks, my sighs, have spoke a thousand times ;
Now, to express it all, my voice must speak.
If but you will look down with gracious favor
Upon the sorrows of your worthless slave,
If in your goodness you will give me comfort
And condescend unto my nothingness,
I'll ever pay you, O sweet miracle,
An unexampled worship and devotion.
Then too, with me your honor runs no risk ;
With me you need not fear a public scandal.
These court gallants, that women are so fond of,
Are boastful of their acts, and vain in speech ;
They always brag in public of their progress ;
Soon as a favor's granted, they'll divulge it ;
Their tattling tongues, if you but trust to them,
Will foul the altar where their hearts have worshipped.
But men like me are so discreet in love,
That you may trust their lasting secrecy.

The care we take to guard our own good name
May fully guarantee the one we love ;
So you may find, with hearts like ours sincere,
Love without scandal, pleasure without fear.

FALSE GODS*

By BRIEUX

Translated by Connie Linton

Satni, a young priest, returning to his own people, finds them still
worshipping their false gods. Since he is unable to perform
miracles, his people refuse to follow the new God.
His father, mortally wounded, implores him to command his "new
faith" to save him.

Satni   My father. . .

Pakh   You are there, my son. . . It is well. . . I am glad that
that maker of spells has gone. . . [*Simply*]   Cure me.

Satni   Yes, father, you will be cured, but you must have
patience.

Pakh   [*Simply*]   Cure me at once.

Satni   I cannot do it.

Pakh   Why do you not wish to cure me?   Do you not see that
I am wounded?   I am suffering, relieve me! . . .

Satni   I would give everything were it within my power.

Pakh   You know prayers of which our priests are ignorant.

Satni   I know no prayers.

Pakh   [*In anguish*]   You are not going to let me die?

Satni   You will not die.   Have confidence.

Pakh   Confidence? . . . In what? . . . [*A silence*]   You do
not want to cure me?

Satni   I cannot.

Pakh   All your knowledge, is it then only to know how to destroy?   My son, I pray of you . . . my blood flows away with
my life. . I do not want to die. . . I beg of you. . . Give me
your hand. . It seems that I am sinking into the night. . .
Hold me back. . . You are not going to let me die? . . . Your

* Translated for the author by Connie Linton.

father . . . I am your father. . . I gave you life. . . Hold me
back ! . . . All grows dim around me ! . . . But at least do
something, speak. . . Say the incantations. [*He sits upright.*]
No ! No ! I do not accept death ! I am not old ! [*With
strength*] I will not ! I will not ! Do not let go of my hand !
I want to live ! to live. . . All my life I have worked, I have
grieved, I have suffered, Satni . . . are you going to let me go
away without benefit from the peace and happiness which you
have promised me . . .

Satni Oh ! my father.

Pakh You cry . . . I am lost then. . . Yes . . . I just saw it
in your eyes. And the stillness grows around me. . . To die.
. . To die. . . [*A long silence*] And afterwards ? . . . [*A
silence*] You do not answer me. . . That then is the life
of a poor man ? Work from childhood, blows. Then work,
always work without profit, only for sustenance. And still
work . . . for others. No joy. One dies. . . And it is
ended ! . . . You have come back to teach me of that. . . Of
work, of blows, of misery. . . The end. To be born, to suffer,
to die. All existence hangs on these three words. [*Silence*]
What have you come here to do ? Is that your work ? [*With
strength*] Satni ! Satni ! Give me my faith, I want it ! . . .
Ah ! Why were you born, destroyer ? . . . It is that, your
truth ? You have been able to convince me that all was false.
Prove to me now that you were lying ! I want it ! Give me
back my faith ; my artlessness ! Give me back the simplicity
which will soothe me. Give me back my faith !

Satni Do not give up hope !

Pakh I give up hope because they do not exist, those happy
fields.

Satni Nevertheless, my father, they exist.

Pakh You lied then ?

Satni I lied.

Pakh They exist. . . And if I die ?

Satni If you die, you will go to Osiris, you will become of
Osiris.

Pakh That is not true ! It is now that you are lying. . .
There is no Osiris ! There is no Osiris ! Nothing ! There is
nothing . . . except the living ! I curse you, you who have
taught me that ! My faith ! Give me back my faith ! [*He*

starts to fall from the bed. Satni piously lifts him and places him back again] Ah! Accursed one! Accursed one! I die in hatred, in rage, in terror! Wicked son! Wicked man! I curse you! I would like to harm you. . . Come closer to me. . . [*He seizes his throat*] Oh if I were only strong enough! I would like my fingernails to penetrate your throat. Wait! Wait! Accursed one! . . . [*He loosens him*] Ah! My whole life lost! All my suffering is useless. . . For ever. . . Never! Never will I know. . . What a pity! [*He stretches his arms toward Satni and falls. He is dead.*]

Satni [*Terified*] He is dead! . . . [*He lifts him up reverently.*] Poor father! . . . For myself also in this moment the lie would have been more comfortable.

CYRANO DE BERGERAC*

By EDMOND ROSTAND

Translated by Brian Hooker

Cyrano, the intellectual wit, is cruelly sensitive about his repulsive appearance, especially his "blue cucumber" of a nose. A meddler tries to insult him by deliberately referring to *Cyrano's* incredible nose.

Cyrano Ah, no, young sir!
You are too simple. Why, you might have said —
Oh, a great many things! Mon dieu, why waste
Your opportunity? For example, thus : —
Aggressive : I, sir, if that nose were mine,
I'd have it amputated — on the spot!
Friendly : How do you drink with such a nose?
You ought to have a cup made specially.
Descriptive : 'Tis a rock — a crag — a cape —
A cape? say rather, a peninsula!
Inquisitive : What is that receptacle —
A razor-case or a portfolio?
Kindly : Ah, do you love the little birds
So much that when they come and sing to you,
You give them this to perch on? *Insolent* :
Sir, when you smoke, the neighbors must suppose
Your chimney is on fire. *Cautious* : Take care —

* Cyrano de Bergerac, copyrighted by Henry Holt and Company. By permission.

A weight like that might make you topheavy.
Thoughtful : Somebody fetch my parasol —
Those delicate colors fade so in the sun !
Pedantic : Does not Aristophanes
Mention a mythologic monster called
Hippocampelephantocamelos ?
Surely we have here the original !
Familiar : Well, old torchlight !   Hang your hat
Over that chandelier — it hurts my eyes.
Eloquent : When it blows, the typhoon howls,
And the clouds darken.   *Dramatic* : When it bleeds —
The Red Sea !   *Enterprising* : What a sign
For some perfumer !   *Lyric* : Hark — the horn
Of Roland calls to summon Charlemagne ! —
Simple : When do they unveil the monument ?
Respectful : Sir, I recognize in you
A man of parts, a man of prominence —
Rustic : Hey ?   What ?   Call that a nose ?   Na, na —
I be no fool like what you think I be —
That there's a blue cucumber !   *Military* :
Point against cavalry !   *Practical* : Why not
A lottery with this for the grand prize ?
Or — parodying Faustus in the play —
"Was this the nose that launched a thousand ships
And burned the topless towers in Ilium ?"
These, my dear sir, are things you might have said
Had you some tinge of letters, or of wit
To color your discourse.   But wit, — not so,
You never had an atom — and of letters,
You need but three to write you down — an Ass.
Moreover, — if you had the invention, here
Before these folk to make a jest of me —
Be sure you would not then articulate
The twentieth part of half a syllable
Of the beginning !   For I say these things
Lightly enough myself, about myself,
But I allow none else to utter them.

CYRANO DE BERGERAC *

By Edmond Rostand

Translated by Brian Hooker

Cyrano — poet, fighter, intellectual wit, is in love with *Roxane,* as is his young, inarticulate friend, *Christian. Cyrano* promises *Christian* that he will hide beneath *Roxane's* balcony one moonlight night, and make love to her for him.

Cyrano   [*More and more overcome by emotion*]
> Let me enjoy
> The one moment I ever — my one chance
> To speak to you . . . unseen!

Roxane   Unseen? —

Cyrano   Yes! — yes. . .
> Night, making all things dimly beautiful,
> One veil over us both — You only see
> The darkness of a long cloak in the gloom,
> And I the whiteness of a summer gown —
> You were all light — I am all shadow! . . . How
> Can you know what this moment means to me?
> If I was ever eloquent —

Roxane   You were
> Eloquent —

Cyrano   — You have never heard till now
> My own heart speaking!

Roxane   Why not?

Cyrano   Until now.
> I spoke through . . .

Roxane   Yes? —

Cyrano   — through that sweet drunkenness
> You pour into the world out of your eyes!
> But to-night. . . But to-night, I indeed speak
> For the first time!

Roxane   For the first time — Your voice,
> Even, is not the same.

Cyrano   [*Passionately; moves nearer*]
>   How should it be?
> I have another voice to-night — my own,
> Myself, daring —

35

[*He stops, confused ; then tries to recover himself*]

                    Where was I ? . . . I forget ! . . .
Forgive me.   This is all sweet like a dream. . .
Strange — like a dream. . .

Roxane   How, strange ?

Cyrano   Is it not so
To be myself to you, and have no fear
Of moving you to laughter ?

Roxane   Laughter — why ?

Cyrano [*Struggling for an explanation*]
Because . . . What am I. . . What is any man,
That he dare ask for you ?   Therefore my heart
Hides behind phrases.   There's a modesty
In these things too — I come here to pluck down
Out of the sky the evening star — then smile,
And stoop to gather little flowers.

Roxane   Are they
Not sweet, those little flowers ?

Cyrano   Not enough sweet
For you and me, to-night !

Roxane   [*Breathless*]
              You never spoke
To me like this. . .

Cyrano   Little things, pretty things —
Arrows and hearts and torches — roses red,
And violets blue — are these all ?   Come away,
And breathe fresh air !   Must we keep on and on
Sipping stale honey out of tiny cups
Decorated with golden tracery,
Drop by drop, all day long ?   We are alive ;
We thirst — Come away, plunge, and drink, and drown
In the great river flowing to the sea !

Roxane But . . . Poetry ?

Cyrano   I have made rimes for you —
Not now —   Shall we insult nature, this night,
These flowers, this moment — shall we set all these
To phrases from a letter by Voiture ?
Look once at the high stars that shine in heaven,
And put off artificiality !
Have you not seen great gaudy hothouse flowers,

Barren, without fragrance ? — Souls are like that :
Forced to show all, they soon become all show —
The means to Nature's end ends meaningless !

Roxane   But . . . Poetry ?
Cyrano   Love hates that game of words !
It is a crime to fence with life — I tell you,
There comes one moment, once — and God help those
Who pass that moment by ! — when Beauty stands
Looking into the soul with grave, sweet eyes
That sicken at pretty words !

Roxane   If that be true —
And when that moment comes to you and me —
What words will you ? . . .

Cyrano   All those, all those, all those
That blossom in my heart, I'll fling to you —
Armfuls of loose bloom !   Love, I love beyond
Breath, beyond reason, beyond love's own power
Of loving !   Your name is like a golden bell
Hung in my heart ; and when I think of you,
I tremble, and the bell swings and rings —
                              Roxane ! . . .
Roxane ! . . . along my veins, *Roxane !* . . .
                                   I know
All small forgotten things that once meant You —
I remember last year, the First of May,
A little before noon, you had your hair
Drawn low, that one time only.   Is that strange ?
You know how, after looking at the sun,
One sees red suns everywhere — so, for hours
After the flood of sunshine that you are,
My eyes are blinded by your burning hair !

Roxane   [*Very low*]
                    Yes . . . that is . . . Love —
Cyrano   Yes, that is Love — that wind
Of terrible and jealous beauty, blowing
Over me — that dark fire, that music. . .
                              Yet
Love seeketh not his own !   Dear, you may take
My happiness to make you happier,
Even though you never know I gave it you —
Only let me hear sometimes, all alone,

The distant laughter of your joy! . . .
                              I never
Look at you, but there's some new virtue born
In me, some new courage.   Do you begin to
Understand, a little?   Can you feel
My soul, there in the darkness, breathe on you?
— Oh, but to-night, now, I dare say these things —
I . . . to you . . . and you hear them! . . . It is too much!
In my most sweet unreasonable dreams,
I have not hoped for this!   Now let me die,
Having lived.   It is my voice, mine, my own,
That makes you tremble there in the green gloom
Above me — for you do tremble, as a blossom
Among the leaves — You tremble, and I can feel,
All the way down along these jasmine branches,
Whether you will or no, the passion of you
Trembling. . .
         [*He kisses wildly the end of a drooping spray of
         jasmine*]

Roxane   Yes, I do tremble . . . and I weep. . .
And I love you . . . and I am yours . . . and you
Have made me thus!

CYRANO DE BERGERAC*

By EDMOND ROSTAND

Translated by Brian Hooker

Cyrano — old, wounded, and dying, talking deliriously to the once
beautiful *Roxane* who is now a nun in the Park of the Convent,
occupied by the "Ladies of the Cross."

Cyrano   Yes — that has been my life.
Do you remember that night Christian spoke
Under your window?   It was always so!
While I stood in the darkness underneath,
Others climbed up to win the applause — the kiss! —
Well — that seems only justice — I still say,
Even now, on the threshold of my tomb —
"Molière has genius — Christian had good looks —"
         [*The chapel bell is ringing.   Along the avenue of
         trees above the stairway, the Nuns pass in pro-
         cession to their prayers*]

They are going to pray now ; there is the bell.

Roxane   *[Raises herself and calls to them]*
Sister ! — Sister ! —

Cyrano   *[Holding on to her hand]*
No, — do not go away —
I may not still be here when you return. . .
*[The Nuns have gone into the chapel. The organ
   begins to play]*
A little harmony is all I need —
Listen. . .

Roxane   You shall not die ! I love you ! —

Cyrano   No—
That is not in the story ! You remember
When Beauty said "I love you" to the Beast
That was a fairy prince, his ugliness
Changed and dissolved, like magic. . . But you see
I am still the same.

Roxane   And I — I have done
This to you ! All my fault — mine !

Cyrano   You ? Why, no,
On the contrary ! I had never known
Womanhood and its sweetness but for you.
My mother did not love to look at me —
I never had a sister — Later on,
I feared the mistress with a mockery
Behind her smile. But you — because of you
I have had one friend not quite all a friend —
Across my life, one whispering silken gown ! . . .
      *   *   *
[More and more delirious]
"Very well,
But what the devil was he doing there ?
What the devil was he doing there, up there ?" . . .
  [He declaims]
Philosopher and scientist,
Poet, musician, duellist —
  He flew high, and fell back again !
A pretty wit — whose like we lack —
A lover . . . not like other men . . .
  Here lies Hercule — Savinion
De Cyrano de Bergerac —
  Who was all things — and all in vain !

Well, I must go — pardon — I cannot stay !
My moonbeam comes to carry me away. . .
   [*He falls back into the chair, half fainting. The
      sobbing of Roxane recalls him to reality. Grad-
      ually his mind comes back to him. He looks at
      her, stroking the veil that hides her hair*]
I would not have you mourn any the less
That good, brave, noble Christian ; but perhaps —
I ask you only this — when the great cold
Gathers around my bones, that you may give
A double meaning to your widow's weeds
And the tears you let fall for him may be
For a little — my tears. . .

Roxane   [*Sobbing*]   Oh, my love ! . . .
Cyrano   [*Suddenly shaken as with a fever fit, he raises him-
              self erect and pushes her away*]
— Not here ! —
Not lying down ! . . .
       [*They spring forward to help him ; he motions
          them back*]
Let no one help me — no one ! —
Only the tree. . .
       [*He sets his back against the trunk. Pause*]
                            It is coming . . . I feel
Already shod with marble . . . gloved with lead. . .
       [*Joyously*]
Let the old fellow come now !   He shall find me
On my feet — sword in hand —
       [*Draws his sword*]
Le Bret   Cyrano ! —
Roxane   [*Half fainting*]
                                 Oh,
Cyrano !
Cyrano   I can see him there — he grins —
He is looking at my nose — that skeleton
— What's that you say ? Hopeless ? — Why, very
well ! —
But a man does not fight merely to win !
No — no — better to know one fights in vain ! . . .
You there — Who are you ?   A hundred against one —
I know them now, my ancient enemies —
       [*He lunges at the empty air*]

Falsehood ! . . . There ! There ! Prejudice —
Compromise — Cowardice —
    [*Thrusting*]
                    What's that ? No ! Surrender ? No !
Never — never ! . . .
                        Ah, you too, Vanity !
I knew you would overthrow me in the end —
No ! I fight on ! I fight on ! I fight on !
    [*He swings the blade in great circles, then pauses,
        gasping. When he speaks again, it is another
        tone*]
Yes, all my laurels you have riven away
And all my roses ; yet in spite of you,
There is one crown I bear away with me,
And to-night, when I enter before God,
My salute shall sweep all the stars away
From the blue threshold ! One thing without stain,
Unspotted from the world, in spite of doom
Mine own ! —
    [*He springs forward, his sword aloft*]
And that is . . .
        [*The sword escapes his hand ; he totters, and falls
            into the arms of Le Bret and Ragueneau*]
Roxane   [*Bends over him and kisses him on the forehead*]
                    — That is . . .
Cyrano   [*Opens his eyes and smiles up at her*]
                        My white plume. . .

PATRIE *

By VICTORIEN SARDOU

Translated by Barrett H. Clarke

In betraying her husband, *Rysoor*, and his cause to the *Duke*,
Dolorès unwittingly deceives her lover *Karloo*. As reward for her
betrayal, the *Duke* gives her two passports out of the country and
her husband and his revolutionists are put to death. *Dolorès* and
Karloo are about to leave the country when he discovers that she
was the woman who had betrayed his cause.

Karloo [*Sobbing, as he steps back from the window*] You
are right, Dolorès, this is ghastly. They are now standing on the

---

* Patrie, reprinted through the courtesy of B. H. Clarke. From "Plays for College Theatres" by Garrett H. Leverton.

faggot heap ! Bakkerzeel — and poor Galèna ! My friends. Oh, I can't look ! I can't. Take me away ! [*He staggers down as far as the table*]

Dolorès [*Triumphantly, as she runs to open the garden door*] At last !

Karloo [*Worn out, leans upon the table, and says in a whisper, his eyes are always turned toward the* Place] Let us leave this house — this city.

Dolorès [*Returning to him — also in a whisper*] Yes — both of us !

Karloo [*With the table still between them*] Together.

Dolorès Together — yes — now, come.

Karloo But can we leave the city ?

Dolorès You have your passport ?

Karloo Yes, but you ?

Dolorès I have mine.

Karloo [*Trembling, as he still clutches the edge of the table. He turns suddenly toward her*] Yours ?

Dolorès Like yours — to Lille.

Karloo To Lille ?

Dolorès Yes.

Karloo You ?

Dolorès I am telling you ! Come, now.

Karloo [*Looking wildly at her*] How did you get it ?

Dolorès I went to the Palace for it.

Karloo This morning ?

Dolorès Yes.

Karloo [*Stepping back, thunderstruck*] Great God ! how horrible !

Dolorès What *is* the matter ?

Karloo That woman — at the Duke's — this morning ! That woman — at the Duke's — last night !

Dolorès Last night ?

Karloo It is she.

Dolorès No !

Karloo It's you. It's you ! You have betrayed us ! You miserable ———— ! Dare you deny that you are the one ?

Dolorès   Ah, Karloo!

Karloo   Leave me — don't touch me!   [*He disengages himself and darts toward the right, where he falls into a chair*]

Dolorès   Pity me.

Karloo   God's vengeance!   And I have been looking for her! And here she is.   Who else?

Dolorès   [*Who has fallen to the floor*]   Ah, Karloo!   Don't curse me!   Let the others do that — not you.

Karloo   Fiend — traitress — coward — coward!

Dolorès   [*On her knees, making her way toward him*]   You don't know all, my Karloo.   He wanted to kill you.   When he left me he said : "I am going to kill him!"   I was mad with terror — stark mad — Karloo!   I swear I was raving mad!   I only tried to save you — I loved you so much!   It was for your sake, for you!

Karloo   [*Taking her hands in his*]   Your love.   Your love has made me a perjurer and a traitor!   Your fatal love has brought these poor wretches to the scaffold, and a whole nation to its ruin!   Your love is hellish, deadly!   I *do* curse you!   I execrate, I hate you!   [*He casts her to the floor*]

Dolorès   Ah, Karloo, you are killing me!

Karloo   No, not yet!

Dolorès   What are you going to do?

Karloo   [*Dragging her to the window*]   Come here, Madam! First, look at your work.

Dolorès   Pity me!   [*The windows are red with the reflected light of the faggots.   Screams and murmurs of horror are heard from the Place*]

Karloo   Look at it!   Look at your faggot heap — it's burning!

Dolorès   Pity me!

Karloo   Look — count your victims!

Dolorès   Karloo — ungrateful —

Karloo   [*Raising her and forcing her to look*]   You must accustom yourself to flames — you must have some notion of what hell is like — hell, where your love is dragging us!

Dolorès   Mercy!

Karloo   Listen!   They have caught sight of me!   Listen now, listen!

The Prisoners   Karloo — traitor !   Traitor !

Karloo   Do you hear ?

Dolorès   My God !

Karloo   And do you not also hear the dead man crying out :
"Remember your oath ?"

Dolorès   [*Rising in terror*]   No.   No.

Karloo   "No matter who the guilty one may be, strike, have no
mercy !"

Dolorès   Karloo, would you strike me ?

Karloo   [*Drawing the dagger*]   My oath !

Dolorès   [*Wild with terror, as she struggles to free herself*]
With your own hand — no !   You wouldn't do that !   Pity me
— I'm afraid !

Karloo   [*Losing his self-control*]   I have sworn !

Dolorès   No, no — don't — leave me !

Karloo   I have sworn, I have sworn !   [*He plunges the dagger into her*]

Dolorès   [*Falling to the floor*]   Now go — you have killed me.
And I loved you so !   I loved you so.—   [*Karloo throws his
dagger down*]

Karloo   [*Nearly out of his mind*]   I have killed you !   I !   I !

Dolorès   At least you can join me, now !   Come.

Karloo   [*Falling to his knees before her, an inanimate mass,
and covering her with kisses, while he sobs*]   I will come with
you — I am so miserable !   Dolorès, my sweetest love !   O
God !   O God !

Dolorès   Come, then.

Karloo   [*Standing*]   Wait !   I am coming !   [*He runs to the
window, stands in it, and cries out*]   Executioner — [*Excitement in the Place*] — you lack one man !   Make way for me
on your faggot heap !

Dolorès   [*Rising in order to see him*]   Ah !

Karloo   [*To Dolorès, his voice full of loving tenderness*]   You
see ?   I am coming, I am coming !   [*He goes swiftly from the
room.   Dolorès dies*]

HERNANI*

By VICTOR HUGO

Translated by Claude C. Spiker

Juan of Aragon has just regained his title and estates and has married the beautiful *Dona Sol*, who loved him when he was *Hernani*, an exile and mountain bandit.

His life is pledged to *Don Ruy Gomez, Dona Sol's* aged kinsman, who loves her too, and who comes to claim his pledge on the night of their marriage.

Doña Sol [*To Don Ruy Gomez*] It would be more fitting even, that you go snatch from the tigers their little ones than from me the one whom I love!

Do you truly know Doña Sol? For a long time through pity for your age, for your sixty years, I have been to you a daughter, gentle, innocent and timid.

But do you see these eyes moist with tears of rage?

[*She draws a dagger from her bosom*]

Do you see this dagger? —

Ah! Mad old man, do you fear not the steel blade when the eye has threatened?

Take care, Don Ruy! — I am of your lineage, my uncle! — Listen to me. Were I your daughter, misfortune be to you if you laid hands on my husband! [*She throws away the dagger, and falls on her knees before the Duke*] Ah! I fall at your feet! Have pity on us! Mercy! alas! my lord, I am only a woman. I am weak. My strength evaporates within my soul. I give way easily! I fall at your knees! Ah! I beg you, have pity on us!

Don Ruy Gomez Doña Sol!

Doña Sol Pardon! We Spanish women, you know that sorrow drives us to the use of sharp words. Alas! You were not wicked! Pity! You kill me, my uncle, when you touch him. Oh have pity! I love him so much!

Don Ruy Gomez [*Gloomy*] You love him too much!

Hernani You are weeping.

Doña Sol No, no, I am not willing, my love, that you die! No, I am not willing!

* Hernani, translated for the author by Claude C. Spiker.

45

[*To Don Ruy*]
Pardon to-day!
I shall love you well also.

Don Ruy Gomez   After him! with these remnants of love, with friendship, — less still, do you believe that you appease the thirst which devours me?   [*Designating Hernani*]   He is alone, he is all in your love!   But I receive only your compassion!   What can I do with your friendship?   O rage!   He would have your heart, your love, and the throne.   And he would permit me one of your glances as alms to a beggar!   And if my mad love still demands a word, it is he who will bid you: "Say that, that and no more!" while he curses in subdued voice the thirsty beggar to whom one feels obliged to offer the dregs from a glass already drained!   Shame!   Derision!   No!   It must be finished. Drink.

Hernani   He has my word, and I must keep it.

Don Ruy Gomez   Come!   [*Hernani raises the vial toward his lips.   Doña Sol seizes his arm*]

Doña Sol   Oh!   Not yet!
Both of you deign to hear me.

Don Ruy Gomez   The sépulcher is open, and I cannot wait.

Doña Sol   One moment! — my Lord!   My Don Juan! — Ah!   You are both very cruel!   What is it I am asking?   One moment, that is all, all that I request!   Finally, that a poor woman be permitted to say what she has on her heart! . . . Oh!   Let me speak!

Don Ruy Gomez   [*To Hernani*]   I am in haste.

Doña Sol   My lords, you make me tremble!   What have I done to you?

Hernani   Ah!   Her cry rends my soul.

Doña Sol   [*Still holding him by the arm*]   Don't you see that I have a thousand things to say!

Don Ruy Gomez   [*To Hernani*]   It is necessary to die.

Doña Sol   [*Still clinging to Hernani's arm*]   Don Juan, after I have spoken, all that you may wish, you may then do it. [*She snatches from him the vial*]   I have it!   [*She holds the vial up before the eyes of Hernani and the astonished old man*]

Don Ruy Gomez   Since I have here to deal with only two women, Don Juan, it is necessary that I seek elsewhere worthy souls. You swear fine oaths on the blood of your fathers, and I go to speak to your father about it in the realm of the dead!— Farewell. [*He takes a few steps as if to leave when Hernani detains him*]

Hernani Duke, stop! [*To Doña Sol*]
Alas! I entreat you, do you wish to see me a falsifier, a perjurer, a felon? Do you wish that wherever I go I bear the brand of treason on my forehead? For pity, that poison, give it back to me! In the name of love, in the name of our immortal souls, I beg you!

Doña Sol [*Gloomy*] You wish? [*She drinks from the vial*] Take it now.

Don Ruy Gomez [*Aside*] Ah! It was for her then!

Doña Sol [*Returning to Hernani the half-empty vial*] Take it, I say.

Hernani [*To Don Ruy*] There you see, wretched old man!

Doña Sol Don't blame me, I have left you your share.

Hernani [*Taking the vial*] God!

Doña Sol You would not have left me my share.
You do not have the heart of a Christian wife.
You are incapable of loving as a Silva loves.
But I have drunk first and I am tranquil.
Go! Drink if you wish!

Hernani Alas! What have you done, unfortunate one?

Doña Sol It is you who wished it.

Hernani It is a terrible death!

Doña Sol No, why so?

Hernani This philtre leads to the tomb.

Doña Sol Were we not to have slept together tonight?
What matters in what bed?

Hernani My father, you are wreaking vengeance on me for forgetting you? [*He raises the vial to his lips*]

Doña Sol [*Throwing herself on him*] Heavens! what strange suffering! Ah! Throw this philtre far from you! My reason wanders. Stop! Alas! My Don Juan, this poison is strong. It hatches in the heart a thousand-toothed hydra which gnaws and devours! Ah! I did not know that one could suffer so! What is that? It's fire. Do not drink! Oh! you will suffer too much!

Doña Sol   What are you doing?

Hernani   What have you done?

Doña Sol   Come, O my young lover, into my arms.   [*They sit down close beside each other*]   Does one not suffer horribly?

Hernani   No.

Doña Sol   Behold, our wedding night has begun!   I am very pale, am I not, for a bride?

Hernani   Ah!

Don Ruy Gomez   Inexorable destiny accomplishes its end.

Hernani   Despair!   Oh!   What   torment!   Doña   Sol   to suffer, and me to behold it!

Doña Sol   Calm yourself.   I am better.   Presently we will fly away together ascending into brighter realms.   Let us depart on even wing toward a better world.   Only a kiss, a kiss! [*They kiss*]

Don Ruy Gomez   O sorrow!

Hernani   [*In a weak voice*]   Oh!   Blessed be heaven which has given to me a life surrounded by abysses and pursued by spectres, but which permits that, worn and weary on its rough road, I can fall asleep, my lips pressed against your hand!

Don Ruy Gomez   How happy they are!

Hernani   [*In a voice more and more feeble*]   Come, come — Doña Sol — it is growing dark.   Are you suffering?

Doña Sol   [*In voice equally faint*]   I suffer no more.

Hernani   Do you see fires among the shadows?

Doña Sol   Not yet.

Hernani   See. . . [*He falls*]

Don Ruy Gomez   [*Lifting the head of Hernani, which falls back again*]   Dead!

Doña Sol   [*Disheveled, and half rising to a sitting position*] Dead!   No!   Only sleeping.   He sleeps.   He is my husband, you see, we love each other.   We are sleeping here.   It is our wedding night.   [*In a dying voice*]   Do not wake him, Sir Duke of Mendoza.   He is weary.   [*She turns her face towards Hernani*]   My love, turn your face towards me.   Nearer . . . nearer still. . . [*She falls back again*]

Don Ruy Gomez   She is dead!   Oh I am damned.   [*He kills himself*]

SPANISH SELECTIONS

LA MALQUERIDA*

By JACINTO BENAVENTE

Translated by John Garrett Underhill

Acacia is engaged to *Faustino*, who is mysteriously shot. Her cousin *Norbert*, to whom she was formerly engaged, is accused and tried, but is acquitted. Later, *Acacia's* step-father confesses to having instigated the murder because of his own love for her, though she has always hated him violently. His wife, *Raimunda*, *Acacia's* mother, resolves to stand by him, and they are discussing plans for his exoneration. "*Acacia* can go to the nuns for a few days at Encinar, then to *Andrada* and live with her *Aunt Eugenia*. She might marry, who knows?"

Acacia I heard what you said. You want to send me to the convent at Encinar and shut me up, I suppose, for the rest of my life.

Raimunda How can you say such a thing? Didn't you tell me yourself that you wanted to go there and stay for a few days with the nuns? Didn't I refuse to let you go for fear that you would never come back, if you once saw the inside of the cloister? How often have you begged me to let you go to your Aunt Eugenia? Now, when it would be a good thing for us all, for the good of the family, which is your family — I tell you that we must hold our heads high — now what do you want me to do? Do you expect me to give up my husband — the man it was your duty to love as a father?

Acacia You are as bad as Juliana. I suppose it was all my fault?

Raimunda I don't say that. But he never looked on you as a daughter, because you were never a daughter to him.

Acacia I suppose I flaunted myself in his face? I suppose I made him kill Faustino?

Raimunda Not so loud! Somebody might hear!

Acacia Well, this time you won't find it so easy to have your

way. You want to save this man and hush it up, but I am
going to tell what I know to the judge — to everybody. I have
only my honor to think of, not that of a man who hasn't any,
who never had any — who is a criminal!

Raimunda Silence! Not so loud! It freezes my heart to
hear you. You hate him — and I had almost forgiven him!

Acacia Yes, I do hate him. I always did hate him, and he
knows it. If he doesn't want me to speak, to denounce him,
let him kill me. I can die — that is what I can do — die. Let
him kill me! Then, perhaps, once for all, you might learn to
hate him.

Raimunda Hush, I say! — Here he comes. [*Esteban enters*]
Esteban!

Esteban She is right. She is not the one who ought to go.
Only I don't want her to give me up. I will do it myself. I
am strong now. I will go out on the road to meet them. Let
me go, Raimunda. You have your child. You forgive me, but
she never will. She hated me from the beginning.

Raimunda No, Esteban, don't you go! Esteban, my life!

Esteban No, let me go, or I will call Norbert's father. I will
tell him. . .

Raimunda [*To Acacia*] Now you see what you have done.
It was your fault. Esteban! Esteban!

Acacia Mother, don't let him go!

Raimunda Ah!

Esteban No, she wants to betray me. Why did you hate me
like this? You never once called me father. You don't know
how I loved you!

Acacia Mother, mother —

Esteban *La Malquerida!* The Passion Flower! I hang my
head. But once — once how I could have loved you!

Raimunda For once, call him father.

Esteban She will never forgive me.

Raimunda But she must! Throw your arms about his neck.
Call him father. Even the dead will forgive us then, and be
happy in our happiness.

Esteban Daughter!

Acacia Esteban! . . . My God! Esteban!

Esteban Ah!

Raimunda But you don't call him father. Has she fainted? Ah! Lip to lip, and you clutch her in your arms! Let go, let go! Now I see why you won't call him father. Now I see that it was your fault . . . and I curse you!

Acacia Yes, it was. Kill me! It is true, it is true! He is the only man I ever loved.

Esteban Ah!

Raimunda What do you say? What is that? I will kill you — yes, and be damned with it!

Esteban Stand back!

Acacia Save me!

Esteban Stand back, I say!

Raimunda Ah! Now I see! It is plain to me now. And it is just as well! What is one murder to me? We can all die. Here! Come, everybody! The murderer! I have the murderer! Take this wicked woman, for she is not my child!

Acacia Run! Get away!

Esteban Yes, together — to hell! For I am damned for love of you. Come! They can hunt us like wild beasts among the rocks. To love you and hold you, I will be as the wild beasts, that know neither father nor mother!

Raimunda Help! Help! Come quick! The murderer! The murderer!

[*Rubio, Bernabé and Juliana appear simultaneously at different doors, followed by others from the village*]

Esteban Out of my way! Take care who crosses me!

Raimunda Stay where you are! The murderer!

Esteban Out of my way, I tell you!

Raimunda Over my dead body!

Esteban Yes — [*Raising his gun, he shoots Raimunda*]

Raimunda Ah!

Juliana God in heaven! — Raimunda!

Rubio What have you done?

A Man Kill him!

Esteban Yes, kill me! I don't defend myself.

Bernabé No! Put the law on him!

Juliana It was this man, this wretched man! Raimunda!— He has killed her—Raimunda! Don't you hear?

Raimunda Yes, Juliana. Don't let me die without confession. I am dying now. This blood. . . No matter—Acacia! Acacia!

Juliana Acacia!—Where is she?

Acacia Mother, mother!

Raimunda Ah, then, you are not crying for him? It consoles me.

Acacia No, mother! You are my mother!

Juliana She is dying! Quick—Raimunda!

Acacia Mother, mother.

Raimunda This man cannot harm you now. You are saved. Blessed be the blood that saves, the blood of our Lord Jesus Christ!

KINGDOM OF GOD *

By G. Martinez Sierra

Translated by Helen G. Barker and H. G. Barker

Hungry and depressed, the boys and girls of the Orphanage have revolted against the injustice of the world. *Sister Gracia*, "an old lady of seventy," supported by a stick, comes on the scene. She persuades them that their problem can't be solved by seeking vengeance on those who have plenty.

Sister Gracia Ah, no, no . . . all that can be done for this wicked world is to help make it good.

Felipe And who's going to?

Sister Gracia You . . . you . . . not by hating but through love. Yes, all of you will help do that. For, when you are men . . . and go away from here, it will be because you have suffered from injustice that you'll know how to make . . . and want to make . . . laws that are just. Oh yes, my sons, yes . . . the world is yours . . . for you have won it by hunger and by suffering and pain. So when you hold it in your hands, make it what it ought to be. God is watching you . . . his hopes are all in you. You suffer now that you may succour his

---

* Taken from *Kingdom of God,* by G. Martinez Sierra. Published and copyrighted by E. P. Dutton and Co., Inc., New York.

world then. God sees you. . . God hears you. Now say with
me. Lord, Lord, we thank thee for this food which is given
us in thy name. There is not much of it, it is not very good,
and we will not forget the taste of this bitter bread. And by
thy precious love we swear that thy children on this earth shall
eat of it no more . . . say it with me . . . say it. . . [*The
boys repeat after her solemnly and quietly*]

Sister Gracia Jesus, Son of God . . . Christ, son of man, by
the divine blood that thou didst shed for us we swear to spend
our own to the last drop when we are men . . . that children
may not be forsaken any more . . . that no more mothers may
be wronged and go hungry and be ashamed to carry their children in their arms. My sons . . . my sons, promise me that
when you are men you'll try to bring these things to pass . . .
that you'll help to build on earth the Kingdom of God. [*Very
quietly, very solemnly, they murmur "Yes"*]

Sister Gracia Thank you, my children . . . thank you. And
now . . . supper's over . . . go to bed and sleep in peace.
[*The boys go slowly out. Only Felipe does not move. He is
sitting on his bench, head buried in his arms, and crying. Sister
Gracia goes to him and puts a hand upon his shoulder*]

Sister Gracia Don't cry . . . for men don't cry, you know.
And they don't complain. They suffer . . . but they work
and hope.

A SUNNY MORNING*

By SERAFIN AND JOAQUIN ALVAREZ QUINTERO
Translated by Robert Ashburn

The scene is "laid in a retired part of a park in Madrid, Spain . . .
on a sunny morning in Autumn. *Doña Laura,* handsome lady of
about 70, with white hair and very refined appearance", is seated
on a bench throwing bread crumbs to the birds, which flock
around her, when *Don Gonzalo,* a gouty old gentleman, leaning
upon the arm of his servant, appears for the second time, scaring
away her little friends.

Don Gonzalo Hang it ! [*Looking everywhere perplexed*]
This cursed city administration, that doesn't provide more
benches for these sunny mornings ! Never mind ! I'll have to

* Translated for the author by Robert Ashburn.

be content with that of the old woman. [*Grumbling, he sits at the opposite end of the bench from Doña Laura, and looks at her indignantly*] Good morning.

Doña Laura   Hello! You here?

Don G.   I insist that we are not acquainted.

Doña Laura   Since you greet me, I answer you.

Don G.   To "Good morning", one answers "Good morning", and that is what you should have done.

Doña Laura   Also you should have asked my permission to sit on this bench, which is mine.

Don G.   Here the benches don't belong to anybody.

Doña Laura   Well, you said that the one the priests occupied was yours.

Don G.   All right, all right, all right. . . That's enough. [*Between his teeth*] The old simpleton. She ought to be knitting.

Doña Laura   Don't grumble, for I am not going away.

Don G.   [*Dusting his shoes with his handkerchief*] If they would sprinkle a little more, it wouldn't be so bad.

Doña Laura   What an idea! To dust one's shoes with a handkerchief!

Don G.   Eh?

Doña Laura   Do you blow your nose with the shoe brush?

Don G.   Eh? But, Madam, what right have you to . . . ?

Doña Laura   That of a neighbor.

Don G.   [*Taking heroic means*] Come, Johnny. Give me the book. I don't care to hear more foolishness.

Doña Laura   You are very kind.

Don G.   If you weren't so meddlesome . . .

Doña Laura   I have the fault of saying everything that I think.

Don G.   And that of talking more than is proper. Give me the book, Johnny.

Johnny   Here it is, sir. [*He takes from his pocket a book and gives it to him. Walking, then, towards the rear, he withdraws and disappears*]

Don G.   [*Looking at Doña Laura with irritation, he puts on some prehistoric spectacles, takes out a large reading glass and with the aid of all this glassware he prepares to read*]

Doña Laura I thought that you were going to get out a telescope also.

Don G. The idea!

Doña Laura You must have very good eyesight.

Don G. About four times as good as yours.

Doña Laura Of course, of course.

Don G. Some rabbits and some quail can testify to it.

Doña Laura Are you a hunter?

Don G. I have been. And still . . . still . . . still . . .

Doña Laura Oh, yes?

Don G. Yes, ma'am. Every Sunday, see? I take my shotgun and my dog, see? and I go to one of my farms, near Aracava . . . to kill time, see?

Doña Laura Yes. If you didn't kill time, you wouldn't kill anything.

Don G. You think not? I could show you the head of a wild boar that I have in my office.

Doña Laura Indeed! And I could show you the skin of a tiger that I have in my living room. What an argument!

Don G. All right, Madam. Let me read. I don't care to talk with you any longer.

Doña Laura Well, being silent suits your temperament better.

Don G. First I am going to take a sniff. [*He takes out a box of snuff*] [*Aside*] I'll give her some of this. Will you have some?

Doña Laura That depends. Is it good?

Don G. There isn't any better. You will like it.

Doña Laura It relieves my head a lot.

Don G. Mine, too.

Doña Laura Do you sneeze?

Don G. Yes, ma'am, three times.

Doña Laura And I three, too. What a coincidence! [*After each one takes his sniff, they await the sneezes, making faces, and then they sneeze alternately*]

Doña Laura Kachoo!

Don G. Kachoo!

Doña Laura Kachoo!

Don G. Kachoo!

Doña Laura Kachoo!

Don G. Kachoo!

Doña Laura Heaven help us!

Don G. Thank you. May it do you good.

Doña Laura The same to you. [*The snuff has reconciled them*]

Don G. Now you will excuse me for reading aloud.

Doña Laura Read any way you like. It doesn't bother me.

Don G. [*Reading*]

> "Everything in love is sad;
> But sad and all, it is the best thing that exists."

From Campoamor. It is from Campoamor.

Doña Laura Ah!

Don G. [*Reading*] "The daughters of the mothers that I loved so much, kiss me now as one kisses a saint!"
These are *humoradas*.

Doña Laura Humoradas, yes.

Don G. I prefer the *doloras*.

Doña Laura And I, also.

Don G. There are some of them also in this volume. [*He seeks the* doloras *and reads*] Listen to this one:
"Twenty years pass: he returns. . ."

Doña Laura I can't stand to see you read with so much glassware. . . .

Don G. But, perhaps you can read without glasses?

Doña Laura Of course!

Don G. At your age? I take the liberty of doubting it.

Doña Laura Give me the book. [*She takes it from the hand of Don Gonzalo and reads*]

> "Twenty years pass: he returns,
> And on seeing each other he and she exclaim:
> (Goodness! Is this he?)
> (Heavens! Is this she?)"
>   [*She returns the book to him*]

Don G. In truth, you have enviable eyesight.

Doña Laura [*Aside*] I knew the verses from memory.

ITALIAN SELECTIONS

FRANCESCA DA RIMINI*

By GABRIELE D'ANNUNZIO

Translated by Arthur Symons

The beautiful *Francesca* is unhappily married to *Giovanni*, "The Lame." She is in love with *Paolo*, "The Beautiful," brother of her husband. *Malatestino*, "The One-eyed," the third brother, is cruel, brutal, malicious, and suspicious. He tells *Giovanni* about the love affair between *Paolo* and *Francesca*. *Giovanni*, in order to prove the accusation, leads the lovers to believe that he is going on a journey, but returns unexpectedly the same night.

Paolo [*Voice heard*]
  Francesca! [*She flings the door open vehemently. With a craving as of thirst she throws herself into the arms of her lover*]

Francesca
  Paolo! Paolo! [*He is dressed as at Vespers; his head is bare*]

Paolo
  Life of my life, never was my desire
  So ardent for you. In my heart I felt
  A dying down
  Of the bright spirits that live within your eyes.
  My forces ebbed away into the night,
  Out of my breast, a flood
  Terrible, clangorous,
  And fear took hold upon my soul, as when
  In that sealed hour,
  You put me to the test, God witnessing,
  The test of the arrow,
  And raised me there, whither although he wills it
  No man returns by willing to return.
  Is it not morning, is it not morning yet?
  The stars have all gone down into your hair,

* Francesca da Rimini, by Gabriele D'Annunzio; translated by Arthur Symons. Copyright, 1902. Reprinted by permission of Frederick A. Stokes Company.

Scattered about the confines of the shades,
Where life may never find them !
[*He kisses her hair passionately, again and again*]

* * *

Francesca

Kiss me upon my eyes, upon my brow,
Upon my cheeks, my throat,
So . . . so . . .
Stay, and my wrists, my fingers . . .
So . . . so . . . And take my soul and pour it out,
Because the breath of the night
Turns back my soul again
To things of long ago,
And the low voices of the night turn back
My soul to things that were,
And joys enjoyed are they that now weigh down
My heart, and as you were
I see you still, and not as you shall be,
My fair friend, my sweet friend.

Paolo

I will carry you where all things are forgot,
And no more time made slave
Is lord of our desire.
Then shall the day and night
Be mingled even as one
Upon the earth as upon one sole pillow ;
Then shall the hands of dawn
No more unclasp from one another's holding
The dusky arms and the white arms of them,
Nor yet untwist
The tangles of their hair and veins.

Francesca

It says
Here in the book, here where you have not read :
"We have been one life ; it were a seemly thing
That we be also one death."

Paolo

Let the book
Be closed !
[*He rises, closes the book on the reading-desk, and blows
out the taper*]

And read in it no more.   Not there
Our destiny is written, but in the stars,
That palpitate above as
Your throat palpitates,
Your wrists, your brow,
Perhaps because they were your garland once,
Your necklet when you went
Burningly through the ways of heaven ?
From what
Vineyard of earth were these grapes gathered in ?
They have the smell
Of drunkenness and honey,
They are like veins, they are swollen with delight,
Fruits of the night !   The flaming feet of Love
Shall tread them in the winepress.   Give me your mouth
Again !   Again !

> [*Francesca lies back on the cushions, forgetful of every-
> thing.   All at once, in the dead silence, a violent shock
> is heard on the door, as if some one hurled himself against
> it.   The lovers start up in terror, and rise to their feet*]

The Voice of Gianciotto
Francesca !   Open, Francesca !

> [*Francesca is petrified with terror.   Paolo looks round the
> room, putting his hand to his dagger.   He catches sight
> of the bolt of the trap-door*]

Paolo   [*In a low voice*]
Take heart, take heart, Francesca !
I will get down
By the way of the trap-door.
Go, go, and open to him.
But do not tremble.

> [*He lifts the trap-door.   The door seems to quiver at the
> repeated blows*]

The Voice of Gianciotto
Open, Francesca.   Upon your life, open !

> [*The door being opened Gianciotto, armed, and covered
> with dust, rushes furiously into the room, looking for his
> brother in every direction.   Suddenly he catches sight
> of Paolo, standing head and shoulders above the level of
> the floor, struggling to free himself from the bolt of the
> trap-door, which has caught in a corner of his cloak.*

Francesca utters a piercing cry, while Gianciotto falls upon his brother, seizing him by the hair, and forcing him to come up]

Gianciotto

So, you are caught in a trap,
Traitor! They are good to have you by the hair,
Your ringlets!

Francesca [*Rushing forward*]

Let him go!
Let him go! Me, take me!

[*The husband loosens his hold. Paolo springs up on the other side of the trap-door, and unsheathes his dagger. Gianciotto, drawing back, bares his sword, and rushes upon him with terrible force. Francesca throws herself between the two men; but as her husband has leant all his weight on the blow, and is unable to draw back, her breast is pierced by the sword, she staggers, turns on herself, towards Paolo, who lets fall his dagger, and catches her in his arms*]

Francesca [*Dying*]

Ah, Paolo!

[*Gianciotto pauses for an instant. He sees the woman clasped in the arms of her lover, who seals her expiring life with his lips. Mad with rage and sorrow, he pierces his brother's side with another deadly thrust. The two bodies sway to and fro for an instant without a sound. Then, still linked together, they fall at full length on the pavement. Gianciotto stoops in silence, bends his knee with a painful effort, and, across the other knee, breaks his blood-stained sword*]

RIGHT YOU ARE! (IF YOU THINK YOU ARE) *

By Luigi Pirandello

Translated by A. L. Darby and Josephine Molli

Who is right —
 Signora Frola, who asserts that *Ponza*, her son-in-law, is insane, because he believes that *Lina*, his first wife, and *Signora Frola's*

---

* Translated for the author by A. L. Darby and Josephine Molli.

daughter, is dead; and that *Julia*, the woman he now lives with, is his second wife?

Ponza, who just as passionately asserts the same of *Signora Frola*, because she believes *Lina* and *Julia* to be one and the same person?

The cruelly inquisitive populace, who suspect both of them of being queer?

Laudisi, who asks, "What can we really know about other people — who they are — what they are — what they are doing, or why they are doing it?"

Or all of them?

Ponza [*Approaching Agazzi, in great agitation*] In the name of God, is it she? Is *she* playing?

Agazzi Yes, your mother-in-law! And how well she plays!

Ponza But how is this? They have brought her here again? And they make her play?

Agazzi I do not see what harm there can be in that!

Ponza Why, no, indeed! That music, no! It is what her daughter played!

Agazzi Ah, perhaps it makes you feel badly to hear her play?

Ponza Oh, not I! It hurts her! A hurt you can't realize! I have even told you, signor Councilor, and the other women the condition of that poor unfortunate —

Agazzi [*Trying to calm his ever increasing agitation*] Yes, yes . . . but see . . .

Ponza [*Continuing*] that she ought to be left alone! that she is not able to receive visits nor to make any. I, alone, know, I, alone, know how one ought to deal with her. They are ruining her! They are ruining her!

Agazzi But no, why? The ladies of my family know well even they . . . [*Interrupting himself suddenly, at the ceasing of the music in the drawing-room from which comes now a chorus of applause*] There, look . . . you can listen. . . [*From the other room comes, distinctly, this following conversation*]

Dina But you still play very well, Signora!

Signora Frola I? Ah, my Lina! You should hear my Lina, how she plays!

Ponza [*Quivering, digging his nails into his hands*] Her Lina! Do you hear? She says her Lina!

Agazzi Ah, of course, her daughter.

Ponza But she says, "she plays!" she says, "she plays!" [*Again from the other room, distinctly*]

Signora Frola Oh no, she can play no more from that time on! And, perhaps, that is her greatest sorrow, poor child!

Agazzi It seems natural to me. . . She believes her yet alive. . .

Ponza But she ought not to talk in that fashion! She ought not . . . she ought not to say it. . . Did you hear? "From that time on" . . . she said, "from that time on!" She means that piano, certainly. She does not know! She means the piano of the poor dead one! [*At this point, Sirelli comes in, who, hearing the last words of Ponza and noting the extreme exasperation, stops, amazed. Agazzi, also dismayed, motions him to approach*]

Agazzi I pray you, have the women come in here. [*Sirelli, keeping at a safe distance, goes to the door at the left and calls the women*]

Ponza The women? Here? No, no! Rather . . . [*The women, at the sign of Sirelli, full of dismay, enter alarmed. Signora Frola, observing her son-in-law in this state of excitement, all of a quiver, almost beastly, is frightened. Assailed by him with extreme violence during the scene following, she makes to the women, from time to time, with her eyes, signs expressive of understanding. The scene unfolds rapidly and is tense with excitement*]

Ponza You, here? Here again? What are you doing here?

Signora Frola I came, have patience. . .

Ponza You came here to say again . . . What did you say? What have you said to these women?

Signora Frola Nothing, I swear to you! Nothing!

Ponza Nothing? How nothing? I heard! This gentleman heard with me! [*Indicating Agazzi*] You said she plays! Who plays? Lina plays? You know well that your daughter has been dead for four years!

Signora Frola But yes, dear! Calm yourself! Yes! yes!

Ponza "And she can play no more from that time on!" Of course she is not able to play again from that time on! How do you expect her to play, if she is dead?

Signora Frola There, certainly! And did I not say so, my friends? I said so, that she can not again, from that time. If she is dead!

Ponza And why do you still think about that piano, then?

Signora Frola I? No; I do not think of it any more! I do not think of it any more!

Ponza I broke it! And you know it! When your daughter died! In order not to let this other one touch it, who, besides, does not know how to play! You know that this other one does not play.

Signora Frola But if she does not know how to play! Certainly!

Ponza And what is her name, it is Lina, is it not? Your child. Now say here what is the name of my second wife! Say it here to everybody, since you know it well! What is her name?

Signora Frola Julia! Julia is her name! Yes, yes! It is true indeed! gentlemen; her name is Julia!

Ponza Julia, then, not Lina! And don't try to wink, meanwhile, saying her name is Julia!

Signora Frola I? no! I did not wink!

Ponza I saw it! You winked! I saw it indeed! You wish to ruin me! You wish to maintain the pretence to these ladies and gentlemen that I still wish to keep your daughter all for myself, as if she were not dead. [*He breaks into frightful sobbing*] As if she were not dead!

Signora Frola [*Immediately with infinite tenderness and humbleness, hurrying towards him*] I? Oh no, no, my dear son; Calm yourself! please. I have not ever said that . . . isn't it true? Isn't it true, ladies?

Amalia, S. Sirelli, Dina Why yes! yes!— She has never said it!— She has always said that she is dead!

Signora Frola Isn't it true? I have said, she is dead! Why not? And that you are always good to me! [*To the women*] Isn't it true? Isn't it true? I, ruin you? I hurt you?

Ponza [*Rising, terrible*] But you go searching meanwhile a piano in the houses of others, in order to play tunes of your daughter, and going about saying that Lina plays them thus, and better than that!

Signora Frola   No, it was . . . I did it only . . . only in order to try . . .

Ponza   You can not! You ought not! How can it enter your mind to play what your dead daughter played?

Signora Frola   You are right, yes! Ah poor boy . . . poor boy! [*Moved, she begins to cry*] I'll never do it again! I'll never do it again!

Ponza   [*Assailing her violently, close to her*] Go! Go away! Go away!

Signora Frola   Yes . . . yes . . . I am going, I am going. . . Oh, God! [*She makes a beseeching sigh to all, stopping, to look again at her son-in-law, and retires, weeping*]

DEATH TAKES A HOLIDAY*

By ALBERTO CASELLA

Translated by Walter Ferris

Death is an unexpected guest of *Duke Lambert*. He comes to earth in the guise of *Prince Sirki,* to discover why men fear him so. He falls in love with the beautiful and sensitive *Grazia*. In the moonlight garden *Sirki* declares his love for *Grazia*.

Shadow   Why are you not with the guests? [*In a limpid, happy tone*]

Grazia   For the same reason that you're not, I think.

Shadow   You say that so simply, as though you knew.

Grazia   I do know.

Shadow   It's strange. . . We hardly need to speak, do we?

Grazia   Thoughts are so much clearer than words.

Shadow   Then perhaps you can tell me what I've been doing in the garden?

Grazia   I think I can . . . almost.

Shadow Tell me. I want to hear it from your lips. [*Grazia speaks slowly with a curious clarity and simplicity of voice*]

Grazia I think you have been holding life in your hands, as I do sometimes. . . I think you have been a little afraid of its beauty.

Shadow [*Trembling*] Ah, you do know! You wonderful, exquisite child! [*He kneels and takes her hand. Grazia seems hardly breathing as she looks up into his face*] I have been walking in the garden that was full of you, and under a sky that sang of you. . . Your laughter was in a wind that went by and touched my hair. . . I knelt by a yellow flower, and out of its heart came a sound that was your voice. . . I put my ear to the ground, and heard your footsteps moving toward me, across the world. And the earth was trembling under your little feet. . . I stood looking at the sky, and the night was illumined by the knowledge of you. . . And I was *shaken*.

Grazia [*As though from a distance*] And ever since I saw you, I have been shaken. . . Oh, what is this that has happened? Who . . . are you?

Shadow [*Trembling*] Sirki. . .

Grazia [*Shaking her head*] I don't mean that. . . You seem to come from a distant place —

Shadow I do come from far away . . . but . . .

Grazia When I'm with you I see depths in your eyes that are like the worlds I visit in sleep. . . And beneath your words there is a sound that I've heard in dreams, and sometimes when there is a storm in the mountains. . . And when you leave me the light goes from the sky. [*She gives a little shaken laugh*] You seem like the mystery that is just beyond sight and sound . . . always just beyond my reach. . . Something that draws . . . and frightens me. [*The Shadow puts his arms about her. His voice is shaken with emotion*]

Shadow Oh Grazia . . . Grazia . . . don't be afraid of me! . . . I am Sirki who loves you! . . . More than any man could love you! I am Sirki, who needs your warmth and your beauty more than any man could need them. I say your name over and over, until its music runs through all my being. . . Your hands are white jasmine flowers in the sun. [*He covers her hands with kisses. Grazia is near to fainting*] Grazia. . . Listen to me, I am a great power, and I am humble before you. . . And tonight I must go back to my . . . distant kingdom.

Grazia [*Far away*] Will you take me?

Shadow [*The impact of her words is startling. He rises as though shocked beyond speech*] Take . . . you . . .

Grazia Yes, I should be so unhappy, alone.

Shadow Take . . . you. . . [*With sudden intensity*] No . . . no! Don't tempt me! [*He lifts her and takes her in his arms*] But Grazia, give me one hour of you! Let me hold you once, and feel your life! You are the meaning of beauty that I must know. Grazia, let me hold you, and feel that last ecstasy . . . and know that I have lived!

Grazia Oh, my love, my love!

Shadow My little love! [*He kisses her, a long kiss. Then they go off slowly, his arms about her*]

RUSSIAN SELECTIONS

THE LOWER DEPTHS *

By Maxim Gorki

Translated by Edwin Hopkins

Only the old pilgrim, *Luka*, can justify the meaningless, tragic existence of the group of derelicts at *Kostilioff's* lodging-house.

Luka I am good, you say. Nyah . . . if it is true, all right. . . [*Behind the red wall is heard soft singing and accordion playing*] But you see, my girl — there must be some one to be good. . . We must have pity on mankind. Christ, remember, had pity for us all and so taught us to be likewise. Have pity when there is still time, believe me, it is very good. I was once, for example, employed as a watchman, at a country place which belonged to an engineer, not far from the city of Tomsk, in Siberia. The house stood in the middle of the forest, an out-of-the-way location . . . and it was winter and I was all alone in the country house. . . It was beautiful there . . . magnificent! And once . . . I heard them scrambling up!

Natasha Thieves!

Luka Yes. They crept higher and I took my rifle and went outside. I looked up: two men . . . as they were opening a window and so busy that they did not see anything of me at all. . . I cried to them: Heh there . . . get out of that . . . and would you think it, they fell on me with a hand ax. . . I warned them — Halt, I cried, or else I fire . . . then I aimed first at one and then at the other. They fell on their knees saying, pardon us. I was pretty hot . . . on account of the hand ax, you remember. You devils, I cried, I told you to clear out and you didn't . . . and now, I said, one of you go into the brush and get a switch. It was done: and now, I commanded, one of you stretch out on the ground, and the other thrash him . . . and so they whipped each other at my command. And when they had each had a sound beating, they said to me: Grandfather, said they, for the sake of Christ

* Reprinted by courtesy of Edwin Hopkins.

give us a piece of bread. We haven't a bite in our bodies. These, my daughter, were the thieves [*laughs*] who had fallen upon me with the hand ax. Yes . . . they were a pair of splendid fellows. . . I said to them: If only you had asked for bread! Then they answered: We had gotten past that . . . we had asked and asked and nobody would give us anything . . . endurance was worn out . . . nyah, and so they remained with me the whole winter. One of them, Stephen by name, liked to take the rifle and go into the woods . . . and the other, Jakoff, was constantly ill, always coughing . . . the three of us watched the place, and when spring came, they said farewell, grandfather, and went away — to Russia. . .

THE BEAR *

By ANTON CHEKHOV

It is seven months to the day since the death of her husband, and *Mrs. Popova* is in no mood to discuss with Lieutenant *Smirnov* the twelve hundred dollar indebtedness of her dead husband. *Smirnov*, gruff in speech and manner, demands the money in order that he may pay the interest on a debt of his own, but *Mrs. Popova* unconcernedly leaves him raging.

Smirnov Well, there! "A state of mind." . . . "Husband died seven months ago!" Must I pay the interest, or mustn't I? I ask you: Must I pay, or must I not? Suppose your husband is dead, and you've got a state of mind, and nonsense of that sort. . . And your steward's gone away somewhere, devil take him, what do you want me to do? Do you think I can fly away from my creditors in a balloon, or what? Or do you expect me to go and run my head into a brick wall? I go to Grusdev and he isn't at home, Yaroshevitch has hidden himself, I had a violent row with Kuritsin and nearly threw him out of the window, Mazugo has something the matter with his bowels, and this woman has "a state of mind." Not one of the swine wants to pay me! Just because I'm too gentle with them, because I'm a rag, just weak wax in their hands! I'm much too gentle with them! Well, just you wait! You'll find out what I'm like! I shan't let you play about with me, confound it! I shall jolly well stay here until she pays!

* Reprinted by courtesy of Charles Scribner's Sons, New York.

Brr! . . . How angry I am today, how angry I am! All my inside is quivering with anger, and I can't even breathe. . . Foo, my word, I even feel sick! [*Yells*] Waiter! [*Enter Luka*]
Luka What is it?

Smirnov Get me some kvass or water! [*Exit Luka*] What a way to reason! A man is in desperate need of his money, and she won't pay it because, you see, she is not disposed to attend to money matters! . . . That's real silly feminine logic. That's why I never did like, and don't like now, to have to talk to women. I'd rather sit on a barrel of gun-powder than talk to a woman. Brr! . . . I feel quite chilly — and it's all on account of that little bit of fluff! I can't even see one of these poetic creatures from a distance without breaking out into a cold sweat out of sheer anger. I can't look at them. [*Enter Luka with water*]

Luka Madam is ill and will see nobody.

Smirnov Get out! [*Exit Luka*] Ill and will see nobody! No, it's all right, you don't see me. . . I'm going to stay and will sit here till you give me the money. You can be ill for a week, if you like, and I'll stay here for a week. . . If you're ill for a year — I'll stay for a year. I'm going to get my own, my dear! You don't get at me with your widow's weeds and your dimpled cheeks! I know those dimples! [*Shouts through the window*] Simeon, take them out! We aren't going away at once! I'm staying here! Tell them in the stable to give the horses some oats! You fool, you've let the near horse's leg get tied up in the reins again! [*Teasingly*] "Never mind. . ." I'll give it to you. "Never mind." [*Goes away from the window*] Oh, it's bad. . . The heat's frightful, nobody pays up. I slept badly, and on top of everything else here's a bit of fluff in mourning with "a state of mind." . . . My head's aching. . . Shall I have some vodka, what? Yes, I think I will. [*Yells*] Waiter! [*Enter Luka*]

Luka What is it?

Smirnov A glass of vodka! [*Exit Luka*] Ouf! [*Sits and inspects himself*] I must say I look well! Dust all over, boots dirty, unwashed, unkempt, straw on my waistcoat. . . The dear lady may well have taken me for a brigand. [*Yawns*] It's rather impolite to come into a drawing-room in this state, but it can't be helped. . . I am not here as a visitor, but as a creditor, and there's no dress specially prescribed for creditors. . .

HE WHO GETS SLAPPED*

By Leonid Andreyev

Translated by Gregory Zilborg

The impostor *Count Mancini*, father of the beautiful bareback rider, *Consuelo*, is offering her in marriage to the *Baron Regnard* for a sum of money.

"*He*," 39, ugly — a clown, has fallen in love with *Consuelo* and is persuading her not to marry the Baron because "You'll perish — you'll die, Consuelo."

He Forget Bezano! Consuelo, do you know who can save you? The only one who can save you? — I.

Consuelo [*Laughing*] You, *He*?

He Yes, but don't laugh! Look. Here is the letter H. It is I, *He*.

Consuelo *He* Who Gets Slapped? Is that written here, too?
He That, too. The stars know everything. But look here, what more is written about him. Consuelo, welcome him. *He* is an old god in disguise, who came down to earth only to love you, foolish little Consuelo.

Consuelo [*Laughing and singing*] Some god!

He Don't mock! The gods don't like such empty laughter from beautiful lips. The gods grow lonely and die, when they are not recognized. Oh, Consuelo! Oh, great joy and love! Do recognize this god, and accept him. Think a moment, one day a god suddenly went crazy!

Consuelo Gods go crazy, too?

He Yes, when they are half man, then they often go mad. Suddenly he saw his own sublimity, and shuddered with horror, with infinite solitude, with superhuman anguish. It is terrible, when anguish touches the divine soul!

Consuelo I don't like it. What language are you speaking? I don't understand —

He I speak the language of thy awakening. Consuelo, recognize and accept thy god, who was thrown down from the summit like a stone. Accept the god who fell to the earth in order

---

* He Who Gets Slapped from *Modern Continental Plays*, by S. Marion Tucker, reprinted by permission of The Theatre Guild, Inc.

to live, to play, and to be infinitely drunk with joy. Evoë Goddess!

Consuelo [*Tortured*] He— I cannot understand. Let my hand alone.

He [*Stands up*] Sleep. Then wake again, Consuelo! And when thou wakest — remember that hour when, covered with snow-white sea-foam, thou didst emerge from the sky-blue waters. Remember Heaven, and the slow eastern wind, and the whisper of the foam at thy marble feet.

Consuelo [*Her eyes are closed*] I believe — wait — I remember. Remind me further — [*He is bowed over Consuelo, with lifted arms; he speaks slowly, but in a commanding voice, as if conjuring*]

He You see the waves playing. Remember the song of the sirens, their sorrowless song of joy. Their white bodies, shining blue through the blue waters. Or can you hear the sun, singing? Like the strings of a divine harp, spread the golden rays — Do you not see the hand of God, which gives harmony, light, and love to the world? Do not the mountains, in the blue cloud of incense, sing their hymn of glory? Remember, O Consuelo, remember the prayer of the mountains, the prayer of the sea. [*Silence*] He. [*Commandingly*] Remember — Consuelo!

Consuelo [*Opening her eyes*] No! *He,* I was feeling so happy, and suddenly I forgot it all. Yet something of it all is still in my heart. Help me again, *He,* remind me. It hurts, I hear so many voices. They all sing "Consuelo — Consuelo." What comes after? [*Silence; pause*] What comes after? It hurts. Remind me, *He.* [*Silence . . . in the ring, the music suddenly bursts forth in a tempestuous circus gallop. Silence*] He, [*Opens her eyes and smiles*] that's Alfred galloping. Do you recognize his music?

He [*With rage*] Leave the boy alone! [*Suddenly falls on his knees before Consuelo*] I love you, Consuelo, revelation of my heart, light of my nights, I love you, Consuelo. [*Looks at her in ecstasy and tears — and gets a slap; starting back*] What's this?

Consuelo A slap! You forget who you are. [*Stands up, with anger in her eyes*] You are *He* Who Gets Slapped! Did you forget it? Some god! With such a face-slapped face! Was it with slaps they threw you down from heaven, god?

He Wait! Don't stand up! I — did not finish the play!

Consuelo [*Sits*] Then you were playing?

He Wait! One minute.

Consuelo You lied to me. Why did you play so that I believed you?

He I am *He* Who Gets Slapped!

Consuelo You are not angry because I struck you? I did not want to really, but you were so — disgusting. And now you are so funny again. You have great talent, *He* — or are you drunk?

He Strike me again.

Consuelo No.

He I need it for my play. Strike!

Consuelo [*Laughs, and touches his cheek with her finger tips*] Here, then!

He Didn't you understand that you are a queen, and I a fool who is in love with his queen? Don't you know, Consuelo, that every queen has a fool, and he is always in love with her, and they always beat him for it. *He* Who Gets Slapped.

Consuelo No. I didn't know.

He Yes, every queen. Beauty has her fool. Wisdom, too. Oh, how many fools she has! Her court is overcrowded with enamoured fools, and the sound of slaps does not cease, even through the night. But I never received such a sweet slap as the one given by my little queen. [*Someone appears at the door. He notices it, and continues to play, making many faces*] Clown *He* can have no rival! Who is there who could stand such a deluge of slaps, such a hail-storm of slaps, and not get soaked? [*Feigns to cry aloud*] "Have pity on me. I am but a poor fool!"

BELGIAN SELECTIONS

THE DAWN*

By ÉMILE VERHAEREN

The enemy is upon them — the flaming town of Oppidomagne, the burning farms, the fleeing peasants all give evidence. The beggars shout with the fierce glee of vengeance against the farmers who have turned them out. The old farmer, *Ghislain*, having set the fire with his own hands, which is to destroy his all, comes upon the beggars. The beggar, *Benoit*, wishes to "strike him down." A running peasant shrieks that "the flames bite the very sky."

Old Ghislain
    Well, and what then ? and what has that to do with me ?
    Let all the plain and all the woods begone,
    And let the wind, the air and the sky burn,
    And let the earth itself break as a pebble breaks.
        [*With a change of tone*]
    Just now this beggar talked of killing me.
        [*To the beggar Benoit*]
    Well, do it, then ; be quick with you !
    Here are my hands, here are my arms, that I have sold
    For vain labour ; here too is my obstinate brain ;
    Here is my skin withered in all its pores,
    Here is my back, here are the rags of me,
    The ruin that I drag about
    All the long years, all the long years !
    Truly I ask myself, why is it that I live ?
    I dig a field the frost will reap,
    I farm the meadows that are evil-starred ;
    All that my father hoarded up, farthing by farthing, all
    That he had squeezed, and hid, and burrowed, like a miser,
    I have lost all, eaten it all.
    I have implored my sons : they have devoured me ;
    They have been swallowed up in the unfruitful town,
    They have preferred a life unfruitful, infamous ;

* Reprinted through the courtesy of Dodd, Mead and Company.
73

Hamlets and little towns are dead;
Oppidomagne has snapped the strength of them,
Oppidomagne has drained the blood of them;
And now, behold
In every acre and in every close
Branching abroad the several maladies
Of water and of earth and air and sun!

A Peasant
Your sorrows are ours. We are all equally wretched.

Old Ghislain
When I was but a child, we feasted sowing-time,
The soil was kindly then to folk and to horned beasts,
The flax came up like happiness in flower.
But now, but now men fear the earth.
And surely needs must something have been violated,
Some sacred and some obscure thing;
Now 'tis the coal that all belongs to, kept,
Once, in the covering night.
The netted rails, upon the plains bestarred
With golden signals, swarm;
Trains graze the meadow-lands, and pierce the banks;
The living skies are eaten up with piercing smoke;
The grass bleeds, and the virgin herb, harvest itself,
Feed on the sulphur's poisonous breath.
'Tis now
That, terrible in victory, come forth
Iron, and lead, and fire;
And hell itself comes forth with them!
  [*The beggars recoil, and cease to threaten*]

A Beggar
Poor man!

Old Ghislain
Poor man! But no!
  [*Drawing towards him a peasant, and pointing to an enclosure which is burning*]
You think, do you, that it was the enemy set fire to my
  enclosure? Undeceive yourselves. [*Showing his hands*]
  It was these two hands.
And my woods by "Firefly Pond"? [*Showing his hands*]
  And my granaries and my ricks? These always. No, no,
  Old Ghislain isn't a poor man. It is he, he only perhaps,

who sees clear. We don't respect our fields; we lose
patience with the slow and sure of things; we kill the
germs; we overheat them; we arrange, we reason, we con-
trive. The earth isn't a wife now; it's a kept woman!
And now, see how the enemy annihilates it!
Where it was wounded by the town,
'Tis burnt by war, the torch of war;
Where the wise man had wellnigh drained it dry,
The bullets fire it now.
Alas, alas, this is the death of it!
There is no need of rain or dewfall now,
There is no need of snow about the mountain's head,
Nor yet of sun, nor of months clear and sweet,
And it were better at one stroke
To end, ending the country side.

PELLÉAS AND MÉLISANDE *

By Maurice Maeterlinck

Translated by Charles Mitrani

Lovely, childlike *Mélisande* in her loneliness turns to *Pelléas*,
youthful brother of her husband, *Golaud*, for companionship.
Pelléas, deeply and tenderly in love with her, asks her to meet
him — "tonight, in the park, near Blind Man's Spring."

Pelléas   Yes. . . Yes. . . Long months ago.— Then, I did not
know. . . Do you know why I have asked you to come this
evening?

Mélisande   No.

Pelléas   It is perhaps the last time that I will see you. . . I must
go away for ever. . .

Mélisande   Why do you say that you go away for ever? . . .

Pelléas   I must tell you that which you know already? — You
do not know what I am going to say to you?

Mélisande   Why no, why no; I know nothing. . .

Pelléas   You do not know why I must go away. . . [*He embraces her suddenly*] I love you. . .

Mélisande   [*In a low voice*]   I love you also. . .

Pelléas   Oh! What have you said, Mélisande! . . . I have

* Translated for the author by Charles Mitrani.

almost not heard it! One has broken the ice with red-hot irons! . . . You say this in a voice which comes from the end of the world! . . . I have almost not heard you. . . You love me? — You love me too? . . . How long since you love me?

Mélisande   Always . . . since I have seen you. . .

Pelléas   Oh! how you say that! . . . one would say that your voice has passed over the sea in the springtime! . . . I have never heard it till now . . . one would say that it had rained on my heart! You say that so frankly! . . . Like an angel whom one questions! I cannot believe it, Mélisande! . . . Why would you love me? — But why do you love me? — Is what you say true? — You do not deceive me? — You do not lie a little, in order to make me smile? . . .

Mélisande   No; I never lie; I only lie to your brother. . .

Pelléas   Oh! how you say that! . . . Your voice! your voice. . . It is more cool and more clear than the water! . . . one would say pure water on my lips! One would say pure water on my hands. . . Give me, give me your hands. . . Oh! your hands are little! . . . I did not know that you were so beautiful! . . . I have never seen anything as beautiful, before you. . . I was restless, I sought everywhere in the house. . . I sought everywhere in the country. . . And I did not find beauty. . . And now I have found you! . . . I have found you! . . . I do not believe that there is on earth a more beautiful woman! . . . Where are you? — I no longer hear you breathe. . .

Mélisande   It is because I look at you. . .

Pelléas   Why do you look at me so gravely? — We are already in the shade. — It is too dark under this tree. Come in the light. We will be able to see how happy we are. Come, come; so little time remains to us. . .

Mélisande   No, no; let us remain here. . . I am closer to you, in the darkness. . .

Pelléas   Where are your eyes? — You are not going to flee from me? — You are not thinking of me at this moment.

Mélisande   Why yes, why yes, I only think of you. . .

Pelléas   You were looking elsewhere. . .

Mélisande   I saw you elsewhere. . .

Pelléas   You are absent-minded. . . What is the matter with you, then? — You do not seem happy to me. . .

Mélisande   Yes, yes ; I am happy, but I am sad. . .

Pelléas   One is sad, often, when one loves. . .

Mélisande   I weep always when I think of you. . .

Pelléas   I too . . . I too, Mélisande. . . I am close to you ; I weep for joy and yet . . . [*He embraces her again*] — You are strange when I embrace you thus. . . You are so beautiful that one would say you are going to die. . .

Mélisande   You also. . .

Pelléas   There, there. . . We do not do that which we wish. . . I did not love you the first time that I saw you. . .

Mélisande   Nor I either. . . I was afraid. . .

Pelléas   I could not look at your eyes. . . I wished to go away immediately . . . and then. . .

Mélisande   I, I did not wish to come. . . I did not yet know why, I was afraid to come. . .

Pelléas   There are so many things which one never knows. . . We wait for ever ; and then. . . What is that noise ? — One is closing the gates ! . . .

Mélisande   Yes, one has closed the gates. . .

Pelléas   We cannot reënter ! — Do you hear the bolts ! — Listen ! listen ! . . . the great chains ! It is too late, it is too late !

Mélisande   So much the better ! so much the better ! so much the better !

Pelléas   You ? . . . There it is, there it is ! . . . It is no longer we who wish it ! . . . All is lost, all is saved ! all is saved this evening ! — Come ! come ! . . . My heart beats like a madman even to the back of my throat. . . [*He clasps her*] Listen ! Listen ! my heart is on the point of choking me. . . Come ! Come ! . . . Ah ! how beautiful it is in the darkness ! . . .

Mélisande   There is someone behind us ! . . .

Pelléas   I see no one. . .

Mélisande   I have heard a noise. . .

Pelléas   I only hear your heart in the darkness. . .

Mélisande   I have heard the dead leaves crackle. . .

Pelléas   It is the wind which has become silent all at once. . . It has fallen while we were embracing. . .

Mélisande   How large our shadows are this evening ! . . .

Pelléas   They clasp each other as far as the back of the gar-

den. . . Oh! how they embrace each other far from us!
Look! Look! . . .

Mélisande [*In a stifled voice*] A-a-h —He is behind a tree!

Pelléas Who?

Mélisande Golaud!

Pelléas Golaud?—where then?—I see nothing. . .

Mélisande There at the end of our shadows. . .

Pelléas Yes, yes; I have seen him. . . Let us not turn around
suddenly. . .

Mélisande He has his sword.

Pelléas I do not have mine. . .

Mélisande He has seen that we embrace each other.

Pelléas He does not know that we have seen him. . . Do not
move; do not turn your head around. . . He will rush. . . He
will remain there as long as he believes that we do not know
it. . . He watches us. . . He is still motionless. . . Go away,
go away immediately from here. . . I will await him. . . I will
stop him. . .

Mélisande No, no, no!

Pelléas Go away! go away! He has seen all! . . . He will
kill us!

Mélisande So much the better! so much the better! so much
the better!

Pelléas He comes! he comes! . . . Your mouth . . . Your
mouth! . . .

Mélisande Yes! . . . yes! . . . yes! . . . [*They kiss each
other desperately*]

Pelléas Oh! oh! All the stars are falling! . . .

Mélisande On me also! on me also! . . .

Pelléas Again! Again! . . . give! give! . . .

Mélisande All! all! all! . . . [*Golaud rushes on them sword
in hand, and strikes Pelleas, who falls on the edge of the fountain,
Mélisande flees, frightened*]

Mélisande [*Fleeing*] Oh! oh! I have no courage! . . . I
have no courage! . . . [*Golaud pursues her across the wood, in
silence*]

THE INTRUDER *

By Maurice Maeterlinck

The *Grandfather* is aged, helpless and blind. This evening the family is gathered in a room awaiting some change in the condition of his daughter, who is critically ill. The *Grandfather* "sees" a "stranger" enter and remain in the room, but the others are not conscious of this invisible presence and try to reason with the *Grandfather*.

Grandfather   It is a very long time since I saw my daughter! . . . I took her hands yesterday evening, but I could not see her! . . . I do not know what has become of her . . . I do not know how she is. . . I do not know what her face is like now. . . She must have changed these weeks! . . . I felt the little bones of her cheeks under my hands. . . There is nothing but the darkness between her and me, and the rest of you! . . . I cannot go on living like this . . . this is not living. . . You sit there, all of you, looking with open eyes at my dead eyes, and not one of you has pity on me! . . . I do not know what ails me. . . No one tells me what ought to be told me. . . And everything is terrifying when one's dreams dwell upon it. . . But why are you not speaking?

The Uncle   What should we say, since you will not believe us?

Grandfather   You are afraid of betraying yourselves!

The Father   Come now, be rational!

Grandfather   You have been hiding something from me for a long time! . . . Something has happened in the house. . . But I am beginning to understand now. . . You have been deceiving me too long! — You fancy that I shall never know anything? — There are moments when I am less blind than you, you know! . . . Do you think I have not heard you whispering — for days and days — as if you were in the house of someone who had been hanged — I dare not say what I know this evening. . . But I shall know the truth! . . . I shall wait for you to tell me the truth ; but I have known it for a long time, in spite of you! — And now, I feel that you are all paler than the dead!

* From The Intruder by Maurice Maeterlinck. Copyright, 1895, 1923, by Dodd, Mead and Company, Inc.

The Three Daughters   Grandfather! grandfather!   What is the matter, grandfather?

Grandfather   It is not you that I am speaking of, girls.   No; it is not you that I am speaking of. . . I know quite well you would tell me the truth — if they were not by — !   And besides, I feel sure that they are deceiving you as well. . . You will see. . . Do not I hear you all sobbing?

The Father   Is my wife really so ill?

The Grandfather   It is no good trying to deceive me any longer; it is too late now, and I know the truth better than you. . .

The Uncle   But *we* are not blind; we are not.

The Father   Would you like to go into your daughter's room? This misunderstanding must be put an end to! — Would you?

Grandfather   [*Becoming suddenly undecided*]   No, no, not now — not yet.

The Uncle   You see, you are not reasonable.

Grandfather   One never knows how much a man has been unable to express in his life! . . .

THE BLUE BIRD*

By MAURICE MAETERLINCK

Translated by Warren F. Manning

Mytyl and *Tyltyl* can't sleep tonight — it is Christmas Eve. Knowing that Father Christmas will not visit them this year, they tiptoe to the window to watch the rich children across the way enjoying their Christmas tree.   A knock is heard, and an old *Fairy* comes in.

The Fairy   . . . What were you doing when I knocked?

Tyltyl   We were playing at eating cakes.

The Fairy   Have you any cakes?   Where are they?

Tyltyl   In the palace of the rich children.   Come and look, it's so beautiful!   [*He pulls the Fairy over to the window*]

The Fairy   [*At the window*]   But it's the other people who are eating them.

* Translated for the author by W. F. Manning.

Tyltyl   Yes, but we can see everything.

The Fairy   You don't begrudge them that?

Tyltyl   Why?

The Fairy   Because they're eating everything.   I think it's very wrong not to give you some.

Tyltyl   Why no, since they're rich, what? . . . How beautiful it is in that house!

The Fairy   It's no more beautiful there than in your house.

Tyltyl   Hmph, it's darker in our house, and smaller, and there are no cakes.

The Fairy   It's absolutely the same thing.   It's because you can't see.

Tyltyl   Why yes, I see very well, and I have very good eyes.   I read the time on the church clock, which papa can't see.

The Fairy   [*Suddenly getting angry*]   I tell you, you can't see!   In what light do you see me then?   How am I made then?   [*Embarrassing silence from Tyltyl*]   Well, will you answer that I may know if you see?   Am I beautiful or quite ugly?   [*The silence becomes more and more embarrassed*] Am I young or quite old?   Am I pink or yellow?   Perhaps I have a hump?

Tyltyl   [*Conciliatory*]   No, no, it's not big.

The Fairy   Why, yes, by your expression, one would think it enormous.   Have I a hooked nose?   Is my left eye caved in?

Tyltyl   No, no, I don't say that.   Who would cave it in?

The Fairy   [*More and more irritated*]   But it's not caved in, insolent wretch!   It's much more beautiful than the other. It's larger, brighter, and it's as blue as the sky.   And my hair, do you see?   It's as blond as wheat.   One would say it's like virgin gold!   And I've so much of it, that my head is heavy. It flies in all directions.   Do you see it on my hands?   [*She displays two lean locks of grey hair*]

Tyltyl   Yes, I see some.

Fairy   [*Indignantly*]   Some!   Sprays!   Armsful!   Tufts! Floods of gold!   I know well that people say they do not see it at all; but you're not one of those wicked, blind people, I suppose.

Tyltyl   Oh no; I see very well what is not hidden.

The Fairy   But you should be just as bold to see the rest!

Men are very curious. Since the death of fairies, they don't see any more at all, and they don't even suspect it. Happily, I always have with me all that is necessary to rekindle dead eyes. What am I taking out of my bag?

Tyltyl Oh, what a pretty little green hat! What is it that shines so in the cockade?

The Fairy That is the big diamond that makes you see. . .

Tyltyl Ah? . . .

The Fairy Yes; when you have the hat on your head, you turn the diamond a little, from right to left, for example: look, like this; do you see? . . . It rests then on a bump on your head that nobody knows of and which opens your eyes. . .

Tyltyl Doesn't that hurt? . . .

The Fairy On the contrary, it's fairylike. . . You see at that very moment what there is in things; the soul of bread, of wine, of pepper, for example. . .

Mytyl Do you see the soul of sugar, too? . . .

The Fairy [*Suddenly angry*] That goes without saying. I don't like useless questions. The soul of sugar is no more interesting than that of pepper. Here, I'll give you what I have to help you in the search for the blue bird. I know well enough that the Ring-Which-Makes-One-Invisible or the Flying-Carpet would be more useful to you. But I have lost the key to the cupboard in which I put them away. Ah, I was about to forget! [*Pointing to the diamond*] When you hold it thus, you see, one little turn more, you see the past again. Another little turn and you see the future. It is curious and practical, and it doesn't make any noise.

Tyltyl Papa will take it from me.

The Fairy He won't see it; nobody can see it, as long as it's on your head. Do you wish to try it? [*She puts the little green hat on Tyltyl*] Now, turn the diamond. One turn, and then . . .

AUSTRIAN SELECTIONS

THE SWAN*

By Ferenc Molnar

Translated by Roderick MacEachen

Alexandra is "beautiful and clever — such dignity, such reserve — . . . a proud white swan." She is eager to marry young *Prince Albert*, thus regaining the throne for her family. She and her mother plan to gain the attention of the *Prince*. *Alexandra* must invite the tutor, *Agi*, to a reception given in honor of the *Prince*. She will appear to be in love with *Agi*, hoping to make the *Prince* jealous.

We find *Agi* and *Alexandra* just outside the ballroom.

Agi   If my life were not twofold —   One is external, the other is internal.   It is a fever-ridden and sorrowful life.

Alexandra   Why have I never known this?

Agi   Because your Highness also believes in miracles.

Alexandra   How?

Agi   You believe that I can remain cold and indifferent, even when I am struck in the face.

Alexandra   [*Shocked*]   Someone strikes you in the face?

Agi   Daily.

Alexandra   But who strikes you in the face?   [*Agi does not answer*]

Alexandra   Who?   Do we do this?   Perhaps. . . I too —

Agi   [*Bows his head*]

Alexandra   How was I to know?

Agi   Those were the most painful blows, your Highness.

Alexandra   Dear God! . . . This is more mysterious than the stars.   When did I insult you?

Agi   Your Highness sees here daily this miracle.   That a man's face, his voice and his whole external bearing remains peaceful and serene whilst he burns within with the fire of youthful pride. And you do not seek the cause of this miracle.

* Translated for the author by Roderick MacEachen.

83

Alexandra   The cause ?

Agi   Why do you think, Highness, that I bear all this ? Why do I teach humbly and listen humbly ? Why do you think, Highness, that I repress my own feelings ? Why am I here, where I am ? Why do I live ? For whom do I live here, where I live and as I live. . .

* * *

Alexandra   [*Hesitating*] I am all confused, Professor. The two words . . . I now heard . . . but I do not grasp the meaning. . .

Agi   Now I, too, am sorry that I spoke.

Alexandra   I am extremely sad, now, Professor.   [*Agi bows his head*]

Alexandra   I am not just talking, Professor, I am very, very sad. [*Agi listens*]

Alexandra   I have just come face to face with something. I believe, Professor, it is with that boundlessness of which you spoke.

Agi   This evening . . . this has lifted me out of the depths.

Alexandra   Yes . . . this . . . this evening.

Agi   For months and months . . . all that you said to me . . . was short and sharp. . . False courtesy . . . only the commonplace was sincere . . . and now, at last. . . You suddenly look upon me as though I, too, were a human being. . . A man . . . and uttered a few warm words. . .

Alexandra   I spoke nothing that . . .

Agi   [*With renewed courage*] But all that you said . . . and did . . . and looked . . . stirred me to the soul and caused a glow to arise within me which still continues and . . . and destroys in my soul, the poem of hopelessness. Tonight, I have lost it eternally. It was beautiful indeed. It happened this evening. . . I should never have spoken. . .

Alexandra   Please. . . I do not know what to say to you. I only wish that it might be otherwise.

Agi   But now, Little Princess, that was the end of your power.

Alexandra   How strangely you speak. I cannot bear it further.

Agi   You need not see me again. I shall go away, if you wish. And, even if you should command me to stay, I shall go nevertheless. You see, I can no longer speak consistently. Princess, you have unbalanced my reason a little. But tomorrow . . . tomorrow . . .

Alexandra No, no! We must discuss it now. I do not wish a misunderstanding. I shall tell you everything. I am so filled with shame. . .

Agi Why, Princess?

Alexandra No, it is impossible. . .

Agi But I implore. . . I would not ask, but I see that whatever I begin. . . [*Hopefully*] . . . Perhaps my plea, my fervent plea . . . that you speak . . . will make you be brave and open your heart . . . that you look upon me . . . speak to me . . . and make me happy, by uttering one word.

Alexandra No, no. Again you misunderstand . . . but it is all my fault . . . no, no, I meant something entirely different. But now if I remain silent, it is still worse . . . you understand. Please, we are discussing something terrible.

Agi But what, Princess?

Alexandra Treason.

Agi Treason?

Alexandra You are a man. . . You respect me, do you not?

Agi Your Highness. . .

Alexandra Listen to me.

Agi I am listening.

Alexandra Forever?

Agi Forever.

Alexandra I wish only that you continue to respect me and this I wish, so that I might be at peace . . . as I was only this afternoon. You are a man of honor, and I believe our good friend. Let me tell you the truth. My family — my mother, has one great objective in life. It is that I become the wife of the Crown Prince. That I bring my family back to the throne. Mark well this moment, Professor. Do me the honor now to be attentive to every word . . . because I feel that I speak as blood flows . . . from a wound. — Professor . . . the Crown Prince cares nothing for me. . . And my sweet mother thought that if there were someone. . . A man . . . through whom . . . I might be brought to Albert's attention. Understand, Professor, please understand, how deeply I appreciate your suffering. . . And how clean I wish to wash my own heart. Never, in all my life, have I done harm to another. You are the first human being in the world to whom I have caused pain. Yet I never would have hurt you. I was indeed often harsh toward you, but it was because I felt . . . I guessed . . . that you . . . were disturbed . . . on my account. But I was weak . . . and mother controls me so easily . . . and I, since early childhood, have never refused her slightest wish. She thought that I should invite you here this evening . . . and that I should look upon you. But had I known, dear Professor . . . had I foreseen, though I know it was impossible . . . had I but dimly known how the eyes of a man will glow when once the flame of feeling arises . . . and that there was such courage in the world and that such daring could set the eye afire — [*slight pause, she goes to the table — sits*] Dear Professor, I have told you all . . . and now I breathe freely again, I am relieved and I feel clean . . . you know everything now, and I trust you will respect me for that treason. . . But I am more human than I thought . . . and thanks to my good mother's great love. . . I have found myself. [*Agi bows his head*] [*Pause*]

Alexandra You are silent?

Agi You only obeyed the command of another.

Alexandra I do not wish to excuse myself. I, too, am guilty. It is hateful of me to blame everything on my mother. I, myself, wish to be queen. [*Rests her head on her arm*]

Agi I presume I may go now. . .

LILIOM*

By FERENC MOLNAR

Translated by Roderick MacEachen

Julie, who has lived in the city for a year as servant girl, has just fallen in love. Her friend, *Marie*, "just fresh from the country," thinks she is in love too, and with a soldier at that. But "what sort" says *Julie*. "Hussar, artilleryman, engineer . . . ?"

Julie [*Forcing herself*] But he doesn't like you.

Marie But I have someone who likes me too.

* Translated for the author by Roderick MacEachen.

Julie   What?

Marie   So long as you didn't have anybody, I didn't tell you. But now, I'm going to tell you [*boastfully*]   I'm in love, too.

Julie   Aren't you ashamed of yourself?

Marie   Not I!   I'm sweetly in love.

Julie   Well then, who is it?   What is he?

Marie   A soldier.

Julie   What kind of soldier?

Marie   That's just what I don't know.   Some kind of soldier. How many kinds are there?

Julie   Oh, many kinds.   Hussars, artillery men, wagon-driver soldiers, infantry —

Marie   A conductor on a street car — he's a soldier, too?

Julie   He's no soldier.   He's just a conductor.

Marie   Well, then, a policeman.   Do you say he's no soldier?

Julie   No, he's just a policeman.   Or a watchman, or a constable.

Marie   But he's got a sword.   A conductor doesn't have a sword, and whoever has a sword is a soldier.

Julie   A marcher in a parade has a sword, and still he's no soldier.   A congressman has a sword, and yet he's no soldier.

Marie   Well then, who *is* a soldier?

Julie   I've already told you.   An official, he's a soldier too. And then, a patriot is a soldier.

Marie   A recruit — what is he?

Julie   Yes, he's one.   But not entirely.   Just about half.   We say he's a soldier here, and a recruit there.

Marie   But how am I going to know which is a soldier?

Julie   If he has a sword, so long as he isn't a policeman, that's the way it is.

Marie   [*Very proudly*]   What is a customs officer?

Julie   A customs officer.

Marie   He has a gun, and a sword, too.   Yet, after all, he's no soldier.

Julie   He's just like a recruit.

Marie   He's just green.

Julie   Maybe yours is green!

Marie　You're crazy — he's not green.

Julie　Whoever is green — he's just half soldier.

Marie　Well then, what about the crimson?

Julie　He's a Hussar.　But only his trousers.　The fireman has stripes.　Brown — that's a train soldier — a wagon-driver.　If you'd been a whole year in the city as I have, you'd know, but you're still small-town.

Marie　[*A little bitterly*]　Well, how am I going to know which one is a soldier?

Julie　Well, there's just one way to tell.

Marie　What way?

Julie　One way.　[*She pauses.　Marie begins to sob*]　What are you bawling about?

Marie　What are you making fun of me for?　You're laughing at me because you think you're citified, and I'm still green. How should I know what a soldier is?　If you know so well, why don't you tell me and not laugh at me?

Julie　Listen to me.　There's only one way to know whether a man's a soldier.　That is if he gives the salute.　This is the only way there is to know.

Marie　Very well, then.

Julie　What?

Marie　Very well, I said.　Only because Hugo . . . Hugo . . .

Julie　[*Laughing and ridiculing*]　What are you doing?

Marie　Hugo — that's who it is — Hugo.　That's his name.

Julie　What are you doing?

Marie　Hugo.　[*Weeps bitterly*]

Julie　There you go, whimpering again.　What are you crying about?

Marie　Why do you tease me?

Julie　I'm not teasing you.　But if you say that it is "Hugo" then, I have to laugh.　Well then — what is his name?

Marie　I'm not going to tell you.

Julie　Very well — if you don't tell me, then he's no soldier.

Marie　[*Bashfully*]　Well then, I'll tell you.

Julie　All right.

Marie　I won't tell [*Cries*]

Julie   He's no soldier.   He's certainly nothing more than a letter carrier.

Marie   No, no. . . I'd rather tell you.

Julie   Well then?

Marie   [*Twisting about*]   But don't look at me.   Turn away, and I'll tell you.

Julie   [*Turns her face away*]

Marie   [*Now she can scarcely keep from laughing*]   Hugo [*she laughs*]   That's his honorable name.   Hugo. . . Hugo. The soldier — Hugo.

Julie   What kind of soldier?

Marie   Red.

Julie   His breeches?

Marie   No.

Julie   His coat?

Marie   Nor that.

Julie   Well, what?

Marie   [*Shouting*]   His cap!   [*Long pause*]

Julie   Why, that's a porter, my dear.   You led right up to it. A red cap means a porter.   He has no sword and he has no gun.

Marie   [*Brightening*]   But he gives a salute.   You said that that's the way to know who's a soldier.

Julie   He doesn't give a salute.   He just greets people.

Marie   He always gives me a salute, and so if Hugo does that, he must be a soldier.   He salutes, he wears a red cap, and he stands on the corner all day, and so . . . he must be a soldier.

Julie   And what does he do?

Marie   He spits.

Julie   That's a porter, my dear.   That's his rank — a common porter.

* * *

Julie   Do you still meet him?

Marie   Yes.

Julie   Often?

Marie   Often. . . He's going to take me —

Julie   For his wife?

Marie   For his wife.

Julie Now you see that he's no soldier.

Marie [*Shamefaced, but a bit boastfully*] I've already started to get gay with him.

Julie What do you do together?

Marie He asks me to go to the woods, but I don't go. Then he promises me a kerchief, and still I don't go. Then he takes me home and nothing serious happens.

Julie Is that a nice way to act?

Marie Well, of course, it's forbidden, but if you're in love, you can do it.

Julie Do you ever quarrel?

Marie Only when he gets excited.

Julie And so he gets excited?

Marie He takes my hand and so we walk along. And then he wants to swing my hand, but I don't let him. I tell him to behave. Then he says, "Why are you so contrary?" And then he tries to swing it again and I won't let him. — And for a long time I won't let him, and then after awhile — all at once I let him. Then we swing hands together — up and down — up, down — and this is the excitement. Of course, this is not allowed, but if you're in love you can do it.

Julie And so you live happily?

Marie Yes, happier than anything. It's wonderful to make love.

Julie Is that so?

Marie Yes, that's so. And you know, it begins to get daylight about three in the morning. Well, by that time we have spatted, and have swung hands, made love and all that, and then I sit on the bench and Hugo takes my hand. We don't drink wine, just red lemonade. You see Hugo doesn't get drunk. He just puts his cheek against my face and so we sit quite still. Soon his eyes get heavy and before long he is fast asleep. But still he doesn't let loose my hand — and I just sit there and keep looking around at the beautiful morning light — but he doesn't realize how lovely it is — because he is sound asleep. And I would also like to go to sleep, but I don't. And so there we are — just we two together — and that's what it means to make love. . .

MADONNA DIANORA *

By Hugo Von Hofmannsthal

Translated by Harriet Betty Boas

The scene is in a corner of a "sombre Lombardian Palace" facing
on a garden. "Two windows are visible, each one having a small
angular balcony with a stone railing" — at one of them *Dianora*
appears.

Dianora   [*At the window*]
A harvester I see, and not the last,
No, not the last, descending from the hill.
There are three more, and there, and there!
Have you no end, you never-ending day?
How have I dragged the hours away from you,
Torn them to shreds and cast them in the flood,
As I do now with these poor tattered blooms!
How have I coaxed each minute of this day.
Each bracelet, and each earring was clasped on,
Ta'en off again, then once more tried, until
'Twas thrown aside, exchanged, and others brought —
I slowly dripped the fountain, drop on drop
All through my tresses, dried them languidly ;
With quiet, measured step, out in the sun
I walked me to and fro — oh! to and fro!
But 'twas still damp — the path is narrow there.
I looked among the bushes, for the birds, —
Less than a zephyr's breath I bent them back,
Those swaying branches, sat 'neath rustling trees,
And felt on cheeks and hands in waiting woe
The little flickerings of warm sunshine.
I closed my eyes, and almost thought soft lips
Gently caressing, strayed my clammy brow.
Sometimes hours come when this duplicity,
All this concealment, seems so fruitless, and
I cannot bear it.   I can only gaze
With eyes of steel far up into the sky
Where flocks of wild geese float, or bend me low
O'er some mad, rushing plunging waterfall
That tears my weakling shadow with its flow, —

I will be patient — why, I must, I am! —
Madonna — I will climb the steepest mount
And on my knees will count me every stone
With this, my rosary, if only now,
Oh, soon, — this day will sink into the night.
It is so long! I have its measured tread
With these same beads been scanning o'er and o'er.
And now I talk so fev'rishly, instead
Of counting all the leaves upon that tree.
Oh! I have finished much too soon again.
See! See the yeoman, calling to his dog.
The shadows do upon his garden fall,
For him the night has come, but brings no joy;
He fears it, locks his door and is alone. —
See where the maidens wander to the well.
I know the manner in which each of them
Will fill her bucket — that one's prettiest.
Why does the stranger at the cross roads stay?
Distant's his goal, I warrant. He unwinds
And folds again the cloth about his feet.
What an existence! Draw the thorns, yes, draw
Them quickly out. You must speed. We all
Must hurry on, the restless day must down
And with it take this bright and scarlet glow
That's lingering in radiance on my cheeks.
All that is troubling us cast far away,
Fling wide the thorn into the field
Where waters flow and sheaves of brilliant flow'rs
Are bending, glowing, yearning towards the night. —
I draw my rings from off my fingers, and
They're happy as the naked children are
Who scamper quickly to the brook to bathe. —
Now all the girls have gone —
Only one maiden's left. Oh, what lovely hair!
I wonder if she knows its beauty's power?
Perhaps she's vain — but vanity, thou art
A plaything only for the empty years.
When once she has arrived where I am now,
She'll love her hair, she'll let it clasp her close,
Enwrap her round and whisper to her low,
Like echoing harpstrings throbbing with the touch
Of fev'rish fingers straying in the dark.

LIGHT-O'-LOVE *

By ARTHUR SCHNITZLER

Translated by B. Q. Morgan

Christine, a young and inexperienced girl, has fallen in love with *Fritz Loheimer*. *Fritz* is a handsome young philanderer, who is in love with *Catherine Binder*, "wife of a stocking-maker." He encourages the advances of *Christine*, knowing full well that he cannot return her love. *Toni*, her friend, resents *Fritz'* lack of attention — "he comes late for his appointments; he doesn't take you home; he goes into a theatre box with strangers; he leaves you in the lurch . . . and you take it all calmly, and make sheeps-eyes at him into the bargain."

Christine tells her father of her love for *Fritz*. The father does not think him worthy of her and denounces him so insistently that *Christine* becomes suspicious that something dreadful has happened.

Christine What . . . what is . . . [*No answer. She looks Theodore in the face; he cannot meet her eyes*] Where is he, . . . where is he? . . . [*In the greatest terror. No answer; all faces are embarrassed and sad*] Where is he? [*To Theodore*] Speak, can't you?

Theodore [*Tries to speak*]

Christine [*Looks at him wide-eyed, looks around her, comprehends the look on their faces, her face shows the dawn of this understanding, she utters a terrible cry*] Theodore . . . he is . . .

Theodore [*Nods*]

Christine [*Seizes her forehead, cannot understand it; she goes to Theodore, takes him by the arm, as if demented*] He is . . . dead? [*As if asking herself*]

Vyring My child —

Christine [*Thrusting him away*] Speak, Theodore, speak!

Theodore You know all.

Christine I know nothing. . . I don't know what has happened . . . do you think. . . I can't hear everything now? . . . how did it happen. . . Father. . . Theodore. . . [*To Toni*] You know it too.

* Reprinted by permission of B. Q. Morgan.

93

Theodore An unfortunate accident.

Christine What, what?

Theodore He fell.

Christine What does that mean: he . . .

Theodore He fell in a duel.

Christine [*Shrieks. She is about to fall, Vyring sustains her, motions to Theodore to go. She notes it and seizes him*] Stay here. . . I must know all. Do you think you can keep anything from me now?

Theodore What else do you want to know?

Christine Why — why did he fight a duel?

Theodore I don't know the reason.

Christine With whom, with whom? . . . You surely know who killed him? . . . Well, well, who . . .

Theodore Nobody you know.

Christine Who, who?

Toni Christine!

Christine Who? You tell me! [*To Toni*] . . . Father, you tell me. . . [*No answer. She starts to go out. Vyring holds her back*] Can't I know who killed him, and for what cause?

Theodore It was . . . a trivial cause. . .

Christine You're not telling the truth . . . why, why . . .

Theodore Dear Christine. . .

Christine [*As if about to interrupt, goes up to him; looks at him in silence, then suddenly shrieks*] On account of a woman?

Theodore No —

Christine Yes — for a woman. . . [*Turning to Toni*] for that woman — for that woman that he loved. And her husband — yes, yes, her husband killed him. . And I . . . what am I? What was I to him? . . . Theodore . . . haven't you anything for me at all . . . didn't he write down anything? . . . Didn't he tell you anything for me? Didn't you find anything . . . a letter . . . a note. . .

Theodore [*Shakes his head*]

Christine And that evening . . . when he was here, when you came to get him . . . he knew it, he knew then that he perhaps would never. . . And he went away from here to be killed for another woman. No, no, it is not possible . . . didn't he know what he was to me . . . didn't . . .

Theodore He did know. On the last morning, when we drove out together . . . he spoke of you too.

Christine He spoke of me too! Of me too! And of what else ? Of how many other people, of how many other things, that meant just as much to him as I did ? Of me too! Oh, God ! . . . And of his father and his mother and his room and of the springtime and of the city and of everything, that belonged to his life and that he had to give up just as much as he gave up me — of everything he talked to you . . . and of me too. . .

Theodore [*Moved*] He surely loved you.

Christine Love ? He ? I was nothing to him but a pastime — and he died for another woman ! And I — I worshipped him ! Didn't he know that ? . . . That I gave him everything I could give, that I would have died for him . . . that he was my God and my bliss of Heaven . . . didn't he see that at all ? He could go away from me with a smile, out of my room, and be shot down for another woman. . . Father, father, can you understand that ?

Vyring [*Goes to her*] Christine !

Theodore [*To Toni*] Child, you might have spared me this.

Toni [*Looks at him venomously*]

Theodore I have had enough distress . . . these last days.

Christine [*With sudden resolve*] Theodore, take me to him — I want to see him — once more I want to see him — his face — Theodore, take me to him.

Theodore [*With a gesture, hesitatingly*] No. . .

Christine Why "no?" You can't refuse me that ! Surely I can see him once more ?

Theodore It is too late.

Christine Too late ? To see his corpse . . . is it too late ? Yes . . . yes. . . [*She does not understand*]

Theodore He was buried this morning.

Christine [*With the greatest horror*] Buried. . . And I didn't know about it ? They shot him . . . and put him in his coffin and carried him out and buried him down in the earth

—and I couldn't even see him once more? He's been dead two days—and you didn't come and tell me?

Theodore [*Moved*] In these two days I have . . . You cannot dream all that I . . . Consider that it was my duty to notify his parents—I had to think of many things—and then my own state of mind.

Christine Your . . .

Theodore And then the . . . it was done very quietly. . . Only the closest relatives and friends. . .

Christine The closest—? And I—? . . . What am I?

Toni They would have asked that.

Christine What am I? Less than all the rest—? Less than his relatives, less than—you?

Vyring My child, my child. Come to me, to me. . . [*He embraces her. To Theodore*] Go . . . leave me alone with her.

Theodore I am very . . . [*With tears in his voice*] I never suspected. . .

Christine Never suspected what? That I loved him? [*Vyring draws her to him; Theodore looks down; Toni stands near Christine. Freeing herself*] Take me to his grave!

Vyring No, no—

Toni Don't go, Christine.

Theodore Christine . . . later . . . tomorrow . . . when you are calmer—

Christine Tomorrow? When I shall be calmer? And in a month completely consoled, eh? And in six months I can laugh again, can I? [*Laughing shrilly*] And then when will the next lover come?

Vyring Christine. . .

Christine Stay here, then. . . I can find the way alone. . .

Vyring and Toni [*Together*] Don't go.

Christine It's even better. . . If I . . . let me go, let go.

Vyring Christine, stay here.

Toni Don't go! Perhaps you'll find the other one there—praying.

Christine [*To herself, her eyes fixed*] I won't pray there . . . no. . . [*She rushes out; the others speechless for the moment*]

SCANDINAVIAN
SELECTIONS

THE WILD DUCK*

By Henrik Ibsen

Hialmar has discovered that *Werle*, the man who has been his benefactor, established him in business, encouraged him in the selection of a wife, is the father of his child, fourteen-year-old *Hedvig*. In his humiliation he scorns *Hedvig* and accuses her of merely pretending love for him. *Hedvig*, to prove her sincere love, determines to destroy her dearest possession, a wild duck, the last tie between her family and *Werle*, and she goes into the attic, where the duck is kept, with that intention.

Hialmar Gina, where is she?

Gina [*Sniffs*] Poor dear, she's sitting out in the kitchen, I dare say.

Hialmar [*Goes over, tears open the kitchen door, and says*] Hedvig, come, come in to me! [*Looks around*] No, she's not here.

Gina Then she must be in her own little room.

Hialmar [*Without*] No, she's not here either. [*Comes in*] She must have gone out.

Gina Yes, you wouldn't have her anywhere in the house.

Hialmar Oh, if she would only come home quickly, so that I can tell her — Everything will come right now, Gregers; now I can believe we can begin life afresh.

Gregers [*Quietly*] I knew it; I knew the child would make amends. [*Old Ekdal appears at the door of his room; he is in full uniform, and is busy buckling on his sword*]

Hialmar [*Astonished*] Father! Are you there?

Gina Have you been firing in your room?

Ekdal [*Resentfully, approaching*] So you go shooting alone, do you, Hialmar?

* Reprinted by courtesy of Modern Library, New York.

Hialmar [*Excited and confused*] Then it wasn't you that fired that shot in the garret?

Ekdal Me that fired? H'm.

Gregers [*Calls out to Hialmar*] She has shot the wild duck herself!

Hialmar What can it mean? [*Hastens to the garret door, tears it aside, looks in and calls loudly*] Hedvig!

Gina [*Runs to the door*] Good God, what's that?

Hialmar [*Goes in*] She's lying on the floor!

Gregers Hedvig! lying on the floor! [*Goes in to Hialmar*]

Gina [*At the same time*] Hedvig! [*Inside the garret*] No, no, no!

Ekdal Ho-ho! does she go shooting, too, now? [*Hialmar, Gina and Gregers carry Hedvig into the studio; in her dangling right hand she holds the pistol fast clasped in her fingers*]

Hialmar [*Distracted*] The pistol has gone off. She has wounded herself. Call for help! Help!

Gina [*Runs into the passage and calls down*] Relling! Relling! Doctor Relling; come up as quick as you can! [*Hialmar and Gregers lay Hedvig down on the sofa*]

Ekdal [*Quietly*] The woods avenge themselves.

Hialmar [*On his knees beside Hedvig*] She'll soon come to now. She's coming to—; yes, yes, yes.

Gina [*Who has come in again*] Where has she hurt herself? I can't see anything—

[*Relling comes hurriedly, and immediately after him Molvik; the latter without his waistcoat and necktie, and with his coat open*]

Relling What's the matter here?

Gina They say Hedvig has shot herself.

Hialmar Come and help us!

Relling Shot herself! [*He pushes the table aside and begins to examine her*]

Hialmar [*Kneeling and looking anxiously up at him*] It can't be dangerous? Speak, Relling! She is scarcely bleeding at all. It can't be dangerous?

Relling How did it happen?

Hialmar Oh, we don't know—

Gina   She wanted to shoot the wild duck.

Relling   The wild duck?

Hialmar   The pistol must have gone off.

Relling   H'm. Indeed.

Ekdal   The woods avenge themselves. But I'm not afraid, all the same. [*Goes into garret and closes the door after him*]

Hialmar   Well, Relling,—why don't you say something?

Relling   The ball has entered the breast.

Hialmar   Yes, but she's coming to!

Relling   Surely you can see that Hedvig is dead.

Gina   [*Bursts into tears*]   Oh, my child, my child—

Gregers   [*Huskily*]   In the depths of the sea—

Hialmar   [*Jumps up*]   No, no, she must live! Oh, for God's sake, Relling—only a moment—only just till I can tell her how unspeakably I loved her all the time!

Relling   The bullet has gone through her heart. Internal hemorrhage. Death must have been instantaneous.

Hialmar   And I! I hunted her from me like an animal! And she crept terrified into the garret and died for love of me! [*Sobbing*] I can never atone to her! I can never tell her—! [*Clenches his hands and cries, upwards*] O thou above—! If thou be indeed! Why hast thou done this thing to me?

Gina   Hush, hush, you mustn't go on that awful way. We had no right to keep her, I suppose.

Molvik   The child is not dead, but sleepeth.

Relling   Bosh.

Hialmar   [*Becomes calm, goes over to the sofa, folds his arms, and looks at Hedvig*]   There she lies so stiff and still.

Relling   [*Tries to loosen the pistol*]   She's holding it so tight, so tight.

Gina   No, no, Relling, don't break her fingers; let the pistol be.

Hialmar   She shall take it with her.

Gina   Yes, let her. But the child mustn't lie here for a show. She shall go to her own room, so she shall. Help me, Ekdal. [*Hialmar and Gina take Hedvig between them*]

Hialmar   [*As they are carrying her*]   Oh, Gina, Gina, can you survive this!

Gina We must help each other to bear it. For now at least she belongs to both of us.

PEER GYNT *

By HENRIK IBSEN

Peer Gynt, the romantic dreamer, lover of fancy, and chaser of rainbows — the irresponsible *Peer,* has returned home to be at the bedside of his dying mother. He finds her alone with the old neighbor-woman, *Kari,* who has cared for her during her illness. *Peer* and his mother are in a reminiscent mood.

Peer	No, now we will chat together,
	but only of this and that,—
	forget what's awry and crooked,
	and all that is sharp and sore.
	Are you thirsty? I'll fetch you water.
	Can you stretch you? The bed is short.
	Let me see : — if I don't believe, now,
	It's the bed that I had when a boy !
	Do you mind, dear, how oft in the evenings
	you sat at my bedside here,
	And spread the fur-coverlet o'er me,
	and sang many a lilt and lay ?
Ase	Ay, mind you ? And then we played sledges
	When your father was far abroad.
	The coverlet served for sledge-apron,
	and the floor for an ice-bound fiord.
Peer	Ay, but the best of all, though,—
	mother, you mind that too ?
	The best was the fleet-foot horses.
Ase	Ay, think you that I've forgot ? —
	It was Kari's cat that we borrowed ;
	it sat on the log-scooped chair —
Peer	To the castle west of the moon, and
	the castle east of the sun,
	to Soria-Moria Castle
	the road ran both high and low.
	A stick that we found in the closet,
	for a whip-shaft you made it serve.

* Reprinted by courtesy of Modern Library, New York.

Ase	Right proudly I perked on the box-seat —

Peer	Ay, ay; you threw loose the reins,
	    and kept turning round as we travelled,
	and asked me if I was cold.
	God bless you, ugly old mother,—
	    you were ever a kindly soul —!
	What's hurting you now?

Ase	My back aches, because of the hard, bare boards.
Peer	Stretch yourself; I'll support you. There now, you're lying soft.
Ase	[*Uneasily*] No, Peer, I'd be moving!
Peer	Moving?
Ase	Ay, moving; 'tis ever my wish.

Peer	Oh, nonsense! Spread o'er you the bed-fur.
	    Let me sit at your bedside here.
	There; now we'll shorten the evening
	    With many a lilt and a lay.

Ase	Best bring from the closet the prayer-book; I feel so uneasy of soul.

Peer	In Soria-Moria Castle
	    the King and the Prince give a feast,
	On the sledge-cushions lie and rest you;
	    I'll drive you there over the heath —

Ase	But, Peer, dear, am I invited?

Peer	Ay, that we are, both of us.
	    [*He throws a string round the back of a chair,
	    takes up a stick, and seats himself at the foot
	    of the bed*]
	Gee-up! Will you stir yourself, Black-Boy?
	    Mother, you're not a-cold?
	Ay, ay; by the pace one knows it,
	    When Granë begins to go!

Ase	Why, Peer, what is it that's ringing? —
Peer	The glittering sledge-bells, dear!
Ase	Oh, mercy, how hollow it's rumbling!
Peer	We're just driving over a fiord.

Ase	I'm afraid! What is that I hear rushing and sighing so strange and wild?
Peer	It's the sough of the pine-trees, mother, on the heath. Do you but sit still.
Ase	There's a sparkling and gleaming afar now; whence comes all that blaze of light?
Peer	From the castle's windows and doorways. Don't you hear, they are dancing?
Ase	Yes.
Peer	Outside the door stands Saint Peter, and prays you to enter in.
Ase	Does he greet us?
Peer	He does, with honour, and pours out the sweetest wine.
Ase	Wine! Has he cakes as well, Peer?
Peer	Cakes? Ay, a heaped-up dish. And the dean's wife is getting ready your coffee and your dessert.
Ase	Oh, Christ; shall we two come together?
Peer	As freely as ever you will.
Ase	Oh, deary, Peer, what a frolic you're driving me to, poor soul!
Peer	[*Cracking his whip*] Gee-up; will you stir yourself, Black-boy!
Ase	Peer, dear, you're driving right!
Peer	Ay, broad is the way.
Ase	This journey, it makes me so weak and tired.
Peer	There's the castle rising before us; the drive will be over soon.
Ase	I will lie back and close my eyes then, and trust me to you, my boy!

Peer	Come up with you, Granë, my trotter!
	  In the castle the throng is great;
	they bustle and swarm to the gateway.
	  Peer Gynt and his mother are here!
	What say you, Master Saint Peter?
	  Shall mother enter in?
	You may search a long time, I tell you.

ere you find such an honest old soul.
Myself I don't want to speak of;
   I can turn at the castle gate.
If you'll treat me, I'll take it kindly;
   If not, I'll go off just as pleased.
But her you shall honour and reverence,
   and make her at home always;
there comes not a soul to beat her
   from the parishes nowadays.—
      [Uneasily]
Why, what makes your eyes so glassy?
   Mother! Have you gone out of your wits—?
      [Goes to the head of the bed]
You mustn't lie there and stare so—!
   Speak, mother; it's I, your boy!
      [Feels her forehead and hands cautiously; then
         throws the string on the chair, and says
         softly]
Ay, ay!—You can rest yourself, Granë;
   for even now the journey's done.
      [Closes her eyes and bends over her]
For all your days I thank you,
   For beatings and lullabys!—
But see, you must thank me back, now—
      [Presses his cheek against her mouth]
There; that was the driver's fare.

PEER GYNT *

By HENRIK IBSEN

Peer Gynt, the romantic dreamer, lover of fancy, and chaser of
rainbows — the irresponsible *Peer —*

Peer [*Casts himself down upon the heathery slope; lies for
some time flat on his back with his hands under his head, gazing
up into the sky*] What a strange sort of cloud! It is just
like a horse. There's a man on it too — and saddle — and bridle.
— And after it comes an old crone on a broomstick. [*Laughs
quietly to himself*] It is mother. She's scolding and screaming: You beast! Hei you, Peer Gynt — [*His eyes gradually
close*] Ay, now she is frightened.—Peer Gynt he rides first,

* Reprinted by courtesy of Modern Library, New York.

and there follow him many.—His steed it is gold-shod and crested with silver. Himself he has gauntlets and sabre and scabbard. His cloak it is long, and its lining silken. Full brave is the company riding behind him. None of them, though, sits his charger so stoutly. None of them glitters like him in the sunshine.—Down by the fence stand the people in clusters, lifting their hats, and agape gazing upwards. Women are curtseying. All the world knows him, Kaiser Peer Gynt, and his thousands of henchmen. Sixpenny pieces and glittering shillings over the roadway he scatters like pebbles. Rich as a lord grows each man in the parish. High o'er the ocean Peer Gynt goes a-riding. Engelland's Prince on the seashore awaits him; there too await him all Engelland's maidens. Engelland's nobles and Engelland's Kaiser, see him come riding and rise from their banquet. Raising his crown, hear the Kaiser address him—

GHOSTS *

By HENRIK IBSEN

Oswald Alving has inherited irregular, lustful desires that are proving fatal to him, as they did to his father before him.

Oswald [*Not listening to her*]. Mother, didn't you say, a little while ago, that there was nothing in the world you would not do for me, if I asked you?

Mrs. Alving Yes, to be sure I said it.

Oswald And you'll stick to it, mother?

Mrs. A. You may rely on that, my dear and only boy! I have nothing in the world to live for but you alone.

Oswald All right, then; now you shall hear. Mother, you have a strong, steadfast mind, I know. Now you are to sit quite still when you hear it.

Mrs. A. What dreadful thing can it be—?

Oswald You are not to scream out. Do you hear? Do you promise me that? We'll sit and talk about it quite quietly. Do you promise me this, mother?

Mrs. A. Yes, yes; I promise you that. Only speak!

Oswald Well, you must know that all this fatigue, and my not being able to think of working at all—all that is not the illness itself—

* Reprinted by courtesy of Walter H. Baker Co.

Mrs. A. Then what is the illness itself?

Oswald The disease I have as my birthright [*he points to his forehead and adds very softly*] is seated here.

Mrs. A. [*Almost voiceless*] Oswald! No, no!

Oswald Don't scream. I can't bear it. Yes, it is sitting here, waiting. And it may break out any day — at any moment.

Mrs. A. Oh, what horror!

Oswald Now, do be quiet. That's how it stands with me —

Mrs. A. [*Jumps up*] It is not true, Oswald. It is impossible, it can't be so.

Oswald I have had one attack down there already. It was soon over. But when I got to know what had been the matter with me, then the dread came upon me raging and tearing; and so I set off home to you as fast as I could.

Mrs. A. Then this is the dread — ?

Oswald Yes, for it's so indescribably awful, you know. Oh! if it had been merely an ordinary mortal disease! For I'm not so afraid of death — though I should like to live as long as I can.

Mrs. A. Yes, yes, Oswald, you must.

Oswald But this is so unspeakably loathsome! To become a little baby again! To have to be fed! To have to — Oh! I can't speak of it.

Mrs. A. The child has his mother to nurse him.

Oswald [*Jumps up*] No, never; that's just what I won't have. I can't endure to think that perhaps I should lie in that state for many years — get old and gray. And in the meantime you might die and leave me. [*Sits in Mrs. Alving's chair*] For the doctor said it would not necessarily prove fatal at once. He called it a sort of softening of the brain — or something of the kind. [*Smiles sadly*] I think that expression sounds so nice. It always sets me thinking of cherry-colored velvet — something soft and delicate to stroke.

Mrs. A. [*Screams*] Oswald!

Oswald [*Springs up and paces the room*] And now you have taken Regina from me. If I'd only had her! She would have come to the rescue, I know.

Mrs. A. [*Goes to him*] What do you mean by that, my darling boy? Is there any help in the world that I wouldn't give you?

Oswald   When I got over my attack in Paris, the doctor told me that when it came again — and it will come again — there would be no more hope.

Mrs. A.   He was heartless enough —

Oswald   I demanded it of him.   I told him I had preparations to make.   [*He smiles cunningly*]   And so I had.   [*He takes a little box from his inner breast pocket and opens it*]   Mother, do you see these?

Mrs. A.   What is that?

Oswald   Morphia powder.

Mrs. A.   [*Looks horrified at him*]   Oswald — my boy?

Oswald   I have scraped together twelve pilules —

Mrs. A.   [*Snatches at it*]   Give me the box, Oswald.

Oswald   Not yet, mother.   [*He hides the box again in his pocket*]

Mrs. A.   I shall never survive this.

Oswald   It must be survived.   Now, if I had Regina here, I should have told her how it stood with me, and begged her to come to the rescue at the last.   She would have done it.   I'm certain she would.

Mrs. A.   Never!

Oswald   When the horror had come upon me, and she saw me lying there helpless, like a little new-born baby, impotent, lost, helpless, past all saving —

Mrs. A.   Never in all the world would Regina have done this.

Oswald   Regina would have done it.   Regina was so splendidly light-hearted.   And she would soon have wearied of nursing an invalid like me —

Mrs. A.   Then Heaven be praised that Regina is not here.

Oswald   Well, then, it is you that must come to the rescue, mother.

Mrs. A.   [*Screams aloud*]   I!

Oswald   Who is nearer to it than you?

Mrs. A.   I!   Your mother!

Oswald   For that very reason.

Oswald   I never asked you for life.   And what sort of a life is it that you have given me?   I will not have it.   You shall take it back again.

Mrs. A. Help! Help! [*She runs out into the hall*]

Oswald [*Going after her*] Don't leave me. Where are you going?

Mrs. A. [*In the hall*] . . . To fetch the doctor, Oswald. Let me go.

Oswald [*Also outside*] You shall not go. And no one shall come in. [*The locking of a door is heard*]

Mrs. A. [*Comes in again*] Oswald — Oswald! — my child!

Oswald [*Follows her*] Have you a mother's heart for me, and yet can see me suffer this unutterable dread?

Mrs. A. [*After a moment's silence, commands herself, and says*] Here is my hand upon it.

Oswald Will you — ?

Mrs. A. If it is ever necessary. But it will never be necessary. No, no; it is impossible.

Oswald Well, let us hope so, and let us live together as long as we can. Thank you, mother. [*He sits down in the arm-chair which Mrs. Alving has moved to the sofa. Day is breaking. The lamp is still burning on the table*]

Mrs. A. [*Drawing near cautiously*] Do you feel calm, now?

Oswald Yes.

Mrs. A. [*Bending over him*] It has been a dreadful fancy of yours, Oswald — nothing but a fancy. You have not been able to bear all this excitement. But now you shall have a long rest; at home with your own mother, my own blessed boy! Everything you point to you shall have, just as when you were a little child. There, now! That crisis is over now. You see how easily it has passed. Oh! I was sure it would — and do you see, Oswald, what a lovely day we are going to have? Brilliant sunshine! Now you will really be able to see your home. [*She goes to the table and puts the lamp out. Sunrise. The glacier and the snow-peaks in the background glow in the morning light*]

Oswald [*Sits in the arm-chair with his back toward the landscape, without moving. Suddenly he says*] Mother, give me the sun.

Mrs. A. [*By the table, starts and looks at him*] What do you say?

Oswald [*Repeats, in a dull, toneless voice*] The sun. The sun.

Mrs. A. [*Goes to him*] Oswald, what is the matter with you?
[*Oswald seems to shrink together in his chair; all his muscles
relax; his face is expressionless, his eyes have a glassy stare. Mrs.
Alving is quivering with terror*] What is this? [*Shrieks*]
Oswald, what is the matter with you? [*Falls on her knees be-
side him and shakes him*] Oswald, Oswald! Look at me!
Don't you know me?

Oswald [*Tonelessly as before*] The sun. The sun. [*Mrs.
Alving springs up in despair, intwines her hands in her hair and
shrieks*]

Mrs. A. I can't bear it. [*Whispers as though petrified*] I
can't bear it! Never! [*Suddenly*] Where has he got them?
[*Fumbles hastily in his breast*] Here! [*Shrinks back a few
steps and screams*] No, no, no! Yes!— No, no! [*She
stands a few steps from him with her hands twisted in her hair,
and stares at him in speechless terror*]

Oswald [*Sits motionless as before and says*] The sun. The
sun.

THE FATHER *

By AUGUST STRINDBERG

Translated by N. Ericksen

The Captain: a ruler of men outside of his home, but a simple
child to his ruthless and calculating wife, *Laura*, who drives him
stark mad by planting in his irresolute mind the idea that he is not
the father of his child. The faithful nurse, who has loved the
Captain devotedly, must put him in a strait-jacket.

Nurse Mr. Adolf, do you remember when you were my darling
little child and I tucked you in of nights, and said, "Gentle
Jesus" to you, and do you remember how I got up in the night
and gave you a drink; do you remember how I lighted the
candle and talked about pretty things when you had bad dreams
and couldn't sleep? Do you remember?

Captain Go on talking, Margret, it soothes my head so; go
on talking again.

Nurse Oh, yes, but you must listen to me! Do you remember when you once took the great kitchen knife and wanted to
cut out boats with it, and how I came in and had to get the knife
away by tricking you? You were a little foolish child so I had

* Reprinted by courtesy of John W. Luce & Co., owners of the copyright.

to trick you, for you didn't believe that we meant well by you. "Give me that ugly snake," I said, "or it will bite you!" and then you gave up the knife. [*Takes the revolver out of the Captain's hand*] And then when you had to dress yourself and didn't want to. Then I had to coax you and say that you should have a golden coat and be dressed like a prince. And then I took your little vest that was only made of green worsted, and held it up in front of you, and said, "In with both arms," and then I said, "Sit nice and still while I button it down the back." [*She gets the jacket on*] And then I said, "Get up now, and walk across the floor like a good boy so that I can see whether it's straight. [*She leads him to the sofa*] And then I said, "Now you must go to bed."

Captain What did you say? Was I to go to bed when I was dressed? . . . Damnation! What have you done with me? [*Tries to free himself*] Ah! You infernally cunning woman! Who would have thought that you had so much wit. [*Lies down on sofa*] Trapped, shorn, outwitted, forbidden to die.

* * *

Laura Give me your hand, friend.

Captain My hand! The hand that you have bound! Omphale! Omphale! . . . But I can feel your shawl against my mouth; it is as warm and soft as your arm, and it smells of vanilla, like your hair when you were young! Laura, when you were young, and we walked in the birchwoods, with the oxlips and the thrushes . . . glorious, glorious! Think how beautiful life was, and what it is now. You did not wish to have it so, and neither did I, and yet it happened. Who, then, rules over life?

Laura God alone rules. . .

Captain The God of strife, then! Or perhaps the goddess nowadays. Take away the cat that is lying on me! Take it away. [*Nurse brings in a pillow and takes away the shawl*] *Captain* Give me my uniform coat! Throw it over me! [*Nurse takes the coat from the clothes-pegs and lays it over him*] Ah, my rough lion-skin that you wanted to take away from me! Omphale! Omphale! Thou cunning woman who wast the lover of peace and the deviser of disarmaments! Wake, Hercules, before they take thy club from thee! You will wile our armor off us, too, and make believe that it is tinsel.

No, it was iron, do you hear, before it became tinsel. In olden days the smith made the cuirass ; now it is the needlewoman. Omphale ! Omphale ! Rude strength has fallen before treacherous weakness — out on you, infernal woman, and damnation on your sex ! [*He raises himself to spit at her, but falls back onto the sofa*] What sort of a pillow have you given me, Margret ? It is so hard, and so cold, so cold ! Come and sit here by me on the chair. There now ! May I lay my head on your lap ? Ah, that is warm ! Bend over me so that I can feel your breast ! Oh, it is sweet to sleep on a woman's breast, a mother's or a mistress's, but the mother's is best.

Laura   Would you like to see your child, Adolf ?

Captain   My child ? A man has no children ; it is only women who have children ; and therefore the future is theirs, when we die childless. Oh, God ! who lovest children.

Nurse   Listen, he is praying to God.

Captain   No, to you to put me to sleep, for I am tired, so tired. Good night, Margret, and blessed be you among women. [*He raises himself but falls back on the Nurse's lap with a cry*]

BEYOND HUMAN POWER *

By Björnstjerne Björnson

Translated by John A. Eiesland

Adolf Sang : a man whose utter faith in humanity is so simple, so clearly defined to himself that it is questioned by others. A literary religious character who lives piously. He has the power to perform miracles, but yet he cannot direct supernatural aid to his invalid wife, *Clara.* His children do not share his simple faith, and he is trying to make them understand his creed as the scene opens.

Sang . . . Of Oriental and Greek enthusiasts in a despairing time — a time when the best only were longing for a land of regeneration — away, away. I know it, my child.

Was it there you fell ?

Great God ! as if the land of regeneration wasn't just as true because it was a very old Oriental dream. If it has been waiting a long while to come, so that weak souls call it an impossible dream, and the demands that lead thither impossible ideals, what does that prove ?

* Translated for the author by J. A. Eiesland.

Nothing about the doctrine but much about those who an-
nounce the new doctrine, the preachers. Without mentioning
them, I will only say what happened to myself.

—I saw that Christianity was crawling on its belly — and
still carefully avoiding all the larger pitfalls. Why does it do
that I ask myself? Is it because if it should rouse itself, it
would lift all things off the hinges? Is a Christianity of that
kind possible, or is it men who don't dare?

If only one dared, would there not be thousands who would
dare? And so I felt that I should try to be that one. And I
mean that everyone should make the trial. Yes, without doing
it, he is no longer a believer. For faith means to know that for
faith all things are possible, and then show this faith.

Is it in order to boast that I say this . . . precisely in order
to accuse myself. For although I now have built such a high
structure and have had such a great grace, I fall away from my
God again and again.

Have I not been going here and been thinking it is impossible
for me alone to save her? Have I not doubted and waited for
others to help?

Therefore God took the help away from me. Therefore he
has permitted that I also should fail before the impossible and
come and tell me about it. For thus should His time be prepared. Now He will show us all what's possible.

Oh, I went there and did not understand. Now I understand. I shall do it alone. Now I have got the command.
Now I can.

Therefore for this reason I have had the great grace of prepa-
ration this very day. Everything comes together.

Clara, do you hear that? It is no longer I that speak — it is
the great certainty in myself. And you know from Whom it
comes every time. [*He kneels*]

Clara, my beloved friend, why should not you be as dear to
God as any who believes fully — as if God were not the father
of us all!

God's love is no privilege of the believer. The privilege of the
believer is to feel His love and to rejoice in it — and in its name
to make the impossible possible.

Patient and faithful friend, now I leave to try it. [*He rises*]

I shall go unto the Church, my child, for I want to be alone.
I shall not go out again before I have received from the hands of

God, sleep for Mother, and after sleep, health, so that she can rise again and be among us.

Don't be terrified. I feel He will do it. He is not going to give it to me at once, for this time I had doubted. But I shall wait on the austere and good Lord — Farewell. [*He kisses her and rises*]

Thank you, my children! Now you have helped me, indeed — more than anyone could have anticipated.

Now I'll ring the bell for prayer so that at the first stroke of the bell you'll know that I have commenced to pray for Mother. Peace be with you!

Hannah [*Has mechanically opened the door for him*] [*Sang goes out*] This is . . . this is . . . [*She bursts into tears*]

Elias I must see. . . I must see him go in. [*He goes out*]

Rachel [*Coming forward*] Mother! Mother!

Hannah Don't speak to her. She is looking at you; but don't speak to her!

Rachel I am afraid!

Hannah Where I stand, I can see your father. Now he has almost reached the church. — Come!

Rachel No! . . . No, I can't stand this! I am so afraid! — Mother! She looks at me; but she does not answer me. — Mother!

Hannah Hush, Rachel! [*The bell begins to ring*]

Rachel [*Sinks upon her knees. After a while, she starts up with a suppressed cry*] For God's sake, Hannah!

Hannah What is it?

Rachel Mother is asleep!

Hannah Asleep?

Rachel Mother is asleep!

Hannah Really and truly?

Rachel I must find Elias I must tell Elias!

Hannah She sleeps like a child. Oh, God! [*She kneels down. A rumbling sound is heard, growing louder and louder; rising to terrible power. There are shrieks without. The house trembles. The roar increases to thunder*]

Rachel [*Outside*] The mountain is falling! [*She shrieks, then comes rushing into the room*] The mountain is falling upon the church! Upon us! Right over the church! Upon us! On father, on us! That rushing and roaring!—it is getting dark,—Oh! [*She cowers down, turning her face away*]

Elias [*Outside*] Father!—Father!—Oh!

Hannah [*Bending over her sister's bed*] It is coming! It is coming! [*The uproar has reached its height. Then gradually it abates. Afterwards the church bell can be heard again, above the din*]

Hannah [*Jumping up*] It is still ringing! He is alive.

Rachel He lives!

Elias [*Outside*] Father is alive! [*Nearer*] The church is standing. [*Comes into the room*] The church is standing. Father is alive, right by the church the slide turned aside—went toward the left, he is ringing the bell. Oh, God! [*He throws himself over his mother's bed*]

Rachel [*Comes forward*] Elias! Mother—?

Elias [*Jumps up*] She is asleep?

Rachel Yes, she is asleep— [*The church bell continues to ring*]

Hannah She is sleeping as quietly as before.

JEPPE OF THE HILL *

By HOLBERG

Translated by John A. Eiesland

Jeppe has one love—brandy. He hates his wife, *Nille,* and Master Eric, the switch with which she beats a tune upon his back. Today *Nille* sends him to town with money to buy some soap. At *Jacob the Shoemaker's,* he meets his love and parts with his money. As a result we find *Jeppe* quarreling with his brandied legs outside *Jacob's* inn.

[*Jeppe feels happy and begins to sing*]

A white hen and a speckled hen
Got into a fight with a rooster—

Oh, if I only dared drink for one penny more! Oh, if I only dared drink for one penny more! I think I'll do it. No,

* Translated for the author by J. A. Eiesland.

calamity will come of it. If I could once get the inn out of my sight, it wouldn't be so bad; but it's as if someone were holding me back. I've got to go in again. But what is this you are doing, Jeppe? I seem to see Nille standing in my way with Master Eric in her hand. I must turn round again. Oh, if I only dared drink for one penny more! My stomach says, "Do it"; my back says "Don't." Which one shall I offend? Isn't my stomach more than my back? I think it is. Shall I knock? Hey, Jacob Shoemaker, come out here! But that cursed woman comes to my mind again. If she only didn't break the bones of my back when she beats me. I wouldn't care a devil about it, but she does beat me like! . . . Oh, God preserve me, poor man! What shall I do? Control your nature, Jeppe! Isn't it a shame to get into trouble for a paltry glass of brandy? No, I shan't do it this time; I must go on. Oh, if I only dared drink for one penny more! It was my undoing that I got a taste of it; now I can't get away from it. Get on, you legs! May the devil take you if you don't! No, by George! those rascals will not budge. They want to go back to the inn. My limbs wage war on each other; my stomach and my legs want to go to the inn, and my back to the town. Will ye go ye dogs! ye beasts! ye rascals! The devil take them, they *will* go back to the inn; I have more trouble getting my own legs away from the inn than I have getting my piebald horse out of the stable. Oh, if I only dared to drink for one penny more! Who knows if Jacob Shoemaker might not trust me for a penny or two more, if I begged enough? Hey, Jacob! Another twopenny glass of brandy!

* * *

Jeppe Oh, Jeppe, you are as full as a beast! My legs won't carry me. Will you stand still, you rascals! Let's see, what time is it? Hey, Jacob, you dog of a shoemaker! I want another drink. Will you stay still, you dogs! May the devil take me if they will keep quiet. Thank you, Jacob Shoemaker! I'll have another. Listen, friend! Which way does the road to town go? Stand still, I say! See, the brute is full. You drank like a rogue. Jacob! Is that a farthing's worth of brandy. . . You measure like a Turk. [*As he speaks, he falls and lies on the ground*]

JEPPE OF THE HILL*

By HOLBERG

Translated by John A. Eiesland

Dead drunk and asleep in a ditch, *Jeppe* is discovered by the *Baron* and his retinue, who decide to play a practical joke on him by taking him to the estate and treating him as Baron of the Manor.

Jeppe awakes —

[*Jeppe is lying in the baron's bed with a cloth-of-gold dressing-gown on a chair beside him. He wakes up, rubs his eyes, looks about, and becomes terrified ; he closes them again, takes his head in his hands and finds a gold-embroidered night-cap on it ; he moistens his fingers and wipes his eyes, then rubs them again, turns the cap around and looks at it, at the fine shirt he is wearing, at the dressing-gown and the other fine things in the room, making strange faces all the while. Meanwhile, soft music begins to play, and Jeppe clasps his hands and weeps. When the music stops he speaks*]

Jeppe O my, O my, what's this ? What splendor ! How did I get here ? Am I dreaming, or am I awake ? No, I am entirely awake. Where is my wife, where are my children, where is my house, and where is Jeppe ? Everything is changed, and I am, too — Oh, what does it all mean ? What does it mean ? [*He calls quietly in a frightened voice*] Nille ! Nille ! Nille ! — I think I'm in heaven — Nille ! and that without merit of mine. But am I myself ? Yes, it seems I am, and yet it seems I'm not. When I feel my back, which is still sore from the last beating I got, when I hear myself speak, when I touch my hollow tooth, it seems to me it's I. But when I look at my nightcap, my shirt, and all the glory before my eyes, when I hear the delicious music, then the devil take me if I can get it through my head that it is I. No, it is not I, I'm a thousand times a rascal if it is. But maybe I'm dreaming. I don't think I am. I'll try and pinch my arm ; if it doesn't hurt, I'm dream-ing. Yes, I feel it ; I'm awake, sure enough ; no one could dispute that with me, because if I weren't awake, I couldn't. . . But how can I be awake, when I come to think of it ? There is

* Translated for the author by J. A. Eiesland.

no question that I am Jeppe of the Mountain; I know that I'm
a poor peasant, a serf, a scoundrel, a cuckold, a starving louse,
a worm, a lump of carrion; then how can I also be an emperor
and lord of a castle? No, it's nothing—only a dream. So
I'd better be patient until I wake up. [*The music starts again
and Jeppe bursts into tears*] Oh, can one hear things like that
in his sleep? It's impossible. But if it's a dream, may I never
wake up, and if I'm crazy, may I never be sane again; I'd sue
the doctor that cured me, and curse the man that waked me.
But I'm neither dreaming nor am I mad, for I can remember
everything that has happened to me; I remember that my
blessed father was Niels of the Mountain, my grandfather Jeppe
of the Mountain; my wife's name is Nille; her whip is Master
Eric; my sons are Hans, Christoffer, and Niels. I've got it!
I know what it is; this is the other life, this is paradise, this is
heaven. Maybe I drank myself to death yesterday at Jacob
Shoemaker's, and went straight to heaven. Death can't be as
hard to go through as they say, for I don't feel a thing. Now,
perhaps the pastor is standing this very minute in the pulpit
delivering a funeral sermon over me, and is saying, "So ended
Jeppe of the Mountain. He lived like a soldier, and he died like
a soldier." There might be some doubt as to whether I died on
land or water, for I went out of the world quite wet. Oh,
Jeppe! how different this is from walking four leagues to town
for soap, lying on straw, being beaten by your wife, and having
horns put on you by the deacon. Oh, to what delights are your
troubles and your sour days now turned! Oh, I must weep for
joy, particularly when I think how all this has happened to me
without merit of mine! But one thing bothers me, and that's
that I'm so thirsty that my lips are sticking together. Should I
wish to be alive again, it would be just so I could get a mug of
ale to quench my thirst, for what good is all this finery to my
eyes and ears, if I am going to die all over again of thirst? I
remember, the priest often said that man neither hungers nor
thirsts in heaven, and also that a man finds all his friends there.
But I'm ready to perish with thirst, and I'm entirely alone—I
don't see a soul; I should at least find my grandfather, who was
a very decent sort of a fellow, and didn't owe his lordship a
penny when he died. I'm sure lots of people have lived as good
lives as I have; so wherefore should I be the only one to go to
heaven? Therefore it can't be heaven. But what can it be?
I'm not asleep, I'm not awake, I'm not dead, I'm not alive,

I'm not crazy, I'm not sane, I'm Jeppe of the Mountain, I'm not Jeppe of the Mountain, I'm poor, I'm rich, I'm a lowly peasant, I'm an emperor. O—o—o—! Help! Help! Help! [*He roars loudly*]

THE TRAGEDY OF LOVE*

By GUNNAR HEIBERG

Karen, passionately in love with her husband, *Erling Kruse,* a forester, suspects that he no longer loves her as he once did. *Erling* has not ceased to love his wife ; but insists that he loves her "in a different way." Unhappy at being left alone, and jealous of the trees among which he spends the greater part of his time, *Karen* seeks to keep him with her as long as possible.

Erling [*Rising*] Johannes is ready with the cart.

Karen Oh, sit a little while longer. It will still be light when you get there, even if you don't leave for another hour. Soon enough I shall be alone.

Erling [*Who has seated himself again*] There you see. You ought not to be so very much alone. I do think it is a little lonely here at times.

Karen When you are not in the woods.

Erling Exactly. But why don't you ask one of your sisters up here, or both — or anybody else you may prefer ?

Karen I don't care for company. It was I who wished that we should move up here earlier than both preceding years. It was I who wished it.

Erling [*Rising*] But in the spring we go to Paris.

Karen Not on my account.

Erling Don't you wish to go to Paris either now ?

Karen Oh, no, . . . as we didn't go that time. . .

Erling But I was willing to go at that time, too. . .

Karen Yes, but not until I had — behaved heroically.

Erling Yes, I should say so ! Merely to think of it makes me proud of you. [*Acting it out*] There you swooped like a bird down on the track — put your claws in the child — swooped away again. [*Admiringly*] Then you were happy, Karen, when you had saved that little boy.

* Reprinted by the courtesy of Edwin Bjorkman, translator.

Karen   I didn't care a rap for the boy.

Erling   What are you saying?   [*He laughs out loud*]

Karen   It was for your sake I did it.

Erling   [*Still smiling*]   That's a good one.   [*Having gone over to the window on the left*]   Say, Karen, what are you to do about your shower bath?   The shed is blown down, I see.

Karen   What does it matter?   This window is the only place from which I can be seen.   And there is no one in the whole house but me and the maids.   [*Johannes is heard cracking his whip*]

Erling   [*Goes out on the balcony*]   All right, Johannes, I am coming.   [*Goes back to the window*]   There is plenty of water in the drain now.   That's not a shower.   It's a waterfall.   It would be nice to see you there — right in the cascade.

Karen   You think so?

Erling   In the full sunlight, like now — yes! . . . But now for the serious side of life!   [*Patting her*]   The day after to-morrow you have me back again.

Karen   Convey my regards then.

Erling   To whom?

Karen   The trees.

Erling   I shall bring them regards from the finest tree in the forest.   [*He gives her a kiss*]   Good-bye.

Karen   Good-bye.   [*Erling goes out.   Karen stands for a moment in the middle of the room.   Her features are distorted.   Her eyes stray helplessly*]

Erling   [*Outside*]   Karen!   Good-bye, Karen.   The day after tomorrow.   [*One hears the cart moving*]

Karen   [*Runs to the balcony and cries with all her might*]   Erling!   Erling!   Come back a moment.   [*She walks back and forth.   Erling comes in, whip in hand.   They stand for a moment looking at each other; as he is about to speak, she says:*]

Karen   Don't you love me any longer?

Erling   [*As if it were a joke*]   Good-bye, Karen.   [*He is about to leave*]

Karen   Answer me.   Don't you love me any longer?

Erling   Yes.

Karen   As much as ever?

Erling   [*Thinks a while; then calmly*]   In a different way.

Karen   [*Almost screaming*]   Take the whip and beat me!

[*She walks back and forth a moment; then she stops and seems to wake up as if in surprise; smiles a little; speaks in a subdued voice, slowly, as if talking to herself*]   So you don't love me any longer, Erling Kruse?

Erling   Yes, Karen.   [*He goes up to her*]

Karen   [*As before*]   And when you came to me last night, it was because I begged you.

Erling   Good heavens, Karen — that's the way it always goes.

[*He takes out his pencil and begins to draw on a newspaper lying on the table*]

Karen   In curves.

IRISH SELECTIONS

PLAYBOY OF THE WESTERN WORLD

By JOHN M. SYNGE

Christopher Mahon, believing he has killed his father, flees from
the scene of the murder and finally comes upon the cabin of
Pegeen Mike. *Pegeen* and *Christy* fall in love and plan to marry,
much to the discomfort of *Shawn,* who wants to marry her, and
to the disapproval of her father.

Michael [*To Christy*] The blessing of God and the holy
angels on your head, young fellow. I hear tell you're after
winning all in the sports below ; and wasn't it a shame I didn't
bear you along with me to Kate Cassidy's wake, a fine, stout
lad, the like of you, for you'd never see the match of it for flows
of drink, the way when we sunk her bones at noonday in her
narrow grave, there were five men, aye, and six men, stretched
out retching speechless on the holy stones.

Christy [*Uneasily, watching Pegeen*] Is that the truth ?

Michael It is then, and aren't you a louty schemer to go bury-
ing your poor father unbeknownst to us when you'd a right to
throw him on the crupper of a Kerry mule and drive him west-
wards, like holy Joseph in the days gone by, the way we could
have given him a decent burial, and not have him rotting beyond, and not a Christian drinking a smart drop to the glory
of his soul ?

Christy [*Gruffly*] It's well enough he's lying, for the likes
of him.

Michael [*Slapping him on the back*] Well, aren't you a
hardened slayer ? It'll be a poor thing for the household man
where you go sniffing for a female wife ; and [*pointing to
Shawn*] look beyond that shy and decent Christian I have
chosen for my daughter's hand, and I after getting the gilded
dispensation this day for to wed them now.

Christy And you'll be wedding them this day, is it ?

Michael [*Drawing himself up*] Aye. Are you thinking, if

I'm drunk itself, I'd leave my daughter living single with a little frisky rascal the like of you?

Pegeen [*Breaking away from Shawn*]   Is it the truth the dispensation's come?

Michael [*Triumphantly*]   Father Reilly's after reading it in gallous Latin, and "It's come in the nick of time," says he; "so I'll wed them in a hurry, dreading that young gaffer who'd capsize the stars."

Pegeen [*Fiercely*]   He's missed his nick of time, for it's that lad, Christy Mahon, that I'm wedding now.

Michael [*Loudly with horror*]   You'd be making him a son to me, and he wet and crusted with his father's blood?

Pegeen   Aye. Wouldn't it be a bitter thing for a girl to go marrying the like of Shaneen, and he a middling kind of a scarecrow, with no savagery or fine words in him at all?

Michael [*Gasping and sinking on a chair*]   Oh, aren't you a heathen daughter to go shaking the fat of my heart, and I swamped and drowned with the weight of drink? Would you have them turning on me the way that I'd be roaring to the dawn of day with the wind upon my heart? Have you not a word to aid me, Shaneen? Are you not jealous at all?

Shawn [*In great misery*]   I'd be afeard to be jealous of a man did slay his da.

Pegeen   Well, it'd be a poor thing to go marrying your like. I'm seeing there's a world of peril for an orphan girl, and isn't it a great blessing I didn't wed you before himself came walking from the west or south?

Shawn   It's a queer story you'd go picking a dirty tramp up from the highways of the world.

Pegeen [*Playfully*]   And you think you're a likely beau to go straying along with, the shiny Sundays of the opening year, when it's sooner on a bullock's liver you'd put a poor girl thinking than on the lily or the rose?

Shawn   And have you no mind of my weight of passion, and the holy dispensation, and the drift of heifers I am giving, and the golden ring?

Pegeen   I'm thinking you're too fine for the like of me, Shawn Keogh of Killakeen, and let you go off till you'd find a radiant lady with droves of bullocks on the plains of Meath, and herself bedizened in the diamond jewelries of Pharaoh's ma. That'd be your match, Shaneen. So God save you now! [*She retreats behind Christy*]

Shawn Won't you hear me telling you . . . ?

Christy [*With ferocity*] Take yourself from this, young fellow, or I'll maybe add a murder to my deeds today.

Michael [*Springing up with a shriek*] Murder is it? Is it mad yous are? Would you go making murder in this place, and it piled with poteen for our drink tonight? Go on to the foreshore if it's fighting you want, where the rising tide will wash all traces from the memory of man. [*Pushing Shawn toward Christy*]

Shawn [*Shaking himself free, and getting behind Michael*] I'll not fight him, Michael James. I'd liefer live a bachelor, simmering in passions to the end of time, than face a lepping savage the like of him has descended from the Lord knows where. Strike him yourself, Michael James, or you'll lose my drift of heifers and my blue bull from Sneem.

Michael Is it me fight him, when it's father-slaying he's bred to now? [*Pushing Shawn*] Go on, you fool, and fight him now.

Shawn [*Coming forward a little*] Will I strike him with my hand?

Michael Take the loy is on your western side.

Shawn I'd be afeard of the gallows if I struck him with that.

Christy [*Taking up the loy*] Then I'll make you face the gallows or quit off from this. [*Shawn flies out of the door*]

Christy Well, fine weather be after him. [*Going to Michael coaxingly*] and I'm thinking you wouldn't wish to have that quaking blackguard in your house at all. Let me give us your blessing and hear her swear her faith to me, for I'm mounted on the spring-tide of the stars of luck, the way'll be good for any to have me in the house.

Pegeen [*At the other side of Michael*] Bless us now, for I swear to God I'll wed him, and I'll not renege.

Michael [*Standing up in the centre, holding on to both of them*] It's the will of God, I'm thinking, that all should win an easy or a cruel end, and it's the will of God that all should rear up lengthy families for the nurture of the earth. What's a single man, I ask you, eating a bit in one house and drinking a sup in another, and he with no place of his own, like an old braying jackass strayed upon the rocks? [*To Christy*] It's many would be in dread to bring your like into their house to end them, maybe, with a sudden end; but I'm a decent man of Ireland, and I leifer face the grace untimely and I seeing a score of grandsons growing up little gallant swearers by the name of God, than go peopling my bedside with puny weeds like of what you'd breed, I'm thinking, out of Shaneen Keogh. [*He joins their hands*] A daring fellow is the jewel of the world, and a man did split his father's middle with a single clout, should have the bravery of ten, so may God and Mary and St. Patrick bless you, and increase you from this mortal day.

Christy and Pegeen Amen, O Lord!

RIDERS TO THE SEA

By JOHN M. SYNGE

Maurya has just returned from wishing *Bartley*, her youngest son, "Godspeed" on his way down to the sea for news of *Michael*, who has been reported drowned. *Michael* is *Maurya's* fifth son to be lost at sea.

Maurya I seen Michael himself.

Cathleen [*Speaking softly*] You did not, mother; it wasn't Michael you seen, for his body is after being found in the far North, and he's got a clean burial by the grace of God.

Maurya [*A little defiantly*] I'm after seeing him this day and he riding and galloping. Bartley came first on the red mare; and I tried to say "God speed you," but something choked the words in my throat. He went by quickly; and the "blessing of God on you," says he, and I could say nothing. I looked up then, and I was crying, at the gray pony, and there was Michael upon it — with fine clothes on him, and new shoes on his feet.

Cathleen [*Begins to keen*] It's destroyed we are from this day. It's destroyed, surely.

Nora Didn't the young priest say the Almighty God wouldn't leave her destitute with no son living?

Maurya [*In a low voice, but clearly*] It's little the like of him knows of the sea... Bartley will be lost now, and let you

call in Eamon and make me a good coffin out of the white
boards, for I won't live after them. I've had a husband, and a
husband's father, and six sons in this house — six fine men,
though it was a hard birth I had with every one of them and
they coming to the world — and some of them were found and
some of them were not found, but they're gone now the lot of
them. . . There were Stephen, and Shawn, were lost in the great
wind, and found after in the Bay of Gregory of the Golden
Mouth, and carried up the two of them on the one plank, and in
by that door. [*She pauses for a moment, the girls start as if
they heard something through the door that is half open behind
them*]

Nora [*In a whisper*] Did you hear that, Cathleen? Did
you hear a noise in the north-east?

Cathleen [*In a whisper*] There's someone after crying out by
the seashore.

Maurya [*Continues without hearing anything*] There was
Sheamus and his father, and his own father again, were lost in
a dark night, and not a stick or sign was seen of them when
the sun went up. There was Patch after was drowned out of a
curagh that turned over. I was sitting here with Bartley, and
he a baby, lying on my two knees, and I seen two women, and
three women, and four women coming in, and they crossing
themselves, and not saying a word. I looked out then, and
there were men coming after them, and they holding a thing
in the half of a red sail, and water dripping out of it — it was a
dry day, Nora — and leaving a track to the door. [*She pauses
again with her hand stretched out towards the door. It opens
softly and old women begin to come in, crossing themselves on
the threshold, and kneeling down in front of the stage with red
petticoats over their heads*]

Maurya [*Half in a dream, to Cathleen*] Is it Patch, or
Michael, or what is it at all?

Cathleen Michael is after being found in the far North, and
when he is found there how could he be here in this place?

Maurya There does be a power of young men floating round
in the sea, and what way would they know if it was Michael
they had, or another man like him, for when a man is nine days
in the sea, and the wind blowing, it's hard set his own mother
would be to say what man was it.

Cathleen It's Michael, God spare him, for they're after sending us a bit of his clothes from the far north. [*She reaches out and hands Maurya the clothes that belonged to Michael. Maurya stands up slowly, and takes them in her hands. Nora looks out*]

Nora They're carrying a thing among them and there's water dripping out of it and leaving a track by the big stones.

Cathleen [*In a whisper to the women who have come in*] Is it Bartley it is?

One of the Women It is surely, God rest his soul. [*Two younger women come in and pull out the table. Then men carrying the body of Bartley, laid on a plank, with a bit of a sail over it, and lay it on the table*]

Cathleen [*To the women, as they are doing so*] What way was he drowned?

One of the Women The gray pony knocked him into the sea, and he was washed out where there is a great surf on the white rocks. [*Maurya has gone over and knelt down by the head of the table. The women are keening softly and swaying themselves with a slow movement. Cathleen and Nora kneel at the other end of the table. The men kneel near the door*]

Maurya [*Raising her head and speaking as if she did not see the people around her*] They're all gone now, and there isn't anything more the sea can do to me. . . I'll have no call now to be up crying and praying when the wind breaks from the south, and you can hear the surf is in the east, and the surf is in the west, making a great stir with the two noises, and they hitting one on the other. I'll have no call now to be going down and getting Holy Water in the dark nights after Samhain, and I won't care what way the sea is when the other women will be keening. [*To Nora*] Give me the Holy Water, Nora, there's a small sup still on the dresser. [*Nora gives it to her*]

Maurya [*Drops Michael's clothes across Bartley's feet, and sprinkles the Holy Water over him*] It isn't that I haven't prayed for you, Bartley, to the Almighty God. It isn't that I haven't said prayers in the dark night till you wouldn't know what I'd be saying; but it's a great rest I'll have now, and it's time surely. It's a great rest I'll have now, and great sleeping in the long nights after Samhain, if it's only a bit of wet flour we do have to eat, and maybe a fish that would be stinking. [*She kneels down again, crossing herself, and saying prayers under her breath*]

KING ARGIMENES AND THE UNKNOWN
WARRIOR *

By Lord Dunsany

King Argimenes is overthrown; his god is "broken in three pieces"; he digs with the slaves in the fields of *King Darniak* and sings the "tear-song, the chant of the low-born." Ragged, dirty, and hungry, he has little to hope for, though the slave, *Zarb*, whispers that should he find gold in the field, he might bribe the guard and lead the slaves to freedom.

King Argimenes [*To himself as his spade touches something in the earth*] Metal! [*Feels with his spade again*] Gold perhaps!—It is of no use here. [*Uncovers earth leisurely. Suddenly he drops on his knees and works excitedly in the earth with his hands. Then very slowly, still kneeling, he lifts, lying flat on his hands, a long greenish sword, his eyes intent on it. About the level of his uplifted forehead he holds it, still flat on both hands, and addresses it thus*] O holy and blessed thing! [*Then he lowers it slowly till his hands rest on his knees, and looking all the while at the sword, loquitur*] Three years ago tomorrow King Darniak spat at me, having taken my kingdom from me. Three times in that year I was flogged, with twelve stripes, with seventeen stripes, and with twenty stripes. A year and eleven months ago, come Moon-day, the King's Overseer struck me in the face, and nine times in that year he called me dog. For one month two weeks and a day I was yoked with a bullock and pulled a rounded stone all day over the path, except while we were fed. I was flogged twice that year — with eighteen stripes and with ten stripes. This year the roof of the slave-sty has fallen in and King Darniak will not repair it. Five weeks ago one of his Queens laughed at me as she came across the slave-fields. I was flogged again this year and with thirteen stripes, and twelve times they have called me dog. And these things they have done to a king, and a king of the House of Ithara. [*He listens attentively for a moment, then buries the sword again and pats the earth over it with his hands, then digs again*]

* * *

[*Kneeling, hands outspread downward*] O warrior spirit, wherever thou wanderest, whoever be thy gods, whether they

* From "King Argimenes and The Unknown Warrior," from "Five Plays" by Lord Dunsany. Reprinted by permission of Little, Brown & Company.

punish thee or whether they bless thee, O kingly spirit, that once laid here this sword, behold, I pray to thee, having no gods to pray to, for the god of my nation was broken in three by night. Mine arm is stiff with three years' slavery, and remembers not the sword. But guide thy sword till I have slain six men and armed the strongest slaves, and thou shalt have the sacrifice every year of a hundred goodly oxen. And I will build in Ithara a temple to thy memory wherein all that enter in shall remember thee; so shalt thou be honored and envied among the dead, for the dead are very jealous of remembrance. Ay, though thou wert a robber that took men's lives unrighteously, yet shall rare spices smoulder in thy temple and little maidens sing and new-plucked flowers deck the solemn aisles; and priests shall go about it ringing bells that thy soul shall find repose. Oh, but it has a good blade, this old green sword; thou wouldst not like to see it miss its mark [*if the dead see at all, as wise men teach*], thou wouldst not like to see it go thirsting into the air; so huge a sword should find its marrowy bone. [*Extending his right hand upward*] Come into my right arm, O ancient spirit, O unknown warrior's soul. And if thou hast the ear of any gods, speak there against Illuriel, god of King Darniak.

PROGRESS *

By St. John G. Ervine

Cold, calculating, scientific *Professor Henry Corrie*, D.Sc., completes an experiment which will humanize war — that is, it will kill a greater number with increased rapidity.

His sister, *Mrs. Meldon*, comes to his laboratory to visit him on the anniversary of the death of her son, who was killed in the war.

Mrs. Meldon No one but you knows the secret of your invention, Henry?

Corrie No — not that I am aware of.

Mrs. M. If you were to destroy your invention, never reveal its secrets, thousands of boys like Eddie might live without fear of being destroyed.

Corrie Oh, I don't know. It's a fantastic thought, that, but

* From *Progress*, by St. John G. Ervine. Reprinted by courtesy of The Macmillan Company, publishers.

there's nothing in it. Other people will invent things even
deadlier than my bomb.

Mrs. M. But, Henry, if you were to suppress your invention !

Corrie Suppress it !

Mrs. M. Yes, if you were to destroy your formulæ, and people were to know what you'd done, perhaps you'd do a great
deal to change people's hearts ! . . .

Corrie My dear Charlotte, most sensible people would think
I'd gone off my head. A few cranks and religious maniacs
might praise me, but the average person would think I was a
fool — besides being damned unpatriotic.

Mrs. M. Henry — I beg you to destroy your invention.

Corrie You what ?

Mrs. M. I beg you to destroy it. Let that be your memorial
to Eddie ! . . .

Corrie My dear Charlotte, I begin to believe that grief has
unhinged your mind ! Destroy my invention ! . . .

Mrs. M. Your bomb will destroy life, Henry. I beg of you
to destroy it ! . . .

Corrie Rubbish, woman, rubbish.

Mrs. M. Then I will destroy it for you ! [*She goes to the
table where the retorts are and hurls the table over so that the
retorts are smashed*]

Corrie What the hell are you doing ?

Mrs. M. I'm destroying your foul invention.

Corrie [*Laughing harshly*] That won't destroy it. I've got
it all in my head. All that you've done, Charlotte, is to make
a mess on my floor. Damned silly, I call it. [*He stoops down
and begins to clear up the mess*]

Mrs. M. [*Standing behind him*] It's all in your head !

Corrie Of course it is. Anybody but a fool woman would
have realized that. Making a confounded mess like this ! . . .

Mrs. M. It's all in your head ?

Corrie Yes, yes. Don't keep repeating yourself, but come and
help to clear up this mess you've made.

Mrs. M. Henry, won't you do what I ask you ?

Corrie Don't be a fool. [*Looking around*] Give me that
cloth over there so that I can mop up this stuff. [*He continues*

*to collect the pieces of broken glass, etc., while she goes towards
to the table where the cloth is. When she reaches the table, she
sees a long knife lying there, and half unconsciously she picks it
up and looks at it*]

Corrie [*Impatiently*] Hurry up. What on earth are you
doing?

Mrs. M. I'm looking at something — this knife!

Corrie Well, you can look at it afterwards. Fetch the cloth
now. Here's Eddie's wreath under the table. You've made a
mess of it, too.

Mrs. M. Eddie's wreath! [*She comes towards him, the knife
in her hand*]

Corrie Yes.

Mrs. M. If you were to give up your invention, Henry, I
wouldn't mind about the wreath. Your offering would be better than mine.

Corrie Well, I shan't. Give up my invention for a lot of
damned sentiment! Not likely!

Mrs. M. It'll destroy life, Henry.

Corrie What's that got to do with it? Give me that cloth.
[*He snatches it out of her hand, but does not see the knife in
her other hand*]

Mrs. M. You won't destroy it, Henry?

Corrie [*Almost in a snarl*] No!

Mrs. M. [*Raising the knife above him*] Then I . . . [*With
a queer moan of despair, she drives the knife into his back. He
sways a moment, uttering a choking sound, and then, clutching
at the air, he pitches forward on to his face. She stands above
him, looking down on his body in a dazed way. She is crying
hysterically, and suddenly she stoops and picks up the broken
wreath. She holds it to her breast, and stares distractedly in
front of her*]

Mrs. M. Eddie, dear, I had to, I had to, Eddie! . . .

ENGLISH SELECTIONS

THE RIVALS

By RICHARD BRINSLEY SHERIDAN

Mr. Faulkland had hoped that *Julia*, his sweetheart, would be miserably lonely during his absence but discovers that she had been very gay; for which he reprimands her, and she runs from the room crying.

Faulkland In tears! Stay, Julia; stay but for a moment.— The door is fastened!—Julia!—my soul—but for one moment!—thus I hear her sobbing!—'Sdeath! What a brute am I to use her thus! Yet stay! Ay,—she is coming now; —how little resolution there is in woman!—how a few soft words can turn them!—No, faith!—she is *not* coming either!—Why, Julia,—my love—say but that you forgive me—come but to tell me that.—Now, this is being *too* resentful.—Stay! she *is* coming too—I thought she would—no steadiness in anything; her going away must have been a mere trick then—she shan't see that I was hurt by it.—I'll affect indifference,— [*Hums a tune; then listens*] No—Zounds! She's *not* coming!—nor don't intend it, I suppose.—This is not *steadiness*, but *obstinacy*! Yet I deserve it.—What, after so long an absence to quarrel with her tenderness!—'twas barbarous and unmanly!—I should be ashamed to see her now!— I'll wait till her just resentment is abated—and when I distress her so again, may I lose her for ever! and be linked instead to some antique virago, whose gnawing passions, and long hoarded spleen, shall make me curse my folly half the day and all the night!

THE RIVALS

By RICHARD BRINSLEY SHERIDAN

Mr. Faulkland drops in for a chat with *Captain Absolute* concerning *Julia*, his sweetheart, whom he believes to be still visiting in Devonshire.

Upon the arrival of *Bob Acres*, *Julia's* neighbor, *Faulkland* discovers that she has just returned to gay Bath and its hilarity.

Faulkland Well, well, it may be so! — Pray, Mr. —, what's his d — d name? — Do you remember what songs Miss Melville sung?

Acres Not I, indeed.

Absolute Stay, now, they were some pretty melancholy purling-stream airs, I warrant; perhaps you may recollect; — did she sing, "When absent from my soul's delight"?

Acres No, that wa'n't it.

Absolute Or, "Go, Gentle Dales!"

Acres Oh, no! nothing like it. Odds! now I recollect one of them — "My heart's my own, my will is free." [*Sings*]

Faulkland Fool! fool that I am! to fix all my happiness on such a trifler! 'Sdeath! to make herself the pipe and ballad-monger of a circle to soothe her light heart with catches and glees! — What can you say to this, sir?

Absolute Why, that I should be glad to hear my mistress had been so merry, sir.

Faulkland Nay, nay, nay — I'm not sorry that she has been happy — no, no, I am glad of that — I would not have had her sad or sick — yet surely a sympathetic heart would have shown itself even in the choice of a song — she might have been temperately healthy, and somehow, plaintively gay; — but she has been dancing, too, I doubt not!

Acres What does the gentleman say about dancing?

Absolute He says the lady we speak of dances as well as she sings.

Acres Aye, truly, does she — there was at our last race-ball —

Faulkland Hell and the devil! There! — there — I told you so! I told you so! Oh! she thrives in my absence! Dancing! — but her whole feelings have been in opposition with mine; — I have been anxious, silent, pensive, sedentary — my days have been hours of care, my nights of watchfulness. — She has been all health! Spirit! laugh! song! dance! Oh! — d — ned levity!

Absolute For heaven's sake! Faulkland, don't expose yourself so. — Suppose she has danced, what then? — Does not the ceremony of society often oblige —

Faulkland Well, well, I'll contain myself — Perhaps, as you say — for form sake. — What, Mr. Acres, you were praising Miss Melville's manner of dancing a minuet — hey?

Acres Oh, I dare ensure her for that—but what I was going to speak of was her country dancing.—Odds swimmings! She has such an air with her!

Faulkland Now disappointment on her!—Defend this, Absolute; why don't you defend this?—Country-dances! jigs, and reels! Am I to blame now? A minuet I could have forgiven—I should not have minded that—I say I should not have regarded a minuet—but country-dances! Zounds! had she made one in a cotillon—I believe I could have forgiven even that—but to be monkey-led for a night!—to run the gauntlet through a string of amorous palming puppies!—to show paces like a managed filly!—O Jack, there never can be but *one* man in the world whom a truly modest and delicate woman ought to pair with in a country-dance; and, even then, the rest of the couples should be her great-uncles and aunts!

Absolute Ay, to be sure!—grandfathers and grandmothers!

Faulkland If there be but one vicious mind in the set, 'twill spread like a contagion—the action of their pulse beats to the lascivious movement of the jig—their quivering, warm-breathed sighs impregnate the very air—the atmosphere becomes electrical to love, and each amorous spark darts through every link of the chain!—I must leave you—I own I am somewhat flurried—and that confounded booby has perceived it.

A TRIP TO SCARBOROUGH

By RICHARD BRINSLEY SHERIDAN

Lord Foppington, a vain, pretentious fool, affected in dress and manner, thinks himself quite a dandy, particularly with the ladies, who find him a boorish fop.

Lord Foppington Dear Loveless, I am your most humble servant.

Loveless My Lord, I'm yours.

Lord F. Madam, your Ladyship's very humble slave.

Loveless My Lord, this lady is a relation of my wife's.

Lord F. [*Saluting her*] The beautifullest race of people upon earth, rat me. Dear Loveless, I am overjoyed that you think of continuing here. I am, stap my vitals. [*To Amanda*] For Gad's sake, Madam, how has your ladyship been able to subsist thus long, under the fatigue of a country life?

Amanda   My life has been very far from that, my Lord, it has been a very quiet one.

Lord F.   Why that's the fatigue I speak of, Madam ; for 'tis impossible to be quiet, without thinking ; now thinking is to me the greatest fatigue in the world.

Amanda   Does not your Lordship love reading then ?

Lord F.   Oh, passionately, Madam, but I never think of what I read.

Berinthia   Why, can your lordship read without thinking ?

Lord F.   O, Lard, can your ladyship pray without devotion, Madam ?

Amanda   I must own, I think books the best entertainment in the world.

Lord F.   I am so much of your ladyship's mind, Madam, that I have a private gallery in town, where I walk sometimes, which is furnished with nothing but books and looking glasses.   Madam, I have gilded them, and ranged them so prettily, before Gad, it is the most entertaining thing in the world, to walk and look at them.

Amanda   Nay, I love a neat library too, but 'tis, I think, the inside of a book should recommend it most to us.

Lord F.   That, I must confess, I am not altogether so fond of, for to my mind, the inside of a book is to entertain one's self with the forced product of another man's brain.   Now I think a man of quality and breeding may be much more diverted with the natural sprauts of his own ; but to say the truth, Madam, let a man love reading never so well, when once he comes to know the tawn, he finds so many better ways of passing away the four-and-twenty hours, that it were ten thousand pities he should consume his time in that.   For example, Madam, now my life, my life, Madam, is a perpetual stream of pleasure, that glides through with such a variety of entertainments, I believe the wisest of our ancestors never had the least conception of any of 'em. I rise, Madam, when in town, about twelve o'clock.   I don't rise sooner, because it is the worst thing in the world for the complexion ; not that I pretend to be a beau, but a man must endeavour to look decent, lest he makes so odious a figure in the side-box, the ladies should be compelled to turn their eyes upon the play ; so, at twelve o'clock I say I rise.   Now, if I find it a good day, I resolve to take the exercise of riding, so to drink my chocolate, and draw on my boots by two. On my return, I dress; and after dinner, lounge perhaps to the Opera.

Berinthia Your lordship, I suppose, is fond of music?

Lord F. O, passionately, on Tuesdays and Saturdays, provided there is good company, and one is not expected to undergo the fatigue of listening.

Amanda Does your lordship think that the case at the Opera?

Lord F. Most certainly, Madam; there is my Lady Tattle, my Lady Prate, my Lady Titter, my Lady Sneer, my Lady Giggle, and my Lady Grin,—these have boxes in the front, and while any favourite air is singing, are the prettiest company in the waurld, stap my vitals! Mayn't we hope for the honour to see you added to our Society, Madam?

Amanda Alas, my Lord, I am the worst company in the world at a concert, I'm so apt to attend to the music.

Lord F. Why, Madam, that is very pardonable in the country, or at church; but a monstrous inattention in a polite assembly. But I am afraid I tire the company?

Loveless Not at all; pray go on.

Lord F. Why then, ladies, there only remains to add, that I generally conclude the evening at one or other of the Clubs, not that I ever play deep; indeed I have been for some time tied up from losing above thousand pawnds at a sitting.

Loveless But isn't your Lordship sometimes obliged to attend the weighty affairs of the nation?

Lord F. Sir, as to weighty affairs, I leave them to weighty heads; I never intend mine shall be a burthen to my body.

Berinthia Nay, my lord, but you are a pillar of the state.

Lord F. An ornamental pillar, Madam; for sooner than undergo any part of the burthen, rat me, but the whole building should fall to the ground.

Amanda But, my lord, a fine gentleman spends a great deal of his time in his intrigues; you have given us no account of them yet.

Lord F. [*Aside*] Soh! She would enquire into my amours, that's jealous; poor soul! I see she's in love with me. [*To her*] Why, Madam, I should have mentioned my intrigues, but I am really afraid I begin to be troublesome with the length of my visit.

Amanda Your lordship is too entertaining to grow troublesome anywhere.

Lord F. [*Aside*] That now was as much as if she had said pray make love to me. I'll let her see I'm quick of apprehension. [*To her*] O Lard, Madam, I had like to have forgot a secret I must needs tell your ladyship. [*To Loveless*] Ned, you must not be so jealous now as to listen.

Loveless Not I, my Lord, I am too fashionable a husband to pry into the secrets of my wife.

Lord F. [*To Amanda, squeezing her hand*] I am in love with you to desperation, strike me speechless!

Amanda [*Giving him a box o' the ear*] Then thus I return your passion,—an impudent fool!

Lord F. Gad's curse, Madam, I'm a Peer of the Realm.

Loveless Hey, what the Devil, do you affront my wife, Sir? Nay then— [*Draws and fight*]

Amanda Ah! What has my folly done?—Help! murder! help! Part them, for Heaven's sake.

Lord F. [*Falling back and leaning on his sword*] Ah! quite through the body, stap my vitals!

THE SCHOOL FOR SCANDAL

By RICHARD BRINSLEY SHERIDAN

Young Lady Teazle is a bit extravagant—at least her elderly husband, *Sir Peter,* is of that opinion. When he tries to reprimand her for her lack of thrift she retaliates with this little domestic scene.

[*Enter Sir Peter and Lady Teazle*]

Sir Peter Lady Teazle, Lady Teazle, I'll not bear it!

Lady Teazle Sir Peter, Sir Peter, you may bear it or not, as you please; but I ought to have my own way in everything, and what's more, I will too. What! though I was educated in the country, I know very well that women of fashion in London are accountable to nobody after they are married.

Sir Peter Very well, ma'am, very well; so a husband is to have no influence, no authority?

Lady Teazle Authority! No, to be sure; if you wanted

authority over me, you should have adopted me, and not married me; I am sure you were old enough.

Sir Peter Old enough! — ay, there it is. Well, well, Lady Teazle, though my life may be made unhappy by your temper, I'll not be ruined by your extravagance!

Lady Teazle My extravagance! I'm sure I'm not more extravagant than a woman of fashion ought to be.

Sir Peter No, no, madam, you shall throw away no more sums on such unmeaning luxury. 'Slife! to spend as much to furnish your dressing-room with flowers in winter as would suffice to turn the Pantheon into a Creenhouse, and give a *fête champêtre* at Christmas.

Lady Teazle And am I to blame, Sir Peter, because flowers are dear in cold weather? You should find fault with the climate, and not with me. For my part, I'm sure I wish it was spring all the year round, and that roses grew under our feet!

Sir Peter 'Oons! madam — if you had been born to this, I shouldn't wonder at you talking thus; but you forget what your situation was when I married you.

Lady Teazle No, no, I don't; 'twas a very disagreeable one, or I should never have married you.

Sir Peter Yes, yes, madam, you were then in somewhat a humbler style — the daughter of a plain country squire. Recollect, Lady Teazle, when I saw you first sitting at your tambour, in a pretty figured linen gown, with a bunch of keys at your side, your hair combed smooth over a roll, and your apartment hung round with fruits in worsted, your own working.

Lady Teazle Oh, yes! I remember it very well, and a curious life I led. My daily occupation to inspect the dairy, superintend the poultry, make extracts from the family receipt-book, and comb my aunt Deborah's lap-dog.

Sir Peter Yes, yes, ma'am, 'twas so indeed.

Lady Teazle And then you know, my evening amusements! to draw patterns for ruffles, which I had not materials to make up; to play Pope Joan with the Curate; to read a sermon to my aunt; or to be stuck down to an old spinet to strum my father to sleep after a fox-chase.

Sir Peter I am glad you have so good a memory. Yes, madam, these were the recreations I took you from; but now you must have your coach — *vis-à-vis* — and three powdered footmen before your chair; and, in the summer, a pair of white cats to draw you to Kensington Gardens. No recollection, I suppose, when you were content to ride double, behind the butler, on a docked coach-horse.

Lady Teazle No—I swear I never did that; I deny the butler and the coach-horse.

Sir Peter This, madam, was your situation; and what have I done for you? I have made you a woman of fashion, of fortune, of rank—in short, I have made you my wife.

Lady Teazle Well, then, and there is but one thing more you can make me to add to the obligations, that is—

Sir Peter My widow, I suppose?

Lady Teazle Hem! hem!

Sir Peter I thank you, madam—but don't flatter yourself! for, though your ill conduct may disturb my peace of mind, it shall never break my heart, I promise you; however, I am equally obliged to you for the hint.

THE SCHOOL FOR SCANDAL

By RICHARD BRINSLEY SHERIDAN

"Good nature" may "become him," but *Sir Peter* can not forego the pleasure of constantly bickering with the young *Lady Teazle*.

Lady Teazle I assure you, Sir Peter, good nature becomes you. You look now as you did before we were married, when you used to walk with me under the elms, and tell me stories of what a gallant you were in your youth, and chuck me under the chin, you would; and asked me if I thought I could love an old fellow, who would deny me nothing—didn't you?

Sir Peter Yes, yes, and you were as kind and attentive—

Lady Teazle Ay, so I was, and would always take your part, when my acquaintance used to abuse you, and turn you into ridicule.

Sir Peter Indeed!

Lady Teazle Ay, and when my cousin Sophy has called you a stiff, peevish old bachelor, and laughed at me for thinking of marrying one who might be my father, I have always defended you, and said, I didn't think you so ugly by any means.

Sir Peter Thank you.

Lady Teazle　And I dared say you'd make a very good sort of husband.

Sir Peter　And you prophesied right; and we shall now be the happiest couple —

Lady Teazle　And never differ again?

Sir Peter　No, never! — though at the same time, indeed, my dear Lady Teazle, you must watch your temper very seriously; for in all our little quarrels, my dear, if you recollect, my love, you always began first.

Lady Teazle　I beg your pardon, my dear Sir Peter; indeed, you always gave the provocation.

Sir Peter　Now, see, my angel! take care — contradicting isn't the way to keep friends.

Lady Teazle　Then don't you begin it, my love!

Sir Peter　There, now! you — you are going on. You don't perceive, my life, that you are just doing the very thing which you know always makes me angry.

Lady Teazle　Nay, you know, if you will be angry without any reason, my dear —

Sir Peter　There! now you want to quarrel again.

Lady Teazle　No, I'm sure I don't; but, if you will be so peevish —

Sir Peter　There now! who begins first?

Lady Teazle　Why, you, to be sure. I said nothing — but there's no bearing your temper.

Sir Peter　No, no, madam; the fault's in your own temper.

Lady Teazle　Ay, you are just what my cousin Sophy said you would be.

Sir Peter　Your cousin Sophy is a forward, impertinent gipsy.

Lady Teazle　You are a great bear, I'm sure, to abuse my relations.

Sir Peter　Now may all the plagues of marriage be doubled on me, if ever I try to be friends with you any more!

Lady Teazle　So much the better.

Sir Peter　No, no, madam; 'tis evident you never cared a pin for me, and I was a madman to marry you — a pert, rural coquette, that had refused half the honest squires in the neighborhood!

Lady Teazle　And I am sure I was a fool to marry you — an

old dangling bachelor, who was single at fifty, only because he never could meet with any one who would have him.

Sir Peter Ay, ay, madam ; but you were pleased enough to listen to me ; you never had such an offer before.

Lady Teazle No! didn't I refuse Sir Tivy Terrier, who everybody said would have been a better match? for his estate is just as good as yours, and he has broke his neck since we have been married.

Sir Peter I have done with you, madam! You are an unfeeling, ungrateful — but there's an end of everything. I believe you capable of everything that is bad. Yes, madam, I now believe the reports relative to you and Charles, madam. Yes, madam, you and Charles are, not without grounds —

Lady Teazle Take care, Sir Peter! you had better not insinuate any such thing! I'll not be suspected without cause, I promise you.

Sir Peter Very well, madam; very well! A separate maintenance as soon as you please. Yes, madam, or a divorce! I'll make an example of myself for the benefit of all old bachelors. Let us separate, madam.

Lady Teazle Agreed! agreed! And now, my dear Sir Peter, we are of a mind once more, we may be the happiest couple, and never differ again, you know ; ha! ha! ha! Well, you are going to be in a passion, I see, and I shall only interrupt you — so, bye! bye! [*Exit*]

Sir Peter Plagues and tortures! I can't make her angry either! Oh, I am the most miserable fellow! But I'll not bear her presuming to keep her temper ; no! she may break my heart, but she shan't keep her temper.

SHE STOOPS TO CONQUER

By Dr. Oliver Goldsmith

Mr. Hardcastle wants *Marlow,* the son of an old friend, to win his daughter *Kate's* hand. *Marlow,* accompanied by his friend *Hastings,* is expected for a visit. *Tony Lumpkin,* a mischievous son of *Mrs. Hardcastle,* on his nightly visit to the alehouse, encounters the travelers as they are inquiring the way to the Hardcastle home and decides to play a practical joke at their expense.

Tony No offence, gentlemen. But I'm told you have been inquiring for one Mr. Hardcastle, in these parts. Do you know what part of the country you are in?

Hastings Not in the least, sir, but should thank you for information.

Tony Nor the way you came?

Hastings No, sir; but if you can inform us—

Tony Why, gentlemen, if you know neither the road you are going, nor where you are, nor the road you came, the first thing I have to inform you is, that—you have lost your way.

Marlow We wanted no ghost to tell us that.

Tony Pray, gentlemen, may I be so bold as to ask the place from whence you came?

Marlow That's not necessary towards directing us where we are to go.

Tony No offence; but question for question is all fair, you know. Pray, gentlemen, is not this same Hardcastle a cross-grained, old-fashioned, whimsical fellow, with an ugly face, a daughter, and a pretty son?

Hastings We have not seen the gentleman, but he has the family you mention.

Tony The daughter, a tall, trapesing, trolloping, talkative may-pole; the son, a pretty, well-bred, agreeable youth, that everybody is fond of?

Marlow Our information differs in this. The daughter is said to be well-bred and beautiful; the son, an awkward booby, reared up and spoiled at his mother's apron strings.

Tony He-he-hem! Then, gentlemen, all I have to tell you is, that you won't reach Mr. Hardcastle's house this night, I believe.

Hastings Unfortunate.

Tony It's a damned long, dark, boggy, dirty, dangerous way. Stingo, tell the gentlemen the way to Mr. Hardcastle's. [*Winking at the landlord*] Mr. Hardcastle's of Quagmire Marsh, you understand me.

Landlord Master Hardcastle's! Lack-a-daisy, my masters, you're come a deadly deal wrong! When you came to the bottom of the hill, you should have crossed down Squash-Lane.

Marlow Cross down Squash-Lane!

Landlord Then you were to keep straight forward, 'till you came to four roads.

Marlow Come to where four roads meet?

Tony Ay; but you must be sure to take only one of them.

Marlow Oh, sir, you're facetious.

Tony Then keeping to the right, you are to go side-ways till you come upon Crackskull Common; there you must look sharp for the track of the wheel, and go forward 'till you come to farmer Murrain's barn! Coming to the farmer's barn, you are to turn to the right and then to the left, and then to the right about again, till you find out the old mill —

Marlow Zounds, man! we could as soon find out the longitude!

Hastings What's to be done, Marlow?

Marlow This house promises but a poor reception; though perhaps the landlord can accommodate us.

Landlord Alack, master, we have but one spare bed in the whole house.

Tony And to my knowledge that's taken by three lodgers already. [*After a pause, in which the rest seem disconcerted*] I have hit it. Don't you think, Stingo, our landlady could accommodate the gentlemen by the fireside with — three chairs and a bolster?

Hastings I hate sleeping by the fireside.

Marlow And I detest your three chairs and a bolster.

Tony You do, do you? Then let me see — what if you go on a mile further to the Buck's Head? — the old Buck's Head on the hill — one of the best inns in the whole country?

Hastings Oh, ho! so we have escaped an adventure for this night, however.

Landlord [*Apart to Tony*] Sure, you ben't sending them to your father's as an inn, be you?

Tony Mum, you fool, you. Let *them* find that out. [*To them*] You have only to keep on straight forward, 'till you come to a large old house by the roadside. You'll see a pair of large horns over the door. That's the sign. Drive up the yard, and call stoutly about you.

Hastings Sir, we are obliged to you. The servants can't miss the way?

Tony No, no. But I tell you, though—the landlord is rich and going to leave off business; so he wants to be thought a gentleman, saving your presence, he! he! He'll be for giving you his company, and ecod! if you mind him, he'll persuade you that his mother was an alderman, and his aunt a justice of the peace.

Landlord A troublesome old blade, to be sure; but a keeps as good wines and beds as any in the whole country.

Marlow Well, if he supplies us with these, we shall want no further connection. We are to turn to the right, did you say?

Tony No, no; straight forward. I'll just step, myself, and show you a piece of the way. [*To the Landlord*] Mum!

Landlord Ah, bless your heart, for a sweet, pleasant— damned! mischievous son of—no matter. [*Exeunt*]

THE CIRCLE *

By SOMERSET MAUGHAM

Thirty years ago *Lady Kitty* eloped with the dashing *Lord Porteous* because her love for him was greater than her sense of responsibility to her husband and five-year-old son, *Arnold*. Now she returns, a fluttery "gay little lady with dyed red hair and painted cheeks . . . outrageously dressed." She arrives at the home of *Arnold* and *Elizabeth* with her lover, now an elderly, grumpy, dyspeptic old gentleman.

Lady Kitty Elizabeth! Elizabeth! [*She kisses her effusively*] What an adorable creature! [*Turning to Porteous*] Hughie, isn't she adorable?

Porteous [*With a grunt*] Ugh! [*Elizabeth, smiling now, turns to him and gives him her hand*]

Elizabeth How d'you do?

Porteous Damnable road you've got down here. How d'you do, my dear? Why d'you have such damnable roads in England? [*Lady Kitty's eyes fall on Teddie and she goes up to him with her arms thrown back, prepared to throw them around him*]

Lady Kitty My boy, my boy! I should have known you anywhere!

* From "The Circle," by W. Somerset Maugham, copyright, 1921, by Doubleday, Doran & Company, Inc.

Elizabeth [*Hastily*]   That's Arnold.

Lady Kitty [*Without a moment's hesitation*]   The image of his father!   I should have known him anywhere!   [*She throws her arms about his neck*]   My boy, my boy!

Porteous [*With a grunt*]   Ugh!

Lady Kitty   Tell me, would you have known me again?   Have I changed?

Arnold   I was only five, you know, when—when you—

Lady Kitty [*Emotionally*]   I remember as if it was yesterday. I went up into your room.   [*With a sudden change of manner*] By the way, I always thought that nurse drank.   Did you ever find out if she really did?

Porteous   How the devil can you expect him to know that, Kitty?

Lady Kitty   You've never had a child, Hughie; how can you tell what they know and what they don't?

Elizabeth [*Coming to the rescue*]   This is Arnold, Lord Porteous.

Porteous [*Shaking hands with him*]   How d'you do?   I knew your father.

Arnold   Yes.

Porteous   Alive still?

Arnold   Yes.

Porteous   He must be getting on.   Is he well?

Arnold   Yes.

Porteous   Ugh!   Takes care of himself, I suppose.   I'm not at all well.   This damned climate doesn't agree with me.

Elizabeth [*To Lady Kitty*]   This is Mrs. Shenstone.   And this is Mr. Luton.   I hope you don't mind a very small party.

Lady Kitty [*Shaking hands with Anna and Teddie*]   Oh, no, I shall enjoy it.   I used to give enormous parties here.   Political, you know.   How nice you've made this room!

Elizabeth   Oh, that's Arnold.

Arnold [*Nervously*]   D'you like this chair?   I've just bought it.   It's exactly my period.

Porteous [*Bluntly*]   It's a fake.

Arnold [*Indignantly*]   I don't think it is for a minute.

Porteous   The legs are not right.

Arnold   I don't know how you can say that.   If there is anything right about it, it's the legs.

Lady Kitty   I'm sure they're right.

Porteous   You know nothing whatever about it, Kitty.

Lady Kitty   That's what *you* think.   I think it's a beautiful chair.   Hepplewhite?

Arnold   No, Sheraton.

Lady Kitty   Oh, I know.   "The School for Scandal."

Porteous   Sheraton, my dear, Sheraton.

Lady Kitty   Yes, that's what I say.   I acted the screen scene at some amateur theatricals in Florence, and Ermete Novelli, the great Italian tragedian, told me he'd never seen a Lady Teazle like me.

Porteous   Ugh!

Lady Kitty   [*To Elizabeth*]   Do you act?

Elizabeth   Oh, I couldn't.   I should be too nervous.

Lady Kitty   Oh, I'm never nervous.   I'm a born actress.   Of course, if I had my time over again, I'd go on the stage.   You know, it's extraordinary how they keep young.   Actresses, I mean.   I think it's because they're always playing different parts.   Hughie, do you think Arnold takes after me or after his father?   Of course I think he's the very image of me.   Arnold, I think I ought to tell you that I was received into the Catholic Church last winter.   I'd been thinking about it for years, and last time we were at Monte Carlo I met such a nice Monsignore.   I told him what my difficulties were, and he was too wonderful.   I knew Hughie wouldn't approve, so I kept it a secret.   [*To Elizabeth*]   Are you interested in religion?   I think it's too wonderful.   We must have a long talk about it one of these days.   [*Pointing to her frock*]   Callot?

Elizabeth   No, Worth.

Lady Kitty   I knew it was either Worth or Callot.   Of course, it's line that's the important thing.   I go to Worth myself, and I always say to him, "Line, my dear Worth, line."   What *is* the matter, Hughie?

Porteous   These new teeth of mine are so damned uncomfortable.

Lady Kitty   Men are extraordinary.   They can't stand the smallest discomfort.   Why, a woman's life is uncomfortable from the moment she gets up in the morning till the moment she goes to bed at night. And d'you think it's comfortable to sleep with a mask on your face?

Porteous They don't seem to hold up properly.

Lady Kitty Well, that's not the fault of your teeth. That's the fault of your gums.

Porteous Damned rotten dentist. That's what's the matter.

Lady Kitty I thought he was a very nice dentist. He told me *my* teeth would last till I was fifty. He has a Chinese room. It's so interesting; while he scrapes your teeth he tells you all about the dear Empress Dowager. Are you interested in China? I think it's too wonderful. You know they've cut off their pig-tails. I think it's such a pity. They were so picturesque.

BIRD IN HAND *

By JOHN DRINKWATER

By his own admission *Thomas Greenleaf*, sixty-five and father of twenty-year-old *Jane*, is old-fashioned and behind the times,— and "of yeoman stock." So rigid is his belief in "class distinction" that when *Jane* goes out with *Gerald Arnwood*, "a member of quality," *Thomas* causes a scene. Reprimanded for his narrow beliefs, *Thomas* thus defends himself.

Thomas I've never had but one child — that's 'er. I'm a yeoman, come out of yeoman stock back as far as far. I've seen a deal of change in my time, the coming of a new world as you might say. When I was a boy my father's gig was the fastest traffic on the Oxford turnpike. When Windridge's saw-mill first started to work with a gas-engine, the London newspapers sent down to write about it. I remember farm wages here-abouts being raised from seven to eight shillings a week, and I remember my uncle saying in this bar that the country was ruined because the income tax had gone to four-pence in the pound. If my father could stand at Carfax cross-ing today he'd think he was in Bedlam, and when I went to London last spring, I thought I was. It's all altered — altered they say more than was ever known in the same time. Well, I've never been able to see that the world was any the better for it, or anybody in it any the 'appier. What's more, I've never seen that folks was any different for all the change. I've not

* Reprinted by courtesy of Lee Shubert.

been much of a one for changing with the times myself, and
I've never tried or wanted to understand half the things that
go on. But some things I've seemed to understand, and about
them I've never seen any occasion for altering my opinions.
There's classes today same as there always was, and same as to
my way of thinking there always will be. Sometimes they get
on together, sometimes they don't, that's all. I've always 'ad
as much self-respect as the quality, but I've never wanted to be
the quality. I grew up believing that young people had something to learn from their elders, and if today they think that
they've nothing to learn from anybody, I don't know as there's
anything to show that they're right and I'm wrong. I've
always thought that to forget your place in love-making looks
romantic and pretty enough in story-books, and means nothing but trouble and confusion anywhere else. I still think so,
and I don't believe that for all their free and easy notions about
it folk are any freer or any easier. That's my audit-book of
life, and I've got my girl to hand it on to, and no one else.
And she throws it back in my face. You may think I've took
an odd way of showing it tonight, but I've cherished that girl
in my 'eart; I've wanted 'er to grow up seeing things straight
and simple like I've tried to do. I've looked for 'er to be a
better showing of my own sort, firm out of the flesh and sense
my forbears gave me, and not to have her 'ead turned by any
high-flown theory that comes along about things that don't
want theories anyway. I've believed in 'er, and she's let me
down. She's got 'erself into this mess, and telling me that it's
no mess can't change my beliefs of a life-time. I'm sorry about
what I've done tonight. I shall be sorry for it till the end of
my life. I've behaved so as I ought to be ashamed, I know.
But this business 'as pretty near broke my 'eart.

BERKELEY SQUARE *

By JOHN L. BALDERSTON

Peter Standish, "a nervous and sensitive" youth, is in love with
the 18th century. He finds the diary of his 18th century name-
sake and, as did the first *Peter Standish*, goes to England to woo
his cousin *Kate*, but falls in love with her sister, *Helen*. *Kate*
fears *Peter* because of his uncanny prophecies of the future and his

* From *Berkeley Square*, by John L. Balderston. By permission of The Macmillan
Company, publishers.

mysterious love of the past and breaks the engagement. Helen *has fathomed the mystery that lies behind* Peter's *eyes.*

Peter   . . . [Peter *turns his head as* Helen *again peers into his eyes*] No— [*Shaking his head sadly*] you'd see other pictures now, things that you mustn't see.

Helen   [*Grasps his shoulders*] I will see.

Peter   [*Moans, but turns his head to her*] You cannot bear it!

Helen   Monsters—no, men, in masks over their heads—a yellow mist around them—they fall, they twist in the mud—

Peter   [*With great effort*] If you *must* see, let it be by night!

Helen   Lights, dancing, flashing, everywhere! But this is the most beautiful of all.

Peter   The fireworks of hell.

Helen   Oh! A great flame opens like a flower.

Peter   A dump of shells that blew a score of men to pieces.

Helen   [*Unheeding*] Curving streams of fire—

Peter   Pumped out of hoses to shrivel men up like insects!

Helen   [*Shrinks back; covers face with hands*] Oh!

Peter   [*Leaping up and back behind stool*] We should have stopped with your fairy city.

Helen   Devils, demons, not men! [*She rises; turns from him R. front*] 'Tis not true! God would never have put us here to suffer, for a race of fiends like that to come after us. [*Buries her face in her hands*]

Peter   [*Comes to her and tenderly embraces her; they are R. of settee*] Helen, dear Helen, what were we doing?

Helen   [*She removes her hands from her eyes, turning to* Peter] The mystery, behind your eyes!

Peter   You saw the future there. [*Pause*]

Helen   But there was something else, more wonderful than that! [*They disengage;—he turns away, crossing to L.C. She half turns away, then turns to him again*] And now I will go to Kate and tell her that I have shared your vision, and why it is that people are afraid—

Peter   No, you mustn't tell her. She won't be afraid tomorrow. Nobody will be afraid any more. I'll be different then.

Helen   [*Walks toward door R.—then turns*] But I don't understand why I mustn't talk to Kate—

Peter You think she threw me over tonight just because she was afraid of me ?   It's more hopeless than that, Helen.   She's found that I don't love her.

Helen   [*After pause*]   But you want to marry her.

Peter Don't let's talk about that.   I had to go on with it, that was all.

Helen Then you don't love Kate any more than she loves you now, and it isn't about Kate you're unhappy, but because you feel lost here, and strange, and because people are afraid of you —

Peter Yes, and as everything has closed in around me, your sympathy has kept me from going mad.

Helen You make me very happy.

Peter You know how I feel.   You must know.   But try to believe, even though you can never understand why, what the beauty that is with us and about us now, though it's more lovely than all the real things that ever were, *isn't* real, Helen.   It's only a mirage.   It's like a vision of heaven.   It couldn't exist in this world at all, or in any real world.   It's — it's unnatural !

Helen   [*Walks up to him*]   Unnatural !

Peter Yes, and impossible, *not real*, Helen.   You must forget it all and forget me, for your own dear sake.   [*He turns away a pace up stage to stool*]

Helen You know I can't do that, Peter.

Peter   [*Sits on stool, facing to L. in agony and remorse*]   Oh, what have I done ?

Helen   [*Bewildered, standing in front of him*]   Peter, you know the future !   Tell me ours !

Peter Our future !   [*Looks up at her, startled*]   No, I don't know that.   Oh, Helen, try to understand.   I come to you from — somewhere else.   Another world.   [*Looking away*]

Helen I know   It's all so different, here.   [*Lights begin to dim*]

Peter But I'm not —   [*Rises and steps back*] — one of you !

Helen I've always felt that, Peter.   [*Her hands go out to him*]   Peter, it's something you've done that's like a wild beast in your mind.   [*A thought strikes her*]   Peter ! what price have you paid for the splendor about you ?   [*Crosses to him.*

Makes to embrace him, but hesitates]   You've not sold your soul
to —

Peter   No, my soul's not damned, not what you mean by
damned.   [*Embraces her*]   I love you.   Oh, God, help us
both!   I love you!

Helen   [*Quietly and proudly*]   I loved you before I ever saw
you, in my first dream of you, coming with a candle, from
somewhere far away, to meet me.

Peter   Oh, but, Helen, I'm not playing my part now.   [*Breaks
from her; moves L. in front of Helen*]   I'm myself, you see.
I'm *myself*, and I'm muddling everything up!   This isn't possible, this isn't my world — or yours.   It isn't my life — or
yours!   [*Backs away from her, up L.C. until he is in Moonlight
cast through R. window*]

Helen   Then take me away with you, Peter.

Peter   I can't!   I can't!

Helen   [*With a cry. Runs to him; clings to him*]   Then
don't leave me!

Peter   I won't.   [*Looks wildly behind him to where the picture
hangs in the modern scene — then kisses her*]   When I kissed
Kate, that was *his* kiss to his betrothed!   [*Straining her to him*]
But there's never been a kiss like that since the world began!

DEAR BRUTUS *

By J. M. Barrie

In an enchanted forest, on Midsummer's Eve, old *Lob's* houseguests
have an opportunity to live as they would, if they had another
chance.

Mr. *Dearth*, once an ardent young artist, has become a waster,
which calamity he thinks could have been avoided had he had a
child.   In the enchanted wood, we find him with his little
"might-have-been" daughter, *Margaret*.

Margaret   Daddy, Daddy.   I have won.   Here is the place.
Crack-in-my-eye   Tommy!   [*He   comes.   Crack-in-my-eye
Tommy, this engaging fellow in tweeds, is Mr. Dearth, ablaze in
happiness and health and a daughter.   He finishes his song,
picked up in the Latin quarter*]

Dearth   Yes, that is the tree I stuck my easel under last night

* Reprinted by courtesy of Charles Scribner's Sons.

and behold the blessed moon behaving more gorgeously than ever. I am sorry to have kept you waiting, old moon ; but you ought to know by now how time passes. Now, keep still, while I hand you down to posterity [*The easel is erected, Margaret helping by getting in the way*]

Margaret [*Critical, as an artist's daughter should be*] The moon is rather pale tonight, isn't she ?

Dearth Comes of keeping late hours.

Margaret [*Showing off*] Daddy, watch me, look at me. Please, sweet moon, a pleasant expression. No, no, not as if you were sitting for it ; that is too professional. That is better ; thank you. Now keep it. That is the sort of thing you say to them, Daddy.

Dearth [*Quickly at work*] I oughtn't to have brought you out so late ; you should be tucked up in your cozy bed at home.

Margaret [*Pursuing a squirrel that isn't there*] With the pillow anyhow.

Dearth Except in its proper place.

Margaret [*Wetting the other foot*] And the sheet over my face.

Dearth Where it oughtn't to be.

Margaret [*More or less upside down*] And Daddy tip-toeing in to take it off.

Dearth Which is more than you deserve.

Margaret [*In a tree*] Then why does he stand so long at the door ? And before he has gone she bursts out laughing, for she has been awake all the time.

Dearth That's about it. What a life ! But I oughtn't to have brought you here. Best to have the sheet over you when the moon is about ; moonlight is bad for little daughters.

Margaret [*Pelting him with nuts*] I can't sleep when the moon's at the full ; she keeps calling to me to get up. Perhaps I am *her* daughter, too.

Dearth Gad, you look it tonight.

Margaret Do I ? Then can't you paint me into the picture as well as mamma ? You could call it "A Mother and Daughter" or simply "Two Ladies," if the moon thinks that calling me her daughter would make her seem old.

Dearth O matre pulchra filia puchrior. That means, 'O Moon —more beautiful than any two-penny-halfpenny daughter.'

Margaret [*Emerging in an unexpected place*] Daddy, do you really prefer her?

Dearth Sh! She's not a patch on you; it's the sort of thing we say to our sitters to keep them in good humor. [*He surveys ruefully a great stain on her frock*] I wish to Heaven, Margaret, we were not both so fond of apple-tart. And what's this! [*Catching hold of her skirt*]

Margaret [*Unnecessarily*] It's a tear.

Dearth I should think it is a tear.

Margaret That boy at the farm did it. He kept calling Snubs after me, but I got him down and kicked him in the stomach. He is rather a jolly boy.

Dearth He sounds it. Ye Gods, what a night!

Margaret [*Considering the picture*] And what a moon! Dad, she is not quite so fine as that.

Dearth Sh! I have touched her up.

Margaret Dad, Dad—what a funny man! [*She has seen Mr. Coade with whistle, enlivening the wood. He pirouettes round them and departs to add to the happiness of others. Margaret gives an excellent imitation of him at which her father shakes his head, then reprehensibly joins in the dance. Her mood changes, she clings to him*]

Margaret Hold me tight, Daddy, I'm frightened. I think they want to take you away from me.

Dearth Who, gosling?

Margaret I don't know. It's too lovely, Daddy; I won't be able to keep hold of it.

Dearth What is?

Margaret The world—everything—and you, Daddy, most of all. Things are too beautiful to last.

Dearth [*Who knows it*] Now, how did you find that out?

Margaret [*Still in his arms*] I don't know; Daddy, am I sometimes stranger than other people's daughters?

Dearth More of a madcap, perhaps.

Margaret [*Solemnly*] Do you think I am sometimes too full of gladness?

Dearth My sweetheart, you do sometimes run over with it. [*He is at his easel again*]

Margaret [*Persisting*] To be very gay, dearest dear, is so near to being very sad.

Dearth [*Who knows it*] How did you find that out, child?

Margaret I don't know. From something in me that's afraid. [*Unexpectedly*] Daddy, what is a 'might-have-been?'

Dearth A might-have-been? They are ghosts, Margaret. I dare say I might have been a great swell of a painter, instead of just this uncommonly happy nobody. Or again, I 'might-have-been' a worthless idle waster of a fellow.

Margaret [*Laughing*] You!

Dearth Who knows? Some little kink in me might have set me off on the wrong road. And that poor soul I might so easily have been might have had no Margaret. My word, I'm sorry for him.

Margaret So am I. [*She conceives a funny picture*] The poor old Daddy, wandering about the world without me!

Dearth And there are other 'might-have-beens'—lovely ones, but intangible. Shades, Margaret, made of sad folks' thoughts.

Margaret [*Jigging about*] I am so glad I am not a shade. How awful it would be, Daddy, to wake up and find one wasn't alive.

Dearth It would, dear.

Margaret Daddy, wouldn't it be awful! I think men need daughters.

Dearth They do.

Margaret Especially artists.

Dearth Yes, especially artists.

Margaret Especially artists.

Dearth Especially artists.

Margaret [*Covering herself with leaves and kicking them off*] Fame is not everything.

Dearth Fame is rot! Daughters are the thing.

Margaret Daughters are the thing.

Dearth Daughters are the thing.

Margaret I wonder if sons would be even nicer?

Dearth Not a patch on daughters. The awful thing about a son is that never, never — at least, from the day he goes to school — can you tell him that you rather like him. By the time he is ten you can't even take him on your knee. Sons are not worth having, Margaret. Signed, W. Dearth.

MAKER OF DREAMS *

By OLIPHANT DOWN

Pierrot has gone to the market-place to find a girl "with a fine air and a string of great beads," who took his fancy at the afternoon performance. *Pierrette* is sitting by the fire crying when the door opens and the *Manufacturer* enters.

He is a gentle looking man, old, yet with a seemingly ageless manner. "He is the sort of person children take to instinctively." He might be taken for the village fiddler rather than a prosperous manufacturer.

Knowing that *Pierrette's* love for *Pierrot* has made her unhappy, and wishing to make things right, the *Manufacturer* hustles *Pierrette* off to the market place in order that he may be alone with *Pierrot* upon his return.

Manufac. Well, friend Pierrot, so business is not so very brisk.

Pierrot Brisk ! If laughter meant business, it would be brisk enough, but there's no money. However, I've done one good piece of work today. I've arranged with the editor to put an article in the paper. That will fetch 'em. [*Singing*]

> "Please come one day and see our house that's down
>   among the trees,
> But do not come at four o'clock for then we count
>   the bees,
> And bathe the tadpoles and the frogs, who splash the
>   clouds with gold,
> And watch the new-cut cucumbers perspiring with the
>   cold."

That's a song I'm writing.

Manufac. Pierrot, if you had all the money in the world you wouldn't be happy.

Pierrot Wouldn't I ? Give me all the money in the world and

* Copyright by Gowans and Gray, Ltd. Published in the United States by Walter H. Baker and Company.

I'll risk it. To start with, I'd build schools to educate the people up to high-class things.

Manufac. You dream of fame and wealth and empty ideals, and you miss all the best things there are. You are discontented. Why? Because you don't know how to be happy.

Pierrot [*Reciting*]

> "Life's a running brooklet,
> Catch the fishes there,
> You who wrote a booklet,
> On a woman's hair."

[*Explaining*] That's another song I'm writing. It's the second verse. Things come to me all of a sudden like that. I must run out a third verse, just to wind it up.

Manufac. Why don't you write a song without any end, one that goes on forever?

Pierrot I say, that's rather silly, isn't it?

Manufac. It all depends. For a song of that sort the singer must be always happy.

Pierrot That wants a bit of doing in my line.

Manufac. Shall you and I transact a little business?

Pierrot By all means. What seats would you like? There are the front rows covered in velvet, one shilling; wooden benches behind, sixpence; and, right at the back, the twopenny part. But, of course, you'll have shilling ones. How many shall we say?

Manufac. You don't know who I am.

Pierrot That makes no difference. All are welcome, and we thank you for your courteous attention.

Manufac. Pierrot, I am a maker of dreams.

Pierrot A what?

Manufac. I make all the dreams that float about this musty world.

Pierrot I say, you'd better have a rest for a bit. I expect you're a trifle done up.

Manufac. Pierrot, Pierrot, your superior mind can't tumble to my calling. A child or one of the "people" would in a moment. I am a maker of dreams, little things that glide about into people's hearts and make them glad. Haven't you often wondered where the swallows go to in the autumn? They come to my workshop, and tell me who wants a dream, and what happened to the dreams they took with them in the spring.

Pierrot   Oh, I say, you can't expect me to believe that.

Manufac.   When flowers fade, have you never wondered where their colors go to, or what becomes of all the butterflies in the winter? There isn't much winter about my workshop.

Pierrot   I had never thought of it before.

Manufac.   It's a kind of lost property office, where every beautiful thing that the world has neglected find its way. And there I make my celebrated dream, the dream that is called "love."

Pierrot   Ho! Ho! Now we're talking.

Manufac.   You don't believe in it?

Pierrot   Yes, in a way. But it doesn't last. It doesn't last. If there is form, there isn't soul, and, if there is soul, there isn't form. Oh, I've tried hard enough to believe it, but, after the first wash, the colors run.

Manufac.   You only get hold of a substitute. Wait until you see the genuine article.

Pierrot   But how is one to tell?

Manufac.   There are heaps of signs. As soon as you get the real thing, your shoulder-blades begin to tingle. That's love's wings sprouting. And, next, you want to soar up among the stars and sit on the roof of heaven and sing to the moon. Of course, that's because I put such a lot of the moon into my dreams. I break bits off until it's nearly all gone, and then I let it grow big again. It grows very quickly, as I dare say you've noticed. After a fortnight it is ready for use once more.

Pierrot   This is most awfully fascinating. And do the swallows bring all the dreams?

Manufac.   Not always; I have other messengers. Every night when the big clock strikes twelve, a day slips down from the calendar, and runs away to my workshop in the Land of Long Ago. I give him a touch of scarlet and a gleam of gold, and say, "Go back, little Yesterday, and be a memory in the world." But my best dreams I keep for today. I buy babies, and fit them up with a dream, and then send them complete and carriage paid . . . in the usual manner.

Pierrot   I've been dreaming all my life, but they've always been dreams I made myself. I suppose I don't mix 'em properly.

Manufac. You leave out the very essence of them. You must put in a little sorrow, just to take away the over-sweetness. I found that out very soon, so I took a little of the fresh dew that made pearls in the early morning, and I sprinkled my dreams with the gift of tears.

Pierrot [*Ecstatically*] The gift of tears! How beautiful! You know, I should rather like to try a real one. Not one of my own making.

Manufac. Well, there are plenty about, if you only look for them.

Pierrot That is all very well, but who's going to look about for stray dreams?

Manufac. I once made a dream that would just suit you. I slipped it inside a baby. That was twenty years ago, and the baby is now a full-grown woman, with great blue eyes and fair hair.

Pierrot It's a lot of use merely telling me about her.

Manufac. I'll do more. When I shipped her to the world, I kept the bill of lading. Here it is. You shall have it.

Pierrot Thanks, but what's the good of it?

Manufac. Why, the holder of that is able to claim the goods; you will notice it contains a complete description, too. I promise you, you're in luck.

Pierrot Has she red cheeks and a string of great beads?

Manufac. No.

Pierrot Ah, then it is not she. Where shall I find her?

Manufac. That's for you to discover. All you have to do is search.

Pierrot I'll start at once. [*He moves as if to go*]

Manufac. I shouldn't start out tonight.

Pierrot But I want to find her soon. Somebody else may find her before me.

Manufac. Pierrot, there was once a man who wanted to gather mushrooms.

Pierrot [*Annoyed at the commonplace*] Mushrooms!

Manufac. Fearing people would be up before him, he started out overnight. Morning came, and he found none, so he returned disconsolate to his house. As he came through the garden, he found a great mushroom had grown up in the night by his very door-step.   Take the advice of one who knows, and wait a bit.

Pierrot   If that's your advice. . . But tell me this, do you think I shall find her ?

Manufac.   I can't say for certain.   Would you consider yourself a fool ?

Pierrot   Ah . . . of course . . . when you ask me a direct thing like that, you make it . . . er . . . rather awkward for me.   But, if I may say so, as man to man . . . I mean as man to . . . [*He hesitates*]

Manufac.   [*Waiving the point*]   Yes, yes.

Pierrot   Well, I flatter myself that . . .

Manufac.   Exactly. And that's your principal danger. Whilst you are striding along gazing at the stars, you may be treading on a little glow-worm.   Shall I give you a third verse for your song ?

> "Life's a woman calling,
>   Do not stop your ears,
>   Lest, when night is falling,
>   Darkness brings you tears."

[*The Manufacturer's kindly and impressive tone holds Pierrot as it had held Pierrette some moments before. Whilst the two are looking at each other, a little red cloak dances past the window, and Pierrette enters with her marketing*]

WILL SHAKESPEARE *

By CLEMENCE DANE

Protesting that he never loved her and was tricked into marriage, *Shakespeare* leaves his wife, *Anne*, and goes to London with *Henslowe* and his players ; there to be free and to make his way in the world.   He falls in love with *Mary Fitton*, a maid-in-waiting to *Elizabeth*, but she, while pretending to love him, is really the mistress of his friend *Marlowe*.   Despite the success of his "Romeo and Juliet," *Shakespeare* is bitter and disillusioned, seeking to lose himself in work ; still *Anne*, as in the beginning, seems to come between him and his writing.

* From *Will Shakespeare*, by Clemence Dane. By permission of The Macmillan Company, publishers.

Shakespeare
> I had a word to say.
> Oh, spark that burned but now — !

Anne's Voice
> It dips, it dies —

Shakespeare
> A night-light, fool, and not a star.   I grope
> Giddily in the dark.   I shall grow old.
> What is my sum ?   I have made seven plays,
> Two poems and some sonnets.   I have friends
> So long as I write poems, sonnets, plays.
> Earn then your loves, and as you like it — write !
> Come, what's your will ?
> Three sets of lovers and a duke or two,
> Courtiers and fool — We'll set it in a wood,
> Half park, half orchard, like the woods at home.
> See the house rustle, pit gape, boxes thrill,
> As through the trees, boyishly, hand on hip,
> Knee-deep in grass, zone-deep in margarets,
> Comes to us, — Mary !

Anne's Voice
> Under the apple-trees,
> In the spring, in the long grass — Will !

Shakespeare
> Still the old shame
> Hangs round my neck with withered arms and chokes
> Endeavour.

Anne's Voice
> Will !

Shakespeare
> At right wing enter ghost !
> It should be Marlowe with his parted mouth
> And sweep of arm.   Why should he wake for me ?
> That would be friendship, and what a friend was I !
> Well — to the work !

Anne's Voice
> Will !   Will !

Shakespeare
> What, ghost ? still there ?
> Must I speak first ?   That's manners with the dead ;
> But this haunt lives — at Stratford, by the river.

Maggot, come out of my brain! Girl! Echo! Wraith!
You've had free lodging, like a rat, too long.
I need my room.   Come, show yourself and go!
"Changed?"   "But I knew her!"—say your say and go!
You'd a tongue once.

Anne's Voice

                    You're to be great—

Shakespeare

                    Stale!   Stale!
That's the Queen's catch-word.

Anne's Voice

                    But I know, I know,
I'm your poor village woman, but I know
What you must learn and learn, and shriek to God
To spare you learning—

Shakespeare

                    Ay, like wheels that shriek,
Carting the grain, their dragged unwilling way
Over the stones, uphill, at even, thus,
Shrieking, I learn—

Anne's Voice

                    When harvest comes—

Shakespeare

                    Is come!
Sown, sprouted, scythed and garnered—

Anne's Voice

                    I alone
Can give you comfort, for you reap my pain,
As I your loss—loss—loss—

Shakespeare

                    Anne, was it thus?

Anne's Voice

                    No other way—

Will Shakespeare

                    Such pain?

Anne's Voice

                    Such pain, such pain!

Shakespeare

I did not know.   O tortured thing, remember,
I did not know—I did not know!   Forgive—

Anne's Voice
  Forgiving is forgetting — no, come back !
  I love you.   Oh, come back to me, come back !
Shakespeare
                    I cannot.
Anne's Voice
                    Oh, come back !   I love you so.
Shakespeare
  Be still, poor voice, be still !
Anne's Voice
                    I love you so.
Shakespeare
  What is this love ?
  What is this awful spirit and unknown,
  That mates the suns and gives a bird his tune ?
  What is this stirring at the roots of the world ?
  What is this secret child that leaps in the womb
  Of life ?   What is this wind, whence does it blow,
  And why ?   And falls upon us like the flame
  Of Pentecost, haphazard.   What is this dire
  And holy ghost that will not let us two
  For no prayers' sake nor good deeds' sake nor pain
  Nor pity, have peace, and live at ease, and die
  As the leaves die ?
Anne's Voice
                    I know not.   All I know,
  Is that I love you.
Shakespeare
                    But I know, having learned —
  This I believe, because I know, I know,
  Being in hell, paying the price, alone,
  Licked in the flame unspeakable and torn
  By devils, as in the old tales that are true —
  All true, the fires, the red hot branding irons,
  The thirst, the laughter and filth of shame,
  All true, O fellow men ! all true, all true —
  Down through the circles, like a mangled rat
  A hawk lets fall from the far towers of the sky,
  Down through the wakeful aeons of the night,
  Into the Pit of misery they call
  Bottomless, falling — I believe and know

That the Pit's bottom is the lap of God,
And God is love.

Anne's Voice
　　　　　Is love, is love —

Shakespeare
　　　　　I know,
In knowing I will live my dark days out
And wait for His own evening to give light.
And though I may not fill the mouth I love,
Yet will I sow and reap and bind my sheaves,
Glean, garner, mill my corn, and bake, and cast
My bread upon the waters of the age.
This will I do for love's sake, lest God's eyes,
That are the Judgment, ask her man of her
One day, and she be ashamed — as I am shamed
Ever, in my heart, by a voice witnessing
Against me that I knew not love.

THE IMPORTANCE OF BEING EARNEST *
By OSCAR WILDE

Algernon Moncrieff, a young man about town, slips away from London society into the country and poses as the imaginary brother of *Jack Worthing,* that he may meet *Cecily Cardew, Jack's* eighteen-year-old ward. *Algernon* falls in love with *Cecily* — *Cecily,* with *Jack's* imaginary brother, thus making it impossible for *Algernon* to disclose his true identity.

Algernon   I hope, Cecily, I shall not offend you if I state quite frankly and openly that you seem to me to be in every way the visible personification of absolute perfection.

Cecily   I think your frankness does you great credit, Ernest. If you will allow me I will copy your remarks into my diary. [*Goes over to table and begins writing in diary*]

Algernon   Do you really keep a diary?   I'd give anything to look at it.   May I?

Cecily   Oh, no.   [*Puts her hand over it*]   You see, it is simply a very young girl's record of her own thoughts and impressions, and consequently meant for publication.   When it appears in volume form I hope you will order a copy.   But pray, Ernest, don't stop.   I delight in taking down from dictation.   I have

* Reprinted by courtesy of Walter H. Baker Company.

reached "absolute perfection." You can go on. I am quite ready for more.

Algernon [*Somewhat taken aback*] Ahem! Ahem!

Cecily Oh, don't cough, Ernest. When one is dictating, one should speak fluently and not cough. Besides, I don't know how to spell a cough. [*Writes as Algernon speaks*]

Algernon [*Speaking very rapidly*] Cecily, ever since I first looked upon your wonderful and incomparable beauty, I have dared to love you wildly, passionately, devotedly, hopelessly.

Cecily I don't think you should tell me that you love me wildly, passionately, devotedly, hopelessly. Hopelessly doesn't seem to make much sense, does it?

Algernon Cecily! [*Enter Merriman*]

Merriman The dog-cart is waiting, sir.

Algernon Tell it to come round next week, at the same hour.

Merriman [*Looks at Cecily, who makes no sign*] Yes, sir. [*Merriman retires*]

Cecily Uncle Jack would be very much annoyed if he knew you were staying on till next week, at the same hour.

Algernon Oh, I don't care about Jack. I don't care for anybody in the whole world but you. I love you, Cecily. You will marry me, won't you?

Cecily You silly boy! Of course. Why, we have been engaged for the last three months.

Algernon For the last three months?

Cecily Yes, it will be exactly three months on Thursday.

Algernon But how did we become engaged?

Cecily Well, ever since dear Uncle Jack first confessed to us that he had a younger brother who was very wicked and bad, you of course, have formed the chief topic of conversation between myself and Miss Prism. And of course a man who is much talked about is always very attractive. One feels there must be something in him after all. I daresay it was foolish of me, but I fell in love with you, Ernest.

Algernon Darling! And when was the engagement actually settled?

Cecily On the 4th of February last. Worn out by your entire ignorance of my existence, I determined to end the matter one way or the other, and after a long struggle with myself I accepted you under this dear old tree here.   The next day I bought this little bangle with the true lovers' knot I promised you always to wear.

Algernon   Did I give you this ?   It's very pretty, isn't it ?

Cecily   Yes, you've wonderfully good taste, Ernest.   It's the excuse I've always given for your leading such a bad life.   And this is the box in which I keep all your dear letters.   [*Kneels at table, opens box and produces letters tied up with blue ribbon*]

Algernon   My letters !   But my own sweet Cecily, I have never written you any letters.

Cecily   You need hardly remind me of that, Ernest.   I remember only too well that I was forced to write your letters for you. I wrote always three times a week, and sometimes oftener.

Algernon   Oh, do let me read them, Cecily ?

Cecily   Oh, I couldn't possibly.   They would make you far too conceited.   [*Replaces box*]   The three you wrote me after I had broken off the engagement are so beautiful, and so badly spelled, that even now I can hardly read them without crying a little.

Algernon   But was our engagement ever broken off ?

Cecily   Of course it was.   On the 22nd of last March.   You can see the entry if you like.   [*Shows diary*]   "Today I broke off my engagement with Ernest.   I feel it is better to do so. The weather still continues charming."

Algernon   But why on earth did you break it off ?   What had I done ?   I had done nothing at all.   Cecily, I am very much hurt indeed to hear you broke it off.   Particularly when the weather was so charming.

Cecily   It would hardly have been a really serious engagement if it hadn't been broken off at least once.   But I forgave you before the week was out.

Algernon   [*Crossing to her, and kneeling*]   What a perfect angel you are, Cecily.

Cecily   You dear romantic boy.   [*He kisses her, she puts her fingers through his hair*]   I hope your hair curls naturally. Does it ?

Algernon   Yes, darling, with a little help from others.

Cecily   I am so glad.

Algernon   You'll never break off our engagement again, Cecily ?

Cecily I don't think I could break it off now that I have actually met you. Besides, of course, there is the question of your name.

Algernon Yes, of course. [*Nervously*]

Cecily You must not laugh at me, darling, but it had always been a girlish dream of mine to love some one whose name was Ernest. [*Algernon rises, Cecily also*] There is something in that name that seems to inspire absolute confidence. I pity any poor married woman whose husband is not called Ernest.

Algernon But, my dear child, do you mean to say you could not love me if I had some other name?

Cecily But what name?

Algernon Oh, any name you like — Algernon, for instance. . .

Cecily But I don't like the name of Algernon.

Algernon Well, my own dear, sweet loving little darling, I can't really see why you should object to the name of Algernon. It is not at all a bad name. In fact, it is rather an aristocratic name. Half of the chaps who get into the Bankruptcy Court are called Algernon. But seriously, Cecily. . . [*Moving to her*]. . . If my name was Algy, couldn't you love me?

Cecily [*Rising*] I might respect you, Ernest, I might admire your character, but I fear that I should not be able to give you my undivided attention.

JOURNEY'S END *

By R. C. SHERRIFF

Captain Stanhope appears in the dug-out. "Despite his stars of rank, he is no more than a boy; tall, slimly built, but broad-shouldered. He is good looking — there is a pallor under his skin and dark shadows under his eyes." *Stanhope* is about to direct the most important and dangerous raid of his war career. *Lieutenant Hibbert,* "a small, slightly-built man in the early twenties," comes in. For months he has unsuccessfully tried to be excused from the army. The nervous strain of the forth-coming raid has "broken him." He makes one last plea to *Stanhope.*

* From *Journey's End,* by R. C. Sherriff. Reprinted by Special Permission of Coward-McCann, Inc., publishers. No performance of any kind may be given of this play without permission first having been obtained in writing from Samuel French, Inc., 25 West 45th Street, New York, N. Y.

Stanhope   Hullo! I thought you were asleep.

Hibbert   I just wanted a word with you, Stanhope.

Stanhope   Fire away.

Hibbert   This neuralgia of mine. I'm awfully sorry. I'm afraid I can't stick it any longer —

Stanhope   I know. It's rotten, isn't it? I've got it like hell —

Hibbert   [*Taken aback*]   *You* have?

Stanhope   Had it for weeks.

Hibbert   Well, I'm sorry, Stanhope. It's no good. I've tried damned hard; but I must go down —

Stanhope   Go down — where?

Hibbert   Why, go sick — go down the line. I must go into hospital and have some kind of treatment. [*There is a silence for a moment. Stanhope is looking at Hibbert — till Hibbert turns away and walks towards his dug-out*]   I'll go right along now, I think —

Stanhope   [*Quietly*]   You're going to stay here.

Hibbert   I'm going down to see the doctor. He'll send me to hospital when he understands —

Stanhope   I've seen the doctor. I saw him this morning. He won't send you to hospital, Hibbert; he'll send you back here. He promised me he would. [*There is silence*]   So you can save yourself a walk.

Hibbert   [*Fiercely*]   What the hell —!

Stanhope   Stop that!

Hibbert   I've a perfect right to go sick if I want to. The men can — why can't an officer?

Stanhope   No man's sent unless he's very ill. There's nothing wrong with you, Hibbert. The German attack's on Thursday; almost for certain. You're going to stay here and see it through with the rest of us.

Hibbert   [*Hysterically*]   I tell you, I can't — the pain is nearly sending me mad. I'm going! I've got all my stuff packed. I'm going now — you can't stop me! [*He goes excitedly into the dug-out. Stanhope walks slowly towards the steps, turns, and undoes the flap of his revolver holster. He takes out his revolver, and stands casually examining it. Hibbert returns with his pack slung on his back and a walking-stick in his hand. He pauses at the sight of Stanhope by the steps*]

Hibbert Let's get by, Stanhope.

Stanhope You're going to stay here and do your job.

Hibbert Haven't I *told* you? I *can't*! Don't you under-stand? Let — let me get by.

Stanhope Now, look here, Hibbert. I've got a lot of work to do and no time to waste. Once and for all, you're going to stay here and see it through with the rest of us.

Hibbert I shall die of this pain if I don't go!

Stanhope Better die of pain than be shot for deserting.

Hibbert ` [*In a low voice*]   What do you mean?

Stanhope You know what I mean —

Hibbert I've a right to see the doctor!

Stanhope Good God! Don't you understand! — he'll send you back here. Dr. Preston's never let a shirker pass him yet — and he's not going to start now — two days before the attack —

Hibbert [*Pleadingly*] Stanhope — if you only *knew* how awful I feel — Please do let me go by — [*He walks slowly round behind Stanhope. Stanhope turns and thrusts him roughly back. With a lightning movement Hibbert raises his stick and strikes blindly at Stanhope, who catches the stick, tears it from Hibbert's hands, smashes it across his knee, and throws it on the ground*]

Stanhope God! — you little swine. You know what that means — don't you? Striking a superior officer! [*There is silence. Stanhope takes hold of his revolver as it swings from its lanyard. Hibbert stands quivering in front of Stanhope*] Never mind, though. I won't have you shot for that —

Hibbert Let me go —

Stanhope If you went, I'd have you shot — for deserting. It's a hell of a disgrace — to die like that. I'd rather spare you the disgrace. I give you half a minute to think. You either stay here and try to be a man — or you try to get out of that door — to desert. If you do that, there's going to be an accident. D'you understand? I'm fiddling with my revolver, d'you see? — cleaning it — and it's going off by accident. It often happens out here. It's going off, and it's going to shoot you between the eyes.

Hibbert [*In a whisper*] You daren't —

Stanhope You don't deserve to be shot by accident—but I'd save you the disgrace of the other way—I give you half a minute to decide. [*He holds up his wrist to look at his watch*] Half a minute from now— [*There is silence; a few seconds go by. Suddenly Hibbert bursts into a high-pitched laugh*]

Hibbert Go on, then, shoot! You won't let me go to hospital. I swear I'll never go into those trenches again. Shoot!—and thank God—

Stanhope [*With his eyes on his watch*] Fifteen more seconds—

Hibbert Go on! I'm ready—

Stanhope Ten. [*He looks up at Hibbert, who has closed his eyes*] Five. [*Again Stanhope looks up. After a moment he quietly drops his revolver into its holster and steps towards Hibbert, who stands with lowered head and eyes tightly screwed up, his arms stretched stiffly by his sides, his hands tightly clutching the edges of his tunic. Gently Stanhope places his hands on Hibbert's shoulders. Hibbert starts violently and gives a little cry. He opens his eyes and stares vacantly into Stanhope's face. Stanhope is smiling*]

Stanhope Good man, Hibbert. I liked the way you stuck that.

Hibbert [*Hoarsely*] Why didn't you shoot?

Stanhope Stay here, old chap—and see it through— [*Hibbert stands trembling, trying to speak. Suddenly he breaks down and cries. Stanhope takes his hands from his shoulders and turns away*]

Hibbert Stanhope! I've tried like hell—I swear I have. Ever since I came out here I've hated and loathed it. Every sound up there makes me all—cold and sick. I'm different to—to the others—you don't understand. It's got worse and worse, and now I can't bear it any longer. I'll never go up those steps again—into the line—with the men looking at me —and knowing—I'd rather die here. [*He is sitting on Stanhope's bed, crying without effort to restrain himself*]

THE ROMANTIC AGE *

By A. A. MILNE

Gervase Mallory's car has broken down on the way to a fancy dress ball. He calls at the *Knowles'* home for help, where he sees the beautiful and romantic *Melisande*.

Later, *Gervase* continues his journey to the ball and loses his way in the forest. The next morning we find him still in the fancy dress of a Prince, talking to *Ern*, the little country boy.

Ern   [L.]   Oo-er!   Oo!   [*He circles slowly round Gervase*] Oo!   Look!   [*Now R.C.*]

Gervase   Yes, it is a bit dressy, isn't it?   Come round to the back   [*Ern moves round to the back*]   —take a good look at it while you can.   That's right. . . Been all round?   Good!

Ern   Oo!

Gervase   Well, I can't go on standing here while you say "Oo." Do you mind if I sit down?   [*Gervase is R.C. and Ern L.C.*] I gather that I have your consent.   I thank you.   [*Sits on bank R.*]

Ern   Oo!   Look!   [*He follows up and points at Gervase's legs and then sits on ground*]

Gervase   What is it now?   My legs?   Oh, but surely you've noticed those before?

Ern   Oo!

Gervase   Really, I don't understand you.   I came up here for a walk in a perfectly ordinary blue suit and you do nothing but say "Oo."   What does your father wear when he's ploughing? I suppose you don't walk all way round *him* and say "Oo!" By the way, I wish you'd tell me your name.   [*Ern gazes at him dumbly*]   Oh, come!   They must have told you your name when you got up this morning.

Ern   [*Smiling sheepishly*]   Ern.

Gervase   [*Bowing*]   How-do-you-do?   I am very glad to meet you, Mr. Hearne.   My name is Mallory.   [*Ern grins*] Thank you.

Ern   [*Tapping himself*]   I'm Ern.

Gervase   Yes, I'm Mallory, Ern.   We can't keep on saying this

to each other, you know, because then we never get any farther.
Once an introduction is over, Mr. Hearne, we are —

Ern Ern.

Gervase Yes, I know. I was very glad to hear it. But now
— Oh, I see what you mean. Ern — short for Ernest?

Ern [*Nodding*] They calls me Ern.

Gervase That's very friendly of them. Being more of a
stranger I shall call you Ernest. Well, Ernest [*getting up*]
— just excuse me a moment, will you? Very penetrating bark
this tree has. It must be a Pomeranian. [*He folds his cloak
and sits down again*] That's better. Now we can talk com-
fortably together. I don't know if there's anything you particularly want to discuss — nothing? — well, then, I will
suggest the subject of breakfast.

Ern [*Grinning*] 'Ad my breakfast.

Gervase You've *had* yours? You selfish brute! . . .

Ern Bacon fat. [*He makes reminiscent noises*]

Gervase Don't keep on going through all the courses. Well,
what happened was this. My car broke down. I suppose you
never had a motor-car of your own.

Ern Don't like moty-cars.

Gervase Well, really, after last night I'm inclined to agree
with you. Well, no, I oughtn't to say that, because, if it hadn't
broken down, I should never have seen Her. Ernest, I don't
know if you're married or anything of that sort, but I think
even your rough stern heart would have been moved by that
vision of loveliness which I saw last night. [*He is silent for
a little, thinking of her*] Well, then I lost my way. There I
was — ten miles from anywhere — in the middle of what was
supposed to be a short cut — late at night — Midsummer night
— what would *you* have done, Ernest?

Ern Gone 'ome.

Gervase Don't be silly. How could I go home when I didn't
know where home was, and it was a hundred miles away, and
I'd just seen the Princess? No, I did what your father or your
Uncle George or any wise man would have done, I sat in the car
and thought of Her.

Ern Oo!

Gervase You are surprised? Ah, but if you'd seen her. . .

Have you ever been alone in the moonlight on Midsummer
Night — I don't mean just for a minute or two, but all through
the night until the dawn came?   You aren't really alone, you
know.   All round you there are little whisperings going on,
little breathings, little rustlings.   Somebody is out hunting;
somebody stirs in his sleep as he dreams again the hunt of yesterday; somebody up in the tree-tops pipes suddenly to the
dawn, and then, finding that the dawn has not come, puts his
silly little head back under his wing and goes to sleep again. . .
And the fairies are out.   Do you believe in fairies, Ernest?
You would have believed in them last night.   I heard them
whispering.

Ern   Oo!

Gervase   [*Coming out of his thoughts with a laugh*]   Well,
of course, I can't expect you to believe me.   But don't go about
thinking that there's nothing in the world but bacon fat and
bull's-eyes.   Well, then, I suppose I went to sleep, for I woke
up suddenly and it was morning, the most wonderful sparkling
magical morning — but, of course, *you* were just settling down
to your bacon fat then.

Ern   Oo!   [*He makes more reminiscent noises*]

Gervase   Yes, that's just what I said.   I said to myself, breakfast.

Ern   'Ad my breakfast.

Gervase   Yes, but I 'adn't.   I said to myself, "Surely my old
friend, Ernest, whom I used to shoot bison with in the
Himalayas, has got an estate somewhere in these parts.   I will
go and share his simple meal with him."   So I got out of the
car, and I did what you didn't do, young man, I had a bathe in
the river, and then a dry on a pocket-handkerchief — one of
my sisters, unfortunately — and then I came out to look for
breakfast.   And suddenly, whom should I meet but my old
friend, Ernest, the same hearty fellow, the same inveterate talker
as when we shot dragon-flies together in the swamps of Malay.
[*Shaking his hand*]   Ernest, old boy, pleased to meet you.
What about breakfast?

Ern   'Ad my —

Gervase   S'sh.   Now then — to business.   Do you mind looking the other way while I try to find my purse.   [*Feeling for
it*]   Every morning when you get up, you should say, "Thank

God, I'm getting a big boy now and I've got pockets in my trousers." And you should feel very sorry for the poor people who lived in fairy books and had no trousers to put pockets in. Ah, here we are. Now, then, Ernest, attend very carefully. Where do you live?

Ern 'Ome.

Gervase You mean, you haven't got a flat of your own yet? Well, how far away is your home? [*Ern grins and says nothing*] A mile? [*Ern continues to grin*] Half a mile? [*Ern grins*] Six inches?

Ern [*Pointing L.*] Down there.

Gervase Good. Now, then, I want you to take this — [*Giving him half-a-crown*] —

Ern Oo! [*Rises*]

Gervase [*Rises*] Yes, I thought that would move you — and I want you to ask your mother if you can bring me some breakfast up here. Now, listen very carefully, because we are coming to the important part. Hard-boiled eggs, bread, butter, and a bottle of milk — and anything else she likes. Tell her that it's most important, because your old friend Mallory whom you shot white mice with in Egypt is starving by the roadside. And if you come back here with a basket quickly, I'll give you as many bull's-eyes as you can eat in a week. [*Very earnestly*] Now, Ernest, with all the passion and emotion of which I am capable before breakfast, I ask you : Have you got that?

Ern [*Nodding*] Going 'ome. [*He looks at the half-crown again*]

Gervase Going 'ome. Yes. But — returning with breakfast. Starving man — lost in forest — return with basket — save life. [*To himself*] I believe I could explain it better to a Chinaman. [*To Ern*] Now then, off you go.

Ern [*As he is going off L. turns half-way*] Oo!

Gervase [*Nodding to him*] Yes, I'm still "Oo."

Ern [*As he goes off L.*] 'Ad my breakfast.

Gervase Yes, and I wonder if I shall get mine.

JUSTICE *

By John Galsworthy

William Falder, junior law clerk, in love with *Ruth Honeywill*, forged a check to secure money that he might take her away from her brutal husband. Out of prison, *Falder* finds society unsympathetic toward him and returns to the law firm to secure a position from *Cokeson*, the managing clerk.

Cokeson Sit down! [*Falder sits in the chair at the side of Cokeson's table, on which he places his cap*]

Cokeson Now you are here I'd like you to give me a little account of yourself. [*Looking at him over his spectacles*] How's your health?

Falder I'm alive, Mr. Cokeson.

Cokeson [*Preoccupied*] I'm glad to hear that. About this matter. I don't like doing anything out of the ordinary; it's not my habit. I'm a plain man, and I want everything smooth and straight. But I promised your friend to speak to the partners, and I always keep my word.

Falder I just want a chance, Mr. Cokeson. I've paid for that job a thousand times, and more. I have, sir. No one knows. They say I weighed more when I came out than when I went in. They couldn't weigh me here [*He touches his head*] or here [*He touches his heart, and gives a sort of laugh*] Till last night I'd have thought there was nothing in here at all.

Cokeson [*Concerned*] You've not got heart disease?

Falder Oh! they passed me sound enough.

Cokeson But they got you a place, didn't they?

Falder Yes; very good people, knew all about it — very kind to me. I thought I was going to get on first rate. But one day, all of a sudden, the other clerks got wind of it. . . I couldn't stick it, Mr. Cokeson, I couldn't, sir.

Cokeson Easy, my dear fellow, easy.

Falder I had one small job after that, but it didn't last.

Cokeson How was that?

Falder It's no good deceiving you, Mr. Cokeson. The fact is, I seem to be struggling against a thing that's all round me. I can't explain it: It's as if I was in a net; as fast as I cut it here,

* Reprinted by courtesy of Charles Scribner's Sons.

it grows up there. I didn't act as I ought to have, about references ; but what are you to do ? You must have them. And that made me afraid, and I left. In fact, I'm — I'm afraid all the time now. [*He bows his head and leans dejectedly silent over the table*]

Cokeson I feel for you — I do really. Aren't your sisters going to do anything for you ?

Falder One's in consumption. And the other —

Cokeson Ye . . . es. She told me her husband wasn't quite pleased with you.

Falder When I went there — they were at supper — my sister wanted to give me a kiss — I know. But he just looked at her, and said : "What have you come for ?" Well, I pocketed my pride and I said : "Aren't you going to give me your hand, Jim ? Cis is, I know," I said. "Look here !" he said, "that's all very well, but we'd better come to an understanding. I've been expecting you, and I've made up my mind. I'll give you twenty-five pounds to go to Canada with." "I see," I said — "good riddance ! No, thanks ; keep your twenty-five pounds." Friendship's a queer thing when you've been where I have.

Cokeson I understand. Will you take the twenty-five pounds from me ? [*Flustered, as Falder regards him with a queer smile*] Quite without prejudice ; I meant it kindly.

Falder They wouldn't let me in.

Cokeson Oh ! Ah ! No ! You aren't looking the thing.

Falder I've slept in the Park three nights this week. The dawns aren't all poetry there. But meeting her — I feel a different man this morning. I've often thought the being fond of her's the best thing about me ; it's sacred, somehow — and yet it did for me. That's queer, isn't it ?

Cokeson I'm sure we're all very sorry for you.

Falder That's what I've found, Mr. Cokeson. Awfully sorry for me. [*With quiet bitterness*] But it doesn't do to associate with criminals !

Cokeson Come, come, it's no use calling yourself names. That never did a man any good. Put a face on it.

Falder It's easy enough to put a face on it, sir, when you're independent. Try it when you're down like me. They talk about giving you your deserts. Well, I think I've had just a bit over.

Cokeson [*Eyeing him askance over his spectacles*] I hope they haven't made a Socialist of you. [*Falder is suddenly still, as if brooding over his past self; he utters a peculiar laugh*]

Cokeson You must give them credit for the best intentions. Really you must. Nobody wishes you harm, I'm sure.

Falder I believe that, Mr. Cokeson. Nobody wishes you harm, but they down you all the same. This feeling— [*He stares round him, as though at something closing in*] It's crushing me. [*With sudden impersonality*] I know it is.

Cokeson [*Horribly disturbed*] There's nothing there! We must try and take it quiet. I'm sure I've often had you in my prayers. Now leave it to me. I'll use my gumption and take 'em when they're jolly.

TRELAWNY OF THE "WELLS" *

By ARTHUR W. PINERO

Sir William Gower is a tyrannical, conventional old man of seventy. Although strongly opposed to actors and actresses, *Sir William*, in a hasty moment, promises to back a play for *Tom Wrench*. *Sir William* is considerably perturbed when he discovers that the plot centers around his only grandson, *Arthur*. Because of *Arthur's* engagement to *Rose Trelawny*, actress, *Sir William* considers him a "late member" of the *Gower* family.

Tom These are old surroundings for you to find yourself in — [*Imogen comes forward*] Miss Parrott—

Sir William [*Advancing to her, giving her two fingers*] Good morning, ma'am.

Imogen This is perfectly delightful.

Sir William What is?

Imogen Your visit.

* Trelawny of the "Wells." Copyright, 1898, by Charles B. Davis; Copyright 1925, by A. W. Pinero. All rights reserved. Entered at Stationers' Hall. Entered at the Library of Congress, Washington, U. S. A. Caution: This selection is fully protected under the Copyright laws of the United States of America, the British Empire, including the Dominion of Canada, and all other countries of the Copyright Union. The selection may not be produced either in public either by amateurs or professionals, broadcast by radio, or used for motion picture purpose. It is intended solely for the use of students and others, privately or in the classroom, and may not be performed or read publicly without the proper written authority from Samuel French, 25 West 45th St., New York City, or 811 West 7th St., Los Angeles, California, or Samuel French (Canada) Limited, 480 University Avenue, Toronto.

Sir William Ugh! [*Weakly*] Give me a cheer. [*Looking about him*] Have ye no cheers here?

Tom Yes. [*Tom places the throne-chair behind* Sir William *who sinks into it*]

Sir William Thank ye; much obleeged. [*To Imogen*] Sit. [*Imogen hurriedly fetches the stool and seats herself beside the throne-chair. Sir William produces his snuff-box*] You are astonished at seeing me here, I dare say?

Tom Not at all.

Sir William [*Glancing at Tom*] Addressing the lady. [*To Imogen*] You are surprised to see me?

Imogen Very.

Sir William [*To Tom*] Ah! [*Tom retreats, getting behind* Sir William's *chair and looking down upon him*] The truth is, I am beginning to regret my association with ye.

Imogen [*Her hand to her heart*] Oh — h — h — h!

Tom [*Under his breath*] Oh! [*Holding his fist over* Sir William's *head*] Oh — h — h — h!

Imogen [*Piteously*] You — you don't propose to withdraw your capital, Sir William?

Sir William That would be a breach of faith, ma'am —

Imogen Ah!

Tom [*Walking about, jauntily*] Ha!

Imogen [*Seizing Sir William's hand*] Friend!

Sir William [*Withdrawing his hand sharply*] I'll thank ye not to repeat that action, ma'am. But I — I have been slightly indisposed since I made your acqueentance in Clerkenwell; I find myself unable to sleep at night. [*To Tom*] That comedy of yours — it buzzes continually in my head, sir.

Tom It was written with such an intention, Sir William — to buzz in people's heads.

Sir William Ah, I'll take care ye don't read me another, Mr. Wicks; at any rate, another which contains a character resembling a member of my family — a *late* member of my family. I don't relish being reminded of late members of my family in this way, and being kept awake at night, thinking — turning over in my mind —

Imogen [*Soothingly*] Of course not.

Sir William [*Taking snuff*] Pa — a — a — ah! pi — i — i —

sh! When I saw Kean, as Richard, he reminded me of no member of my family. Shakespeare knew better than that, Mr. Wicks. [*To Imogen*] And therefore, ma'am, upon receiving your letter last night, acqueenting me with your intention to commence rehearsing your comedy — [*Glancing at Tom*] *His* comedy —

Imogen [*Softly*] *Our* comedy —

Sir William Ugh — today at noon, I determined to present myself here and request to be allowed to — to —

Tom To watch the rehearsal?

Sir William The rehearsal of those episodes in your comedy which remind me of a member of my family — a *late* member.

Imogen [*Constrainedly*] Oh, certainly —

Tom [*Firmly*] By all means.

Sir William [*Rising, assisted by Tom*] I don't wish to be steered at by any of your — what d'ye call 'em? — your gypsy crew —

Tom Ladies and Gentlemen of the Company, we call 'em.

Sir William [*Tartly*] I don't care what ye call 'em. [*Tom restores the throne-chair to its former position*] Put me into a curtained box, where I can hear, and see, and not be seen; and when I have heard and seen enough, I'll return home — and — and — obtain a little sleep; and tomorrow I shall be well enough to sit in Court again.

AMERICAN SELECTIONS

THE BEAU OF BATH*

By CONSTANCE D'ARCY MACKAY

Beau Nash, the Gentleman of Bath, has grown old with the customs and manners of the age of *Queen Anne* still in his heart. While sitting by his fire, his thoughts drift again to the days of "wits and beauties, fops and gamesters gay — all that made life in Bath, when he held sway."

Beau Nash   Everything passes.   Naught remains of all
Except that portrait smiling from the wall.
   [*He crosses to the portrait, candlestick in hand*]
Disdainful Rosamond, you still look down
As when you were the toast of all the town.
Lips red as holly, eyes so archly bright —
Nay, but your beauty dims the candle's light!
   [*He puts down the candlestick*]
'Tis vain to wish for things that may not be;
Yet could you for one hour come back to me
Would I not say all that I left unsaid
In days gone by?   But you are long since dead,
While I, grown old, above the embers cower,
   [*He goes back to his chair*]
Or play a game to help me pass the hour
When shadows flicker . . . and the candles blink
Until I drowse . . . and . . .
   [*He nods and dozes in his chair. The Lady of the Portrait moves, smiles, slowly and gracefully steps down from the portrait, silently crosses to the table, her eyes on the Beau. She catches up a handful of cards*]

The Lady   'Tis my play, I think
If I see rightly by the candle's gleam.

Beau Nash   [*In a whisper*]
Rosamond!

---

* From *The Beau of Bath and Other One-Act Plays of Eighteenth Century Life*, by Constance D'Arcy Mackay. Copyrighted by Henry Holt and Company, to whom application should be made for performance rights.

The Lady   [*Lightly*]
Well, sir, do you always dream
When you play cards with ladies?   If 'tis so
I think 'twere best to call my chair and go.

Beau Nash   [*Bewildered, passing a hand across his eyes*]
I thought . . . that you were dead . . . and I
       was old!

The Lady   [*Still lightly*]
Fie, sir, to think that hearts like ours grow cold!
And when I hear you call upon my name
 Shall I not step down from that gilded frame
To spend an hour of Christmas night with you?
Come!   Let us gossip of the folk we knew!
Lord Foppington, whose wit I did adore—

Beau Nash   I thought Lord Foppington a monstrous bore!
But Kitty Cavendish—'Faith, one mad night
We drank her health from out her slipper white.

The Lady   [*With spirit*]
I vow then you were tipsy, one and all,
For Kitty's slipper was by no means small.

Beau Nash   Nay, let's have done with thrust and counter thrust!
Ah, Rosamond, in days gone by you must
Have known I loved you, yet you were so cold.

The Lady   [*Very low*]
I had been warmer, sir, had you been bold!

Beau Nash   Bold!   At your feet dukes laid their coronets,
I could but offer you some gambling debts.
These, and the worship of a world-worn heart
Would scarce pass coinage in Dame Fashion's mart.
So I fought down my love for you, and yet
Your slightest gesture in the minuet
Would stir my pulses.   With a covert glance
I watched you through the mazes of the dance,
So fair, so radiant—but what need for me
To tell you of my heart's poor comedy.
Is that a tear which falls for it, my sweet?

The Lady   [*Very sweetly and gently*]
A tear is naught, sir.
   [*She turns to him*]
Ah, must I repeat

My love in *words* before you will believe
That I too loved in vain?
  [*As their eyes meet her meaning grows clear to
    him*]
Now I must leave,
For tis not long until the clock strikes one.

Beau Nash   And you loved me!
The Lady   Our hour is almost done.
I leave you to your firelight and your chair,
And to your game that's always — solitaire!
  [*With delicate tread, moving silently as a ghost,
    the Lady steps back into the portrait. The
    Beau dozes again. The rosy glow of the fire
    dies, leaving the room in utter twilight*]

THE MERRY MERRY CUCKOO *

By JEANNETTE MARKS

Each spring for fifty years *Annie* and her husband, *David,* have listened to the song of the first cuckoo. Now *David* is ill and dying — and his only wish is to hear the cuckoo once more. *Annie,* fearing that this once the cuckoo will not sing, devises a scheme to fulfill her dying husband's wish.

Annie . . . He's wantin' to hear the cuckoo more nor anythin else, dear, dear! Everywhere 'tis green now, an' the lilies will be here before long — but lad, lad, the cuckoo, will it come? [*She goes to left into garden, the wet clothes in a basket under her arm and stands there, looking about*] 'Twas over there it laid its egg in the robin's nest this year ago in May — aye, an' one poor little bird pushed the other out, an' ye picked it up, lad dear, an' were so tender with it. An' they're not wantin' ye, Davy, my old lad darlin', to think the cuckoo will be singin' soon! Dear God, is there to be no cuckoo singin' for the lad again? Just once more, dear God, to sing to him and comfort him? Aye! just the one song? No cuckoo? Aye, there will be a cuckoo singin', there shall be a cuckoo singin'! [*She looks toward the closed windows behind which David lies, and puts down her basket of clothes*] He's asleep! Hush, I'll

* From "The Merry Merry Cuckoo" by Jeannette Marks, from "Representative One-Act Plays by American Authors" by Margaret G. Mayorga. Reprinted by permission of Little, Brown & Company.

be the cuckoo! He'll wake an' think the spring has really come. Here by this tree. They're in the chapel, an' they'll never know. [*Throughout this scene, until Lowry speaks, a cuckoo song is being played very softly. And it is into a few notes of this, several times repeated, that Annie swings when she actually begins her cuckoo song. She opens her mouth to begin, a look of appealing misery on her face*] 'Twas somethin' like this: *Coo-o Coo-o!* Tut, that sounds like a hen. I know, it goes over an' over again, sing-song, sing-song, like this: *cu-cu, cu-cu.* Aye, that's better. [*She rocks herself backwards and forwards practising it and repeating cu-cu, cu-cu*] 'Tis growin᷄ better, but lad, lad, I'm plannin' to deceive ye whatever! [*Brushes tears away impatiently and begins song again*] *Cucu-cu, cucu-cu, cucucu-cu, cu!* Aye, that's fair; aye, 'tis fine! He'll not know me from a real cuckoo. I'll try it loud now, for ye've no long, dearie. [*She holds eagerly on to the tree beside her, so lost in the cuckoo music that she is not aware of a head popping up behind the garden wall and down again. She draws a long breath and begins, softly, slowly, the song sounding as if it came from a distance. She waits a moment,— the heads are well above the wall now in amazement,— and then sings more loudly, making the song sound as if it came from the garden where she is standing*]

David [*Calling*] Annie!

Annie [*Hurrying to open his windows*] Aye, lad dear, I'm comin'.

David [*Ecstatically*] Annie, Annie, dear, I heard the cuckoo singing'; I was dreamin' again, an' all at once I heard the cuckoo singin' in the garden, loud and clear. It sang three times: first, it sounded like somethin' else, 'twas so breathless; then it sang quiet and sweet like a cuckoo; an' the third time it seemed comin' from the old mill wheel.

Annie But, lad darlin', ye've heard it, an' I'm that glad! Three times; yiss, yiss, 'tis a real fine cuckoo. Now ye're happy, darlin', and ye'll sleep well upon it.

David [*Disappointedly*] Did ye no hear it?

Annie I'm thinkin' I did an' thinkin' I didn't.

David Where were ye?

Annie Out in the garden, hangin' out the clothes.

David [*Still more disappointedly*] An' ye didn't hear it?

Annie I'm no certain, darlin'; I heard somethin'—I did, indeed.

David [*Proudly*] 'Twas the cuckoo, Annie, dear; I'm hearin' it first every year; ye must be growin' deaf.

Annie Yiss, yiss. Now go to sleep, an' I'll call ye if I hear the cuckoo sing.

David Will it sing again?

Annie Aye, darlin', if ye heard it once, 'tis sure to sing again.

David I'll be gettin' well, Annie, is it not so?

Annie [*Turning away suddenly*] Indeed, lad dear, ye'll be about among the heather 'fore long.

David [*Speaking quietly, almost to himself*] To think the cuckoo's singin'—singin' for me!

Annie Aye, aye; now go to sleep.

ICEBOUND *

By OWEN DAVIS

Having realized the irresponsibility of her wayward son *Ben*, whom she loved, *Mrs. Jordan* willed her fortune to *Jane*, knowing that she would care for him.

Believing that she has carried out the wishes of *Mrs. Jordan*, and thinking that *Ben* cares nothing for her, *Jane* is about to leave the *Jordan* farm.

Ben, knowing that *Jane* is necessary to his happiness, reproaches her.

Jane Good-by. [*She starts up to door*]

Ben And so you're going to break your word? [*Jane turns, hurt*] I don't know what 't was you promised mother, but you've broke your word. No man ever needed a woman more'n I need you, and you're leaving me.

Jane That isn't fair.

Ben It's true, ain't it; truth ain't always fair— You ain't helped me none, you've hurt me—worse than bein' broke, worse than bein' in jail.

Jane It don't seem like I could stand to have you talk like that.

* Reprinted by permission of Little, Brown & Company. From *Icebound* by Owen Davis.

Ben   What you done you done for her.   I didn't count, I never have, not with you.

Jane   When you've been trying to do a thing as long as I have, it gets to be a part of you.

Ben   You done it all for her — well — she's dead — you'd better go.

Jane   Maybe I had, but if I do it will be with the truth between us.   Here's the letter she left for me, Ben — I got a feeling somehow like she was here with us now, like she wanted you to read it.   [*She holds it out*]   It's like she was guiding us from the grave — read it.   [*Crosses up to window*]

Ben   [*Reads*]   "My dear Jane : The doctor tells me I haven't long to live and so I am doing this, the meanest thing I think I've ever done to you.   I'm leaving you the Jordan money. Since my husband died there has been just one person I could get to care about, that's Ben, who was my baby so long after all the others had forgotten how to love me.   [*He mumbles the letter to himself, then brings out the words*]   Hold out her heart and let him trample on it, as she has on mine."   [*Slowly he breaks down, sobbing bitterly*]

Jane   Don't, Ben —

Ben   Look what I done to her.   Look what I done.

Jane   [*Hand on his shoulder*]   Oh, my dear — my dear !

Ben   I did love her, mor'n she thought, mor'n I ever knew how to tell her !

Jane   [*Kneels beside him*]   It wasn't all your fault — you were a lonely boy — she never said much — she was like you, Ben, ashamed to show the best that's in you.

Ben   [*Bitterly*]   The best in me.   I ain't fit that you should touch me, Jane — you'd better go.

Jane   Not if you need me, Ben, and I think you do.

Ben   I love you — mor'n I ever thought I could — tenderer — truer — but I'm no good — You couldn't trust me — I couldn't trust myself.

Jane   Spring's coming, Ben, everywhere, to you and me, if you would only try.

Ben   Can a feller change — just 'cause he wants to ?

Jane   I don't want you changed.   I want you what you are, the best of you — just a man that loves me — if you do love me, Ben.

Ben   Can't you help me to be fit?

Jane   I'm going to do the thing I always meant to do — good times and bad, Ben, I'm going to share with you.

Ben   God knows I —

Jane   Hush, Ben — I don't want another promise.

Ben   What do you want?

Jane   You said I was a good sport once — you shook hands on what we'd do to bring this old place back — there's plenty to be done. I'll stay and help you if you want me.

Ben   A good sport?   [*He takes her hand*]   I'll say you're all of that.

THE GREEN PASTURES *

By Marc Connelly

Noah's wife, an elderly negress, is preparing dinner in the dining room of their "fairly prosperous" cabin, when *Noah* appears with a stranger.

Noah   Company, darlin'.   [*Noah's wife takes Noah's and God's hats*]   Dis gemman's a preacher, too. He's jest passin' through de country.

God   Good mo'nin', sister.

Noah's Wife   Good mo'nin'. You jest ketch me when I'm gettin' dinner ready. You gonter stay with us?

God   If I ain't intrudin'. Brother Noah suggested —

Noah's Wife   You set right down yere. I got a chicken in de pot an' it'll be ready in 'bout five minutes. I'll go out de back and call Shem, Ham an' Japheth. [*To God*] Dey's our sons. Dey live right acrost de way but always have Sunday dinner wid us. You mens make yo'selves comf'table.

God   Thank you, thank you very kindly.

Noah   You run along, we all right. [*God and Noah seat themselves. Noah's wife exits*]

God   You got a fine wife, Brother Noah.

* From *The Green Pastures*, by Marc Connelly. Published by Farrar and Rinehart. Reprinted by the courtesy of the author.

Noah She pretty good woman.

God Yes, suh, an' you got a nice little home. Have a ten-cent seegar? [*God offers him one*]

Noah Thank you, much obliged. [*Both men lean back restfully in their chairs*]

God Jest what seems to be de main trouble 'mong mankind, Noah?

Noah Well, it seems to me de main trouble is dat de whol' distric' is wide open. Now you know dat makes fo' loose livin'. Men folks spen's all dere time fightin', loafin' an' gamblin', an' makin' bad likker.

God What about de women?

Noah De women is worse dan de men. If dey ain't makin' love powder dey out beg, borrow an' stealin' money for policy tickets. Doggone, I come in de church Sunday fo' last 'bout an hour befo' de meetin' was to start, and dere was a woman stealin' de altar cloth. She was goin' to hock it. Dey ain't got no moral sense. Now you take dat case las' month, over in East Putney. Case of dat young Willy Roback.

God What about him?

Noah Dere is a boy seventeen years old. Doggone, if he didn't *e*lope with his aunt. Now, you know, dat kin' of goin' on is bad fo' a neighborhood.

God Terrible, terrible.

Noah Yes, suh. Dis use' to be a nice, decent community. I been doin' my best to preach de Word, but seems like every time I preach de place jest goes a little mo' to de dogs. De good Lawd only knows what's gonter happen.

God Dat is de truth. [*There is a pause. Each puffs his cigar. Suddenly Noah grasps his knee, as if it were paining him, and twists his foot*]

Noah Huh!

God What's de matter?

Noah I jest got a twitch. My buck-ager I guess. Every now and then I gets a twitch in de knee. Might be a sign of rain.

God That's just what it is. Noah, what's de mos' rain you ever had round dese parts?

Noah Well, de water come down fo' six days steady last April

an' de ribber got so swole it bust down de levee up 'bove Free-
port.   Raise cain all de way down to de delta.

God   What would you say was it to rain for forty days and
nights ?

Noah   I'd say dat was a *complete* rain !

God   Noah, you don't know who I is, do you ?

Noah   [*Puzzled*]   Yo' face looks easy, but I don' think I re-
call de name.   [*God rises slowly, and as He reaches His full
height, there is a crash of lightning, a moment's darkness, and a
roll of thunder.   It grows light again, Noah is on his knees in
front of God*]   I should have known you.   I should have seen
de glory.

God   Dat's all right, Noah.   You didn't know who I was.

Noah   I'm jes' ol' preacher Noah, Lawd, an' I'm yo' servant.
I ain't very much, but I'se all I got.

God   Sit down, Noah.   Don' let me hear you shamin' yo'self,
caize yo' a good man.   [*Timidly Noah waits until God is seated,
and then sits himself*]   I jest wanted to fin' out if you was good,
Noah.   Dat's why I'm walkin' de earth in de shape of a natchel
man.   I wish dey was mo' people like you.   But, far as I kin
see you and yo' family is jest de only respectable people in de
worl'.

Noah   Dey jest all poor sinners, Lawd.

God   I know.   I am your Lawd.   I am a god of wrath and
vengeance an' dat's why I'm gonter destroy dis' worl'.

Noah   [*Almost in a whisper ; drawing back*]   Jest as you say,
Lawd.

God   I ain't gonter destroy you, Noah.   You and yo' family,
yo' sheep an' cattle, an' all de udder things that ain't human I'm
gonter preserve.   But de rest is gotta go.   [*Takes a pencil and
a sheet of paper from His pocket*]   Look yere, Noah.   [*Noah
comes over and looks over His shoulder*]   I want you to build
me a boat.   I want you to call it de "Ark," and I want it to
look like dis.   [*He is drawing on the paper.   Continues to write
as he speaks*]   I want you to take two of every kind of animal
and bird dat's in de country.   I want you to take seeds an'
sprouts an' everything like dat an' put them on dat Ark, because dere is gonter be all dat rain.   Dey's gonter to be a deluge,
Noah, an' dey's goin' to be a flood.   De levees is gonter bust an'
everything dat's fastened down is comin' loose, but it ain't gonter

float long, caize I'm goin' ter make a storm dat'll sink everythin' from a hencoop to a barn. Dey ain't a ship on de sea dat'll be able to fight that tempest. Dey all got to go. Everythin'. Everythin' in dis pretty worl', I made, except one thing, Noah. You an' yo' fam'ly an' de things I said are going to ride dat storm in de Ark. Yere's de way it's to be. [*He hands Noah the paper. Noah takes it and reads*]

Noah [*Pause; looks at paper again*] Yes, suh, dis seems to be complete. Now 'bout the animals, Lawd, you say you want everythin'?

God Two of everythin'.

Noah Dat would include jayraffes an' hippotamusses?

God Everythin' that is.

Noah Deay was a circus in town las' week. I guess I kin' fin' them. Co'se I kin git all de rabbits an' possums an' wil' turkeys easy. I'll send de boys out. Hum, I'm jest wonderin'—

God 'Bout what?

Noah 'Bout snakes. Think you'd like snakes, too?

God Certainly. I want snakes.

Noah Oh, I kin git snakes, lots of 'em. Co'se, some of 'em's a little dangerous. Maybe I better take a kag of likker, too?

God You kin have a kag of likker.

Noah [*Musingly*] Yes, suh, dey's a awful lot of differ'nt kin's of snakes, come to think about it. Dey's water moccasins, cotton-moufs, rattlers — mus' be a hund'ed kin's of other snakes down in de swamps. Maybe I better take two kags of likker.

God [*Mildly*] I think de one kag's enough.

Noah No. I better take two kags. Besides I kin put one on each side of de boat, an' balance de ship wid dem as well as having dem fo' medicinal use.

God You kin put one kag in de middle of de ship.

Noah [*Buoyantly*] Jest as easy to take de two kags, Lawd.

God I think one kag's enough.

Noah Yes, Lawd, but you see forty days — an' forty nights — [*There is a distant roll of thunder*]

God [*Firmly*] One kag, Noah.

Noah Yes, Lawd, one kag.

COUNSELLOR-AT-LAW*

By ELMER RICE

Bessie Green, pretty young telephone operator in the law firm of Simon and Tedesco, divides her time between the switchboard and a movie magazine, being partial to the latter. She is frequently interrupted by the entrance of clients and *Henry,* the office boy.

Bessie Simon and Tedesco— Who is calling, please?— He's not in, yet. Do you want to talk to Miss Gordon?— Well, just a minute, she's on another wire— All right, here she is now— Mr. Simon's brother calling— All rightee, go ahead. [*Turning*] Mail, Henry.

* * *

Bessie Say, listen, how many people's work do you think I'm goin' to do around here? . . . Simon and Tedesco— Oh, it's you, is it?— Why, I thought you was dead and buried— No, I don't look so good in black— Yeah, sure I missed you: like Booth missed Lincoln— Well, what do you think I've been doing: sittin' home embroiderin' doilies? Gee, I'm glad I'm wearin' long sleeves, so's I can laugh in 'em— All right, now I'll tell one— [*A buzz*] Wait a minute— Simon and Tedesco— Mr. Tedesco hasn't come in yet— Any minute— What is the name, please?— How do you spell that?— Napoli Importing Company?— All rightee, I'll tell him— Hello— Yeah, I had another call— No, I can't tonight— I can't, I'm tellin' you— I got another date— Ask me no questions and you'll hear no lies— How do you know I want to break it?— Say, you must have your hats made in a barrel factory—

* * *

Bessie Mind your own business, you! Oh, just a fresh kid in the office, here— No, an' I don't want to see it; I'm sick of gangsters— Wait a minute— All rightee— [*She dials a number*] Hello— I don't know if I do or not— Yeah? Go on, tell me some more— You know all the answers, don't you?— Wait a minute—Simon and Tedesco—Mr. Weinberg?— One moment, please— Hello. National Security Company?— Mr. Welford, please— Mr. George Simon's secretary— Here's Mr. Welford, Miss Gordon— Hello—

CRAIG'S WIFE *

By GEORGE KELLY

By keeping the "destiny of her home" in her own hands, selfish *Mrs. Craig* has realized her sole ambition "of authority over the man I married." *Mr. Craig* has never so interpreted the actions of his conniving wife until his Aunt, *Miss Austen*, warns him of the danger of being dominated by his selfish wife. There is no mistake that the house is *Mrs. Craig's* and that *Craig* "simply went with the house. . ." No smoking is allowed outside the den ; roses are not permitted because the petals fall off and clutter up the floors ; visitors are not welcome ; but let the maids, *Mrs. Harold* and *Mazie,* tell about "snoopin'" *Mrs. Craig.*

Mrs. Harold I've been here nearly a year now, and *I* have my first time to see her do anything— Only a lot of snoopin'—after somebody else has finished.

Mazie It's too bad Miss Austen didn't tell her that while she was at it.

Mrs. Harold [*Raising her hand, with a touch of solemnity*] She told her enough. [*She goes to foot of stairs and looks up*]

Mazie Well, didn't *he* say anything?

Mrs. Harold Not very much ; Miss Austen done most of the talkin'. [*She comes down to Mazie's left, confidentially*] She told him if he didn't do something very soon, his wife 'ud make him look like an echo.

Mazie She will, too.

Mrs. Harold He said she had a peculiar disposition—and that Miss Austen didn't understand her. Well, I felt like sayin' if Miss Austen don't understand her, I do. And I'd soon tell her how well I understand her, too, only that she gives me a wide berth.

Mazie I feel kind of sorry for him sometimes, though.

Mrs. Harold Yes, it's a pity for *him*. [*Lowering her voice,*

* From "Craig's Wife" by George Kelly. Reprinted by permission of Little, Brown & Company.

and speaking with great conviction] She could build a nest in his ear, and he'd never know it. [*She turns to the table and settles the various ornaments*]

Mazie She certainly is the hardest woman to please that I've ever worked for.

Mrs. Harold Well, I don't know whether she's hard to please or not, Mazie, for I've never tried to please her. I do my work, and if she don't like it she has a tongue in her head; she can soon tell me, and I can go somewhere else. I've worked in too many houses to be left out of a place very long. [*Straightening up and resting her left hand on the table*] Did I tell you about wanting me to dust the leaves off that little tree in front of the dining-room window last week?

Mazie Dust the leaves?

Mrs. Harold [*Looking to heaven for witness*] That's the honest God's fact. And me with the rheumatism at the time.

Mazie Can you imagine such a thing?

Mrs. Harold Well, you know how I done it, don't you?

Mazie What'd you say to her?

Mrs. Harold I told her right up; I said, "I'll dust no tree for nobody."

Mazie You done right.

Mrs. Harold She sez, "You mean you refuse to dust it?"—"Yes," I sez, "I refuse," and, I sez, "what's more, I'm goin' to stay refuse." "Well," she sez, "it needs dusting, whether you dust it or not." "Well," I sez, "let it need it," I sez, I sez, "a little dust won't poison it." I sez, "We'll be dust ourselves some day, unless we get drowned." [*She goes to the portières*]

Mazie You done right.

Mrs. Harold Oh, I told her. [*She glances out through the rooms*]

Mazie I think the worst kind of a woman a girl can work for is one that's crazy about her house.

Mrs. Harold I do, too; because I think they *are* crazy half the time. You know, you can go crazy over a house, Mazie, the same as you can over anything else.

Mazie Sure you can.

Mrs. Harold Doctor Nicholson's wife was one of them; although she wasn't as generous a woman as this one.

Mazie No, that's one thing you've got to say for Mrs. Craig; she's not stingy.

Mrs. Harold No, that's true, she isn't.

Mazie I don't think I've ever worked in a house where there was as good a table for the help.

Mrs. Harold That's right; you always get whatever they get.

Mazie And you never have to ask for your wages, neither. [*The doorbell rings*]

Mrs. Harold No, she's very good that way.

Mazie [*Going to answer the door, settling her cap and apron*] I guess that's that gentleman Mr. Craig's expectin'.

Mrs. Harold Come out when you come in, Mazie.

THE EMPEROR JONES *
By EUGENE O'NEILL

Brutus Jones, a fugitive from American justice, after killing two men in the States escapes to an island in the West Indies. Taking advantage of the superstitions of the negroes, he establishes himself there as emperor.

The negroes revolt against the harsh, tyrannical treatment of *Emperor Jones*. He escapes into the Great Forest.

* * *

The end of the plain where the Great Forest begins. The foreground is sandy, level ground dotted by a few stones and clumps of stunted bushes cowering close against the earth to escape the buffeting of the trade wind. In the rear the forest is a wall of darkness dividing the world. Only when the eye becomes accustomed to the gloom can the outlines of separate trunks of the nearest trees be made out, enormous pillars of deeper blackness. A somber monotone of wind lost in the leaves moans in the air. Yet this sound serves but to intensify the impression of the forest's relentless immobility, to form a background throwing into relief its brooding, implacable silence.

[*Jones enters from the left, walking rapidly. He stops as he nears the edge of the forest, looks around him quickly, peering into the dark as if searching for some familiar landmark. Then, apparently satisfied that he is where he ought to be, he throws himself on the ground, dog-tired*]

* Reprinted by permission of Random House, New York.

Well, heah I is. In de nick o' time, too! Little mo' an' it'd
be blacker'n de ace of spades heahabouts. [*He pulls a bandana
handkerchief from his hip pocket and mops off his perspiring
face*] Sho'! Gimme air! I'se tuckered out sho' 'nuff. Dat
soft Emperor job ain't no trainin' fo' a long hike ovah dat plain
in de briling sun. [*Then with a chuckle*] Cheer up, nigger,
de worst is yet to come. [*He lifts his head and stares at the
forest. His chuckle peters out abruptly. In a tone of awe*]
My goodness, look at dem woods, will you? Dat no-count
Smithers said dey'd be black an' he sho' called de turn. [*Turning away from them quickly and looking down at his feet he
snatches at a chance to change the subject—solicitously*] Feet,
you is holdin' up yo' end fine an' I suttinly hopes you ain't
blisterin' none. It's time you git a rest. [*He takes off his
shoes, his eyes studiously avoiding the forest. He feels of the
soles of his feet gingerly*] You is still in de pink—only a
little mite feverish. Cool yo'selfs. Remember you done got a
long journey yit befo' you. [*He sits in a weary attitude, listening to the rhythmic beating of the tom-tom. He grumbles in
a loud tone to cover up a growing uneasiness*] Bush niggers!
Wonder dey wouldn't git sick o' beatin' dat drum. Sound
louder, seem like. I wonder if dey's startin' after me? [*He
scrambles to his feet, looking back across the plain*] Couldn't
see dem now, nohow, if dey was hundred feet away. [*Then
shaking himself like a wet dog to get rid of these depressing
thoughts*] Sho', dey's miles an' miles behind. What you gittin'
fidgety about? [*But he sits down and begins to lace up his
shoes in great haste, all the time muttering reassuringly*] You
know what? Yo' belly is empty, dat's what de matter wid you.
Come time to eat! Wid nothin' but wind on yo' stumach, o'
course you feels jiggedey. Well, we eats right heah an' now,
soon's I gits dese pesky shoes laced up. [*He finishes lacing up
his shoes*] Dere! Now le's see! [*Gets on his hands and
knees and searches the ground around him with his eyes*] White
stone, white stone, where is you? [*He sees the first white stone
and crawls to it with satisfaction*] Heah you is! I knowed
dis was de right place. Box of grub, come to me. [*He turns
over the stone and feels under it—in a tone of dismay*] Ain't
heah! Gorry, is I in de right place or isn't I? Dere's nother
stone. Guess dat's it. [*He scrambles to the next stone and
turns it over*] Ain't heah, neither! Grub, whar is you? Gorry,
has I got to go hungry into dem woods—all de night? [*While

he is talking he scrambles from one stone to another, turning them over in frantic haste. Finally, he jumps to his feet excitedly] Is I lost de place? Must have! But how dat happen when I was followin' de trail across de plain in broad daylight? *[Almost plaintively]* I'se hungry, I is! I gotta git my feed. Whar's my strength gonna come from if I doesn't? Gorry, I gotta find dat grub high an' low somehow! Why it come dark so quick like dat? Can't see nothin.' *[He scratches a match on his trousers and peers about him. The rate of the beat of the far-off tom-tom increases perceptibly as he does so. He mutters in a bewildered voice]* How come all dese white stones come heah when I only remembers one? *[Suddenly, with a frightened gasp, he flings the match on the ground and stamps on it]* Nigger, is you gone crazy mad? Is you lightin' matches to show dem whar you is? Fo' Lawd's sake, use you haid. Gorry, I'se got to be careful! *[He stares at the plain behind him apprehensively, his hand on his revolver]* But how come all dese white stones? And whar's dat tin box o' grub I hid all wrapped up in oilcloth?

[While his back is turned, the Little Formless Fears creep out from the deeper blackness of the forest. They are black, shapeless, only their glittering little eyes can be seen. If they have any describable form at all it is that of a grubworm about the size of a creeping child. They move noiselessly, but with deliberate, painful effort, striving to raise themselves on end, falling and sinking prone again. Jones turns about to face the forest. He stares up at the tops of the trees, seeking vainly to discover his whereabouts by their conformation]

Can't tell nothin' from dem trees! Gorry, nothin' round heah looks like I evah seed it befo'. I'se done lost de place sho' nuff. *[With mournful foreboding]* It's mighty queer! It's mighty queer! *[With sudden forced defiance—in an angry tone]* Woods, is you tryin' to put somethin' ovah on me?

[From the formless creatures on the ground in front of him comes a tiny gale of low mocking laughter like a rustling of leaves. They squirm upward toward him in twisted attitudes. Jones looks down, leaps backward with a yell of terror, yanking out his revolver as he does so—in a quavering voice] What's dat? Who's dar? What is you? Git away from me befo' I shoots you up! You don't?—

[He fires. There is a flash, a loud report, then silence broken only by the far-off, quickened throb of the tom-tom. The formless fears have scurried back into the forest. Jones remains

fixed in his position, listening intently. The sound of the shot, the reassuring feel of the revolver in his hand, have somewhat restored his shaken nerve. He addresses himself with renewed confidence]

Dey're gone. Dat shot fix 'em. Dey was only little animals, little wild pigs, I reckon. Dey've maybe rooted out yo' grub and eat it. Sho' you fool nigger, what you think dey is — ha'nts? [*Excitedly*] Gorry, you give de game away when you fire dat shot. Dem niggers heah dat fo' sutin! Time you beat it in the woods widout no long waits. [*He starts for the forest — hesitates before the plunge — then urging himself in with manful resolution*] Git in, nigger! What you skeered at? Ain't nothin' dere but de trees! Git in! [*He plunges boldly into the forest*]

THE HAIRY APE *

By EUGENE O'NEILL

Robert Smith, "*Yank*," untamed and powerful, animal-like in his fierceness, is respected by all the men in the stoker room for his superior strength — "the grudging respect of fear."

One day *Mildred Douglas* sees "*Yank*," shouting, cursing, furiously pounding the air like a vicious beast. "Paralyzed with horror — terror, she whimpers: 'The filthy beast!'" Tormented by this insult he goes to the city and stands before a cage, facing his "brother" — a gorilla.

Yank [*With a hard, bitter laugh*] Welcome to your city, huh? Hail, hail, de gang's all here! [*At the sound of his voice the chattering dies away into an attentive silence. Yank walks up to the gorilla's cage and, leaning over the railing, stares in at its occupant, who stares back at him, silent and motionless. There is a pause of dead stillness. Then Yank begins to talk in a friendly confidential tone, half-mockingly, but with a deep undercurrent of sympathy*] Say, yuh're some hard-lookin' guy, ain't yuh? I see lots of tough nuts dat de gang called gorillas, but yuh're de foist real one I ever seen. Some chest yuh got, and shoulders, and dem arms and mits! I bet yuh got a punch in eider fist dat'd knock 'em all silly! [*This with genuine admiration. The gorilla, as if he understood, stands upright, swelling out his chest and pounding on it with his fist. Yank grins sympathetically*] Sure, I get yuh. Yuh challenge de whole woild, huh? You

* Reprinted by permission of Random House, New York.

got what I was sayin' even if yuh muffed de woids. [*Then bitterness creeping in*] And why wouldn't yuh get me? Ain't we both members of de same club—de Hairy Apes? [*They stare at each other—a pause—then Yank goes on slowly and bitterly*] So yuh're what she seen when she looked at me, de white-faced tart! I was you to her, get me? On'y outa de cage—broke out—free to moider her, see? Sure! Dat's what she tought. She wasn't wise dat I was in a cage, too—worser'n yours—sure—a damn sight—'cause you got some chanct to bust loose—but me— [*He grows confused*] Aw, hell! It's all wrong, ain't it? [*A pause*] I spose yuh wanter know what I'm doin' here, huh? I been warmin' a bench down to de Battery—ever since last night. Sure. I seen de sun come up. Dat was pretty, too—all red and pink and green. I was lookin' at de sky-scrapers—steel—and all de ships comin' in, sailin' out, all over de oith—and dey was steel, too! De sun was warm, dey wasn't no clouds, dere was a breeze blowin'. Sure, it was great stuff. I got it all right—what Paddy said about dat bein' de right dope—on'y I couldn't get *in* it, see? I couldn't belong in dat. It was over my head. And I kept tinkin'—and den I beat it up here to see what youse was like. And I waited till dey was all gone to git yuh alone. Say, how d'yuh feel sittin' in dat pen all de time, havin' to stand for 'em comin' and starin' at yuh—de white-faced, skinny tarts and de boobs what marry 'em—makin' fun of yuh, laughin' at yuh, gittin' scared of yuh—damn 'em! [*He pounds on the rail with his fist. The gorilla rattles the bars of his cage and snarls. All the other monkeys set up an angry chattering in the darkness. Yank goes on excitedly*] Sure! Dat's de way it hits me, too. On'y yuh're lucky, see? Yuh don't belong wit 'em and yuh know it. But me, I belong wit 'em—but I don't—see? Dey don't belong wit me, dat's what. Get me? Tinkin' is hard— [*He passes one hand across his forehead with a painful gesture. The gorilla growls, impatiently. Yank goes on gropingly*] It's dis way, what I'm drivin' at. Youse can sit and dope dream in de past, green woods, de jungle and de rest of it. Den yuh belong and dey don't. Den yuh kin laugh at 'em, see? Yuh're champ of de woild. But me— I ain't got no past to tink in, nor nothin' dat's comin', only what's now—and dat don't belong. Sure, you're de best off! Yuh can't tink, can yuh? Yuh can't talk neider. But I kin make a bluff at talkin' and tinkin'—a'most git away wit it—

a'most ; — and dat's where de joker comes in. [*He laughs*] I ain't on oith and I ain't in Heaven, get me? I'm in de middle trying to separate 'em, takin' all de woist punches from bot' of them. Maybe dat's what dey call hell, huh? But you, yuh're at de bottom. You belong! Sure! Yuh're de on'y one in de woild dat does, yuh lucky stiff! [*The gorilla growls proudly*] And dat's why dey gotter put yuh in a cage, see? [*The gorilla roars angrily*] Sure! Yuh get me. It beats it when yuh try to tink it or talk it — it's way down — deep — behind — you 'n' me we feel it. Sure! Bot' members of dis club! [*He laughs — then in a savage tone*] What de hell! T'hell wit it! A little action, dat's our meat! Dat belongs! Knock 'em down and keep bustin' 'em till dey croaks yuh wit a gat — wit steel! Sure! Are yuh game? Dey've looked at youse, ain't dey — in a cage? Wanter git even? Wanter wind up like a sport 'stead of croakin' slow in dere? [*The gorilla roars an emphatic affirmative. Yank goes on with a sort of furious exaltation*] Sure! Yuh're reg'lar! Yuh'll stick to de finish! Me 'n' you, huh? — Bot' members of dis club! We'll put on one last star bout dat'll knock 'em offen deir seats! Dey'll have to make de cages stronger after we're trou! [*The gorilla is straining at his bars, growling, hopping from one foot to the other. Yank takes a jimmy from under his coat and forces the lock on the cage door. He throws this open*] Pardon from de governor! Step out and shake hands. I'll take yuh for a walk down Fif' Avenoo. We'll knock 'm offen de oith and croak wit' de band playin'. Come on, Brother. [*The gorilla scrambles gingerly out of his cage. Goes to Yank and stands looking at him. Yank keeps his mocking tone — holds out his hand*] Shake — de secret grip of our order. [*Something, the tone of mockery, perhaps, suddenly enrages the animal. With a spring he wraps his huge arms around Yank in a murderous hug. There is a crackling snap of crushed ribs — a gasping cry, still mocking, from Yank*] Hey, I didn't say kiss me! [*The gorilla lets the crushed body slip to the floor; stands over it uncertainly, considering; then picks it up, throws it in the cage, shuts the door, and shuffles off menacingly into the darkness at left. A great uproar of frightened chattering and whimpering comes from the other cages. Then Yank moves, groaning, opening his eyes, and there is silence. He mutters painfully*] Say — dey oughter match him — wit Zybsko. He got me, aw right. I'm trou. Even him didn't tink I belonged. [*Then, with sudden passionate despair*] Christ, where do I get off at? Where do I fit in? [*Checking himself as suddenly*] Aw, what de hell! No squawkin', see! No quittin', get me! Croak wit your boots on! [*He grabs hold of the bars of the cage and hauls himself painfully to his feet — looks around him bewilderedly — forces a mocking laugh*] In de cage, huh? [*In the strident tones of a circus barker*] Ladies and gents, step forward and take a slant at de one and only — [*His voice weakening*] — one and original — Hairy Ape from de wilds of — [*He slips in a heap on the floor and dies. The monkeys set up a chattering, whimpering wail. And, perhaps, the Hairy Ape at last belongs*]

THE GIANTS' STAIR *
By W. D. STEELE

John Weatherburn has been murdered. *Sheriff Bane* tries to throw suspicion on *Mrs. Weatherburn* and her sister *Til*. *Til* is "queer," always hearing the giant spirit walking around on stormy nights. "She is large, putty-fleshed, and colorless." "*Til* is what would be called, in Oriental countries, 'inspired.'" She sits motionless . . . her hands, pallid, puffy, inert-looking . . . her eyes staring fixedly ahead of her at nothing at all.

Til — Banes' — Tolleys' — Jetherses' — Whites' — Us!

Mrs. Weatherburn [*Who has the receiver with the last signal*] Yes, me! [*After an instant she puts out a hand to the wall to steady her. She turns to the others, still holding the receiver to her ear*] They've found his — body.

Bane Where? [*Blanching*] I — I demand you tell me where?

* * *

Til [*In the same eerie note*] Ha-ha-ha-ha —

Bane [*Choking*] I'll kill ye, Til Jessup! I'll strangle ye 'f you don't leave off that — Here! Where ye goin' *now*? [*As Til moves, or, rather, seems to be pulled toward the door*] Til, if you open that door, I vow — Quit it! Mis' Weatherburn, make her quit it, the crazy, ravin' thing! [*Til lifts the latch with a trancelike deliberation, pulls open the door, and stands on the sill, framed by the darkness, cringing and hugging her body with her fleshy arms*] I vow! That's the end!

* *Giants' Stair*, by W. D. Steele, reprinted by courtesy of D. Appleton-Century Company, publishers.

Mrs. W. What you carryin' on so for, Til?

Til [*Peering into the night*] To *horrify* myself. I got to look. To *horrify* me. I see him! [*Crouching a little*] Black as pitch it is, and yet I see him. 'Nunder the trees he is; 'nunder the meadow rise he is, and yet I see him — comin' on — comin' on up the road toward Whites'. [*She crouches yet a little lower. The backwash of the wind in the house's lee lifts the strings of her unkempt hair*]

Bane [*Almost in a whisper*] That's the end! That's enough!

Til Coming on, comin' on. He's up the hill to Whites' now. He's under the aspen trees, up by the lower gate to Whites' now. Comin' on under the aspen trees. In the black dark there, inunder the aspen trees at the bend; in under the drippin' aspen trees. The dead eyes shinin' pale in his head, pale as ashes in his blowed-out head — shinin' pale in the drippin' dark inunder the aspen trees. You'd think he'd drag his feet, but he don't drag his feet. His feet's not on the ground. Inches above the ground his feet is, and he comes on floatin' against the wind, sailin' against the black wind and rain. Not against the wind! Betwixt the wind! Betwixt the flakes of the wind! Comin' on out — out from inunder the aspen trees.

* * *

[*Til stands as though untouched by all this, inert, entranced, staring at the door as if its panels were no barrier to her occult vision*]

Til Comin' on swifter now, he is. Comin' on, comin' on. He's been by Whites' now, and they've seen him. Mis' White's see him; in the light from the porch she see him. Now she's goin' back through the hall, white's a sheet. Now she's goin' acrost the dinin' room. Now she's to the telephone — [*Til's head swings irresistibly in the direction of the phone. As irresistibly the others' gazes follow. The bell begins to ring*] Banes' — [*She glances at Mrs. Weatherburn who does not move*] Tolleys' — Jetherses' — [*Throwing off the Sheriff's hand, she runs to the instrument and puts the receiver to her ear*] Yes? Yes? Quick, Mis' White! Yes? Quick — [*Bane is upon her. Wresting the receiver from her hand, he thrusts her aside*]

* * *

[*Turning around with a hand to his head, his eyes fall on* Til, *back at the door again, holding it wide, staring out*]

* * *

Til He's on the farm now. I hear the gate just now. In the roar and moan of the wind I hear the gate. [*Lifting her voice to a nerve-struck scream*] John! John!

Mrs. W. Oh, Til!

Bane [*Advancing*] Oh, "Til?" I'll "Til" her! I'll "Til" the crazy! [*Dragging her back, he casts her violently on the floor. He slams the door with a force sufficient to carry away the latch, which falls in a clatter of bits about his feet*]

Mrs. W. You broke the latch!

Til [*From the floor*] You broke the latch. Now you *can't* keep it shut.

Bane [*Deep in his throat*] I guess I can! I guess I can! [*He stands facing it, his two hands spread against it, his feet propped out solidly behind. Silence follows, the clock-tick silence of the room enclosed in the outer shell of storm. . . Bane remains propped and motionless, breathing heavily. Mrs. Weatherburn sinks into a chair and holds her hands crossed on her breast. Til, still on the floor to one side of the door, holds her head erect and attentive*]

Til [*After a time*] That's the other gate. The near one.

Bane [*His breath rasping*] I never hear a thing! [*The hush runs on again for seconds*]

Til You hear that, then? On the gravel? He's come out of the wind now. He's got his feet on the ground now. Hear that?

Bane No! No! No! [*Another moment*]

Til On the step. There. Standin'. Standin' still. [*The hush returns. After a space of it a voice becomes audible, racked, thin, almost falsetto. It is the voice of Bane, to the door*]

Bane Go 'way! Go 'way, I tell ye! [*Beating the panel*] Go 'way!

Til He ain't gone. Still standin'.

Bane [*After a moment, putting his lips nearer the wood*] I'll tell ye somethin' there! Ye listenin'? I'll tell ye somethin' I got a gun here. It's your own gun, John, and it's loaded with bird shot. Right here to my hand I got it. [*Removing one hand cautiously from the door, he gropes out blindly to the right, where the shot gun rests against the wall beside the chair]* Right here I got it, John! *[Finding he cannot reach it, he takes his other hand from the door, and is about to take the furtive, necessary step, when the door begins to swing inward, slowly. A cackle emerges from Til's open mouth; a kind of high, tight, tittering of the palate. Bane flings himself against the door again, slamming it tight]* No, ye don't!

* * *

[As from the tail of his eye he perceives something scuttling past him on the floor and out of the door]
Mrs. W. That's only Til. Til, where you goin' to?
Til [Lost in the darkness without] To — horrify myself!
[And fainter, still further off] John! John!

THE GAME OF CHESS*

By KENNETH SAWYER GOODMAN

His excellency, *Alexis Alexandrovitch*, is awaiting the arrival of *Boris Ivanovitch Shamrayeff*. *Shamrayeff* enters *Alexandrovitch's* luxurious room, wearing "the clothes of a respectable artisan. He is, apparently, somewhat younger than *Alexis*, strongly built, and has rather a fine, but stolid face."

Boris has come to kill *Alexis*, but hesitates to shoot him when *Alexis* tells him that they are foster-brothers. Finally they agree to die together by drinking poison.

Alexis To your easy death, brother. *[He lifts the glass and drinks]*
Boris Ah! So you're a brave man after all! *[He lifts the glass and pauses]* What if I were to leave you now, eh?
Alexis My men have orders to seize you the moment you leave the room.
Boris In that case! *[He lifts the glass]* To your final redemption, brother!
Alexis Sit down! *[Boris sits down]*
Boris How long have we to wait?
Alexis Perhaps five minutes; it's a Chinese concoction. They call it the draught of final oblivion. I believe it to be painless.

* Reprinted by the courtesy of The Northern Trust Co., Chicago.

I'm told that one becomes numb. Do you find yourself becoming drowsy?

Boris　No. My senses seem to be becoming more alert. Your voice sounds very sharp and clear.

Alexis　Lift your hand.

Boris　It seems very heavy. Are you afraid of Death, excellency?

Alexis　[*Eyeing him sharply*]　No, I am not afraid of Death, brother, not in the least.

Boris　Nor I!

Alexis　Good! Now, move your feet.

Boris　I don't seem to be able to. That's strange. I can't feel anything.

Alexis　Nor I! Can you get out of your chair?

Boris　[*Slowly*]　I — I can hardly move my hand. I might move by supreme effort but I haven't the will. I — I feel no pain, only a ringing in my head.

Alexis　So? Well, well! Can you still hear perfectly?

Boris　Yes — yes, I can still hear.

Alexis　H'm, h'm.

Boris　Tell me, on your hope of redemption, was what you said to me just now the truth?

Alexis　On my hope of redemption, eh?

Boris　If it was, I ask you to forgive me.

Alexis　I have nothing to forgive.

Boris　Thanks!

Alexis　On my hope of redemption, Boris Shamrayeff, everything I told you was lies! Lies! Lies! [*Boris struggles painfully to his feet and lurches painfully toward the table where he has laid the pistol. Alexis springs to the table, seizes the pistol, and tosses it out of the window. Boris supports himself against the edge of the table, half sitting, half leaning against it, his mouth open, his eyes staring. He sways dizzily. Alexis stands before him*]

Alexis　Well, you can still speak, can't you?

Boris　You fiend! You dog! You liar! Ha, ha, ha! At least you can't escape! No need for me to strike you!

Alexis　Ha, ha!

Boris Well! Sneer at me if you like. You're feeling the agony too, Alexis Alexandrovitch. You can't deny it.

Alexis I am not dying, Boris Shamrayeff.

Boris But I know! I saw! I saw you drink! You're dying, excellency!

Alexis Yes, we drank together, didn't we? Well, well! And your eye wasn't off me an instant, was it? And you didn't lift your cup till I'd drained the last drop of mine, did you? Well, well, well!

Boris I saw you drink what I drank.

Alexis Yes, I did drink it, Boris Ivanovitch, didn't I? But what is sending you down to fry in Hell with the stupid ghosts of your bestial ancestors is only embarrassing me with the slightest of headaches. [*He chuckles*]

Boris It — it is not possible!

Alexis Eh? An oriental trick. A man in constant fear of poison may accustom himself, little by little, to a dose that would blast the life of an ordinary man. A fantastic precaution these days, only interesting to an antiquarian like myself. Well, well, you can hear me, can't you? I tell you I could have taken the entire mess; half of it seems to have been enough for you. [*Boris makes an effort to get at Alexis but almost sinks to the floor*] No use, Boris Shamrayeff! I advise you to hold fast to the table.

Boris Why? Why have you done this thing to me?

Alexis Body of St. Michael! I am of one order, you of another. You are a terrorist, a Red; the blood of my brother, shot down in the streets of Kronstadt, the lives of my friends, the preservation of the sacred empire — are these nothing? Nothing — beside your dirty petitions of right? Pah! God has delivered *you* into *my* hands. I, and not you, am the instrument of God today! Boris Ivanovitch, can you still hear me? *Eh?*

Boris Yes!

Alexis So! So! One thing more! Why did I risk my own life to get yours? You would like to know that, wouldn't you? Why did I let you in here at all? You'd ask that if you could. Ha, ha! Well, it was because men were thinking that Alexis Alexandrovitch wasn't what he used to be; because I was beginning to think so myself. Because I had begun to doubt my own wits. I had to let myself be brought to bay. I had to look into the muzzle of your pistol.   I had to pit my life against yours in a struggle, where I had no other weapon, no other help, than this.   [*He taps his forehead*]   I think it unlikely that Constantine will check-mate me in five moves today !

Boris   Fiend !   Fiend !   Fiend !   [*He crumples up and falls to the floor*]

Alexis   So, it's over, is it ?   Well, well, well !   [*He takes a cover from the couch and throws it over Boris and stands over him*]

HELL-BENT FER HEAVEN *
By HATCHER HUGHES

Sid, a healthy mountaineer, and *Rufe,* a religious fanatic "with a pale face and shifty, uncertain manner," are both in love with *Jude,* who favors *Sid.*   During a fierce thunderstorm, *Rufe* decides that God has ordered him to blow up a dam which *Sid* has gone to, that an example might be made of "this blasphemer." *Sid* accuses *Rufe* of the attempted murder.

Sid   So !   I'm right !   You *wus* at the bottom of it.   Did you do it apurpose ?

Rufe   God forgive you, Sid, fer sich a thought !

Sid   An' God damn you !   [*He hurls Rufe into a corner of the room and rushes out at the front.   A blinding flash of lightning envelops him.   Rufe lies on his elbow, cowering in fear, till the thunder crashes and reverberates.   Then suddenly he rises to his knees and clasps his hands in prayer*]

Rufe   Did you hear what he said, God ?   I can put up 'ith his insults to me, but when it comes to blasphemin' Thy holy name it does look like it's time to call a halt.   But You know what You're a-doin', God, an' I don't.   I'm only a ignerunt sinner. You know more in a minit 'n I could ever know in a million years.   It bothers me, though, Lord, that You let the wicked prosper more'n the righteous.   They git the best o' everything in this world now.   It wusn't so in Bible times, Lord.   Then You cut the wicked down afore the congregation o' Israel.   An' the dread o' You an' the fear o' You wus on all people.   But now Your name is a byword among sinners.   You hyeard that

* From *Hell-Bent Fer Heaven*, by Hatcher Hughes.   Reprinted by courtesy of the author and Harper and Brothers, publishers.

Yourself jist now. [*His voice has been gradually increasing in volume till it culminates in an emotional climax. He rises and goes to the door, trembling in every limb*] I ain't presumin' to give You advice, Lord! You know Your own business. But if You'd make an edzample o' this blasphemer — if You'd strike him down in the abomination of his wickedness by a bolt o' lightnin' it'ld serve as a warnin' to all like him. An' they'd be sich another revival o' ole-time religion in these mountains as You've never seed sence the earthquake. [*He pauses again as if struck by a new thought. His knees gradually give way beneath him and he sinks to the floor*] In Your Holy Word, Lord, I know You commanded Your servants to slay all blasphemers. Mebby You think that's enough. An' mebby it ought to be. [*He pleads with great fervor*]

But I'd druther You'd do it Yourself, Lord. You can do it better 'n I can. An' it 'ld have more effect. But I want You to understand, God, that I ain't no coward. If it don't suit You to do it Yourself — I'll do it fer You — I don't keer if they hang me. You died fer me once, an' I'm willin' to die fer You if You want me to. They wus a time, Lord, when my proud heart said, "All o' self an' none o' Thee." Then You come — a-knockin' at the door o' my sinful soul an' I whispered, "Some o' self an' some o' Thee." But that's all changed now, Lord. I'm Yourn an' You are mine. An' the burden o' my song now is, "None o' self an' all o' Thee." You can do with me what You please, Lord. If it's Your will that this blasphemer shall die, I've got a whole box o' dynamite out in the store, with a time fuse long enough so I can git back here afore it explodes. I can blow up the dam while he's under thar a-telephonin', an' the waters o' Your wrath'll sweep over him like they did over Pharaoh an' his hosts in olden times! An' the fear o' You an' the dread o' You'll be on all nations ag'in! [*A heavy gust of wind strikes the house, followed by terrific thunder and lightning. Rufe rises to a standing position, his knees trembling. As the noise of the thunder dies away his fear is transformed into joy. He stands firmly on his feet and looks toward heaven, his voice ringing out triumphantly*] I hear You, Lord! An', like Joshua o' old, I go to do Your will! [*He rushes out*]

* * *

[*Rufe has confessed his plans, and fearing the consequences, rushes into the cellar in which the flood waters are rising*]

Rufe Oh God, save me! You can save me if You will! I dunno how, but I know You can! I've got faith in You! I never have doubted You, an' I ain't a-goin' to doubt you jist because I'm in a tight place! But everybody ain't like me, God! They's lots o' folks that has to have proof! An' if You save the others an' don't save me, like the fool, they're a-goin' to say in their hearts they ain't no God! [*There is a moment's silence. He opens the cellar door and peeps out cautiously. Seeing that the room is empty, he rushes to the front door and looks out, then shrinks back, terrified by what he sees*] They're right! [*His voice drops to a hoarse whisper*] They ain't no God! [*A malignant expression sweeps over his face*] If they is He hain't got no use fer folks like me! He's fer them that's on top! That's what He is! [*He suddenly rises on his toes, as if impelled by some power outside himself, and hurls defiance toward heaven*] Damn You, God! [*He gradually collapses, muttering brokenly in a fit of terror*] Now I've done it! I've committed the unpardonable sin! [*Then he screams hysterically as the curtain falls*] Help! Help! Come here, everybody, come here!

IN ABRAHAM'S BOSOM *

By PAUL GREEN

Abraham McCranie, negro son of *Colonel McCranie*, a southern gentleman, has dreamed of great things for his race.

His latest attempt to start a negro school is thwarted by a mob of white men who beat him and drive him away. The beaten and half-crazed negro, escaping the angry mob, meets *Lonnie McCranie*, legitimate son of the *Colonel*. They quarrel, and *Abe* kills *Lonnie*. *Abe* rushes to his home to persuade *Goldie*, his wife, and his aunt, *Muh Mack*, to escape for their lives while he remains to meet the lynching party.

Abe . . . I cain't, cain't quite think — yeh, they was a crowd of white men at de door with dough-faces over their faces. Said wa'nt going to be no meeting. Dey beat me, run me off. And dey give me till tomorrow to git outen de country. You got to git away, foh it's worse'n dat — oh, it is! [*Calmly and without bitterness*] Who you reckon set 'em on me? Who you think it was tole 'em about de trouble I been in before? Yeh, and he

* From *The Field God* and *In Abraham's Bosom*, by Paul Green. Reprinted through the courtesy of Robert M. McBride and Co., 1927.

made it out terribler'n it was.   Douglass told 'em. . . He done
it.   My own flesh and blood.   No!   No!   He was but ain't
no more!   [*Gloomily*]   But I don't blame him — dey ain't no
blaming nobody no longer.

* * *

. . . Dey drove me away from de meeting.   I come back by
the road mad.   [*He gasps*]   Every white man's hand ag'in' me
to de last.   And Mr. Lonnie come out to de road when I passed
his house and begun to abuse me about de crop.   He struck
at me, and I went blind all of a sudden and hit him wid my fist.
Den we fou't.   [*His voice growing shrill*]   And I hit him and
hit him.   I beat his head in.   I killed him dead, dead!   I beat
on and on until all de madness went out o' me and de dark was
everywhere.   Den I seed a sight —   [*He stops, aghast at the
remembrance*]   I left him dere in de night dead on de ground.
Dey done found 'im — I heah 'em crying up dere in de night.
Dey's coming to git me.   [*He holds out his bruised hands*]
His blood's still shining on dem hands.   [*He turns his head
away in fear*]
Muh Mack   [*In a high whine of terror*]   My God a-mighty!
You kilt yo' own flesh!
Abe   [*Turning wrathfully upon her*]   Yeh, yeh, some bitch
went a-coupling wid a white man!   And I seed it — seed it!
[*He drops his hands helplessly.   A sort of terror comes upon
him*]   Oh Lawd God!   I'm anudder Cain.   I tell you I — I
scrushed his head in and beat it until I put out de stars wid
blood.   Mercy!   Mercy!   [*With his hands still held before
him, he stands with bowed head.   After a moment he looks up
and speaks calmly, almost resignedly, his dignity coming back
to him*]   This is the way it was meant to be, and I'm glad it's
ended.   [*He stands with his fists to his temples, and then flings
out his arms in a wide gesture*]   Oh, but damn 'em!   Don't
dey know I want to do all for de best.   [*Shaking his fist at the
shadows*]   I tell you, I tell you what I wanted — I've tried to
make it come right.   [*Lowering his head*]   And now it's come
to dis.

* * *

. . . Tell me, what is it, Goldie!   What ails you, gal?
[*She sits looking dumbly at him and he draws away from her.
Presently there is a sound of stamping feet outside, and voices
slip in like the whispering of leaves.   A stone is thrown against*

the house, then another and another. One crashes through the window and strikes the lamp. The room is left in semi-darkness. Abe with a sob of overwhelming terror falls upon his knees. Twisting his great hands together, he casts up his eyes and cries in a loud voice]

God, God, where is you now! Where is you, God! [*He begins half sobbing and chanting*] You has helped befo', help me now. Is you up dere? Heah my voice! [*Fear takes possession of him*] Blast me, Lawd, in yo' thunder and lightning, if it is yo' will! Ketch me away in de whirlwind, foh I'm a sinner. Yo' will, yo' will, not mine. Let fiah and brimstone burn me to ashes and scatter me on de earf. [*Gasping*] I've tried, I've tried to walk de path, but I'm po' and sinful. . . Give me peace, rest — rest in yo' bosom — if it is dy will. Save me, Jesus, save me!

KISMET *

By EDWARD KNOBLOCK

Driven always by the urge within him to avenge the cruelty of *Jawan*, who years ago stole his wife and killed his only son, *Hajj* has contrived to rise from beggary to wealth and power. The joy of his life is *Marsinah*, daughter by a second wife, whom *Mansur*, *Chief Wazur*, agrees to marry if *Hajj* will kill his enemy, the *Caliph*. The attempted murder fails, and *Hajj* is beaten into unconsciousness and thrown into prison.

Hajj [*After some groans, slowly returning to consciousness, in the whining tone of the beggar, not realising where he is*] Alms for the love of Allah! For the love of — [*He awakes slowly to his surroundings; with a cry of horror*] Ah! I am here! I am here. 'Tis over — is it? Is it over?

Jawan He! He! He! 'Tis not yet begun.

Hajj 'Tis not? [*Coming to the full realisation of things*] Thou! Now I know. Thou! Oh! The sun is setting! Red! Red! [*With a sudden cry*] Mansur! — Thou fiend of lowest hell! "Even as the day ends red, so shall she end red this day!" O Marsinah! O Marsinah! And I in prison — in chains!"

Jawan He! He! He!

Hajj Laugh! Thou canst laugh? Thou the beginning —

thou the end of my sufferings! [*Tugging at the chains*] O Allah! Give me strength! Make these strong arms doubly, trebly strong! Put all the power of a lifetime into these sinews ; only for once, O Allah, that I may snap these maddening chains in twain!

Jawan Never! Never! [*He laughs jeeringly*] He! He! He!

Hajj Once! Only once! [*He tugs, he twists, then with a wild cry of delight he has broken himself free*] Free! Free! The Granter hath granted!

Jawan [*With terror — breathless*] Wah —

Hajj [*Sitting up, very quietly*] At last!

Jawan [*Trembling*] What — what art thou thinking?

Hajj [*Rises*] What — what? [*He crouches slightly and slowly, step by step, like a wild beast, creeps over to Jawan's corner*]

Jawan No nearer! I have a knife.

Hajj A knife — hast thou?

Jawan 'T has served me a thousand times. Luck's written on the blade.

Hajj Luck? I take my luck. [*With a cry*] Allah is all great! [*He springs into the dark at Jawan. A fierce struggle as of two panthers fighting. Groans, hisses, heavings and cries. After a minute — silence. Then Hajj emerges from the dark*]

Hajj [*Breathless and fervently*] O Allah mine, thou hast given me this hour. Behold my sacrifice to thee. At last, at last, I am avenged! Avenged! [*Laughing bitterly*] But my Marsinah! — O spare her, O Lord of justice, spare her from Mansur and the horror of his harim. [*A thought striking him*] The Harim! Kut-al-Kulub! The Wife of wives! Even now she is waiting for me! If I could reach her! She'd help me to save Marsinah! She'd — [*He goes to the door pounding on it desperately*] Free! Free! Free! — [*He stops and turns hopelessly*] Madness! [*Looking at Jawan's body*] They'll find him the minute the litter comes, and then — [*With sudden inspiration*] The litter! Allah! Dost Thou open the door of escape? Dost Thou? [*Wildly*] Ha! Ha! Ha! If it succeed! If it succeed! [*He goes into the corner to the body*] The cloak! the turban! The purse! In his sleeve, — his breast? [*He comes across the chain on his breast*] The chain! The broken hand of Fatimah! [*Imitating*

Jawan] "I shall see my son again! I shall find him!" Wilt thou? [*He takes off the chain*] Wilt thou? [*Putting it over his own neck*] Hang thou here on my neck now thou broken hand of Fatimah! I shall find him, so Allah will it. I shall! Ha! [*He finds the purse and chinks it*] Fifty dinars! For the gaoler! Good! Now off with thy cloak. What? [*He stops and listens*] Nothing. Nothing. Keep thine eyes cool and clear, O Hajj. Cool and clear. [*He returns to the body*] So! So! Thou shalt play the Moorman now, O my king. Dead. Ha! Ha! Thou art dead, dost thou hear? And yet, O dead one, 'tis thou shalt draw me out of my grave — me thy slayer! [*He drags the body to where he lay fainting when the gaoler went out and covers it with his own cloak*] So! Lie thou there! Quiet! Budge not, I pray thee. Faint! [*He turns to Jawan's cloak and turban*] Now for mine own beautifying! [*As he picks up the garments he sees the knife which he discarded*] The knife! Luck's written on the blade. [*He puts the knife into his belt*] Luck! So be it. Luck shall carry me into the street. Luck let me leap from the litter! Luck bring me to the harim and to thee, O my Marsinah, O my— [*The door outside is unlocked. Hajj, throwing the cloak over himself, hurries into Jawan's corner and lies down. Kutayt reappears with a lanthorn, followed by two men with a rough stretcher*]

Kutayt The stretcher, O my Lord.

Hajj [*Coughing and imitating Jawan's voice*] Here! [*He throws the purse*]

Kutayt [*Picking it up and examining it by the light of the lanthorn*] Allah bless thy journey. [*To the men as they lift up Hajj*] Carefully. Lift the Sheikh of Sheikhs carefully. [*He chinks the purse and turns to the dead body*] How? Still fainted! Hoo! Hoo! Look, O my lord— [*He goes to the body and raises up an arm*] Still fainted!

Hajj [*As the litter is lifted up and carried out, imitating Jawan's laugh*] He! He! He! [*He is carried through the door*]

Kutayt [*Dropping the arm*] Rose water! [*Kicking the body*] Rose water! Hoo! Hoo!

Hajj [*From the staircase without*] He! He! He!

[*Kutayt turns slowly and follows the litter, slamming the door behind him*]

THE MELTING POT *

By ISRAEL ZANGWILL

After the persecution of his family in Russia, *David*, a Russo-Jewish lad, comes to America. Here he becomes engaged to *Vera*, a Christian settlement worker. Her father, the *Baron*, hearing of this engagement, comes to dissuade his daughter. The *Baron's* prejudice against *David* convinces *Vera* of her unquenchable love for him.

Vera Father, I will be calm. I will speak without passion or blindness. I will tell David the truth. I was never absolutely sure of my love for him — perhaps that was why I doubted his love for me — often after our enchanted moments there would come a nameless uneasiness, some vague instinct, relic of the long centuries of Jew-loathing, some strange shrinking from his Christless creed —

Baron [*With an exultant cry*] Ah! She is a Revendal.

Vera But now — [*She rises, and walks firmly toward David*] Now, David, I come to you, and I say in the words of Ruth, thy people shall be my people, and thy God my God! [*She stretches out her hands to David*]

Baron You shameless —! [*He stops as he perceives David remains impassive*]

Vera [*With agonized cry*] David!

David [*In low, icy tones*] You cannot come to me. There is a river of blood between us.

Vera Were it seven seas, our love must cross them.

David Easy words to you. You never saw that red flood bearing the mangled breasts of women and the spattered brains of babes and sucklings. Oh! [*He covers his eyes with his hands. The Baron turns away in gloomy impotence. At last David begins to speak quietly, almost dreamily*] It was your Easter, and the air was full of holy bells and the streets of holy processions — priests in black and girls in white and waving palms and crucifixes, and everybody exchanging Easter eggs and

* From *The Melting Pot*, by Israel Zangwill. Reprinted by the courtesy of The Macmillan Company, publishers.

kissing one another three times on the mouth in token of peace
and good will, and even the Jew-boy felt the spirit of love
brooding over the earth, though he did not then know that this
Christ, whom holy chants proclaimed re-risen, was born in the
form of a brother Jew.   And what added to the peace and holy
joy was that our own Passover was shining before us.   My
mother had already made the raisin wine, and my greedy little
brother Solomon had sipped it on the sly that very morning.
We were all at home — all except my father — he was away in
the little Synagogue at which he was cantor.   Ah, such a voice
he had — a voice of tears and thunder — when he prayed it was
like a wounded soul beating at the gates of Heaven — but he
sang even more beautifully in the ritual of home, and how we
were looking forward to his hymns at the Passover table,— [*He
breaks down.   The Baron has gradually turned round under the
spell of David's story and now listens hypnotised*]   I was playing my cracked little fiddle.   Little Miriam was making her
doll dance to it.   Ah, that decrepit old china doll — the only
one the poor child had ever had — I can see it now — one eye, no
nose, half an arm.   We were all laughing to see it caper to my
music. . . My father flies in through the door, desperately
clasping to his breast the Holy Scroll.   We cry out to him to
explain, and then we see that in that beloved mouth of song
there is no longer a tongue — only blood.   He tries to bar the
door — a mob breaks in — we dash out through the back into
the street.   There are the soldiers — and the Face — [*Vera's
eyes involuntarily seek the face of her father, who shrinks away
as their eyes meet*]

Vera   [*In a low sob*]   O God !

David   When I came to myself, with a curious aching in my
left shoulder, I saw lying beside me a strange shapeless Something — [*David points weirdly to the floor, and Vera,
hunched forward, gazes stonily at it, as if seeing the horror*]
By the crimson doll in what seemed a hand I knew it must be
little Miriam.   The doll was a dream of beauty and perfection
beside the mutilated mass which was all that remained of my
sister, of my mother, of greedy little Solomon —   Oh !   You
Christians can only see that rosy splendour on the horizon of
happiness.   And the Jew didn't see rosily enough for you, ha !
ha ! ha ! the Jew who gropes in one great crimson mist.   [*He
breaks down in spasmodic, ironic, long-drawn, terrible laughter*]

Vera [*Trying vainly to tranquillise him*] Hush, David! Your laughter hurts more than tears. Let Vera comfort you. [*She kneels by his chair, tries to put her arms around him*]

David [*Shuddering*] Take them away! Don't you feel the cold dead pushing between us?

Vera [*Unfaltering, moving his face toward her lips*] Kiss me.

David I should feel the blood on my lips.

Vera My love shall wipe it out.

David Love! Christian love! [*He unwinds her clinging arms; she sinks prostrate on the floor as he rises*] For this I gave up my people — darkened the home that sheltered me — there was always a still, small voice at my heart calling me back, but I heeded nothing — only the voice of the butcher's daughter. [*Brokenly*] Let me go home, let me go home. [*He looks lingeringly at Vera's prostrate form, but overcoming the instinct to touch and comfort her, begins tottering with uncertain pauses toward the door leading to the hall*]

Baron [*Extending his arms in relief and longing*] And here is *your* home, Vera! [*He raises her gradually from the floor; she is dazed, but suddenly she becomes conscious of whose arms she is in and utters a cry of repulsion*]

Vera Those arms reeking from that crimson river! [*She falls back*]

Baron [*Sullenly*] Don't echo that babble. You came to these arms often enough when they were fresh from the battlefield.

Vera But not from the shambles! You heard what he called you. Not soldier — butcher! Oh, I dared to dream of happiness after my nightmare of Siberia, but you — you — [*She breaks down for the first time in hysterical sobs*]

Baron [*Brokenly*] Vera! Little Vera! Don't cry! You stab me!

Vera You thought you were ordering your soldiers to fire at the Jews, but it was my heart they pierced. [*She sobs on*]

Baron . . . And my own. . . But we will comfort each other. I will go to the Czar myself — with my forehead to the earth — to beg for your pardon! . . . Come, put your wet face to little father's. . .

Vera [*Violently pushing his face away*] I hate you! I curse the day I was born your daughter! [*She staggers toward the*

*door leading to the interior. At the same moment David, who
has reached the door leading to the hall, now feeling subcon-
sciously that Vera is going and that his last reason for lingering
on is removed, turns the door-handle. The click attracts the
Baron's attention, he veers round]*

Baron *[To David]* Halt! *[David turns mechanically.
Vera drifts out through the door, leaving the two men face to
face. The Baron beckons to David, who as if hypnotised moves
nearer. The Baron whips out his pistol, slowly crosses to David,
who stands as if awaiting his fate. The Baron hands the pistol
to David]* You were right! *[He steps back swiftly with a
touch of stern heroism into the attitude of the culprit at a military execution, awaiting the bullet]* Shoot me!

David *[Takes the pistol mechanically, looks long and pen-
sively at it as with a sense of its irrelevance. Gradually his arm
droops and lets the pistol fall on the table, and there his hand
touches a string of his violin, which yields a little note. Thus
reminded of it, he picks up the violin, and as his fingers draw
out the broken string he murmurs]* I must get a new string.
*[He resumes his dragging march toward the door, repeating
maunderingly]* I must get a new string.

THE SERVANT IN THE HOUSE *

By CHARLES RANN KENNEDY

The Reverend William Smythe finds it imperative that the drains
be fixed if he is to keep his church open. Although he would
rather not have his undesirable brother visit his parish, he has no
choice in the matter because "Drains," sewers, are *Robert's* business. *Robert* consents to come, as he wishes to see his small
daughter, who is being reared by the *Vicar*.

We see the brusque, rude, loud-mouthed *Robert* with *Manson*,
the silent, soft-spoken, mysterious servant, "dressed in his native
Eastern costume."

Robert Oh, Jeeroosalem! . . . 'Ere, 'elp us orf, comride: I'm
wet through. Rainin' cats an' dorgs dahn at the Junction!
'Ere, I cawn't . . . Wot oh! The very identical! . . .
*[Manson has helped him off with his coat, and now hands him
the cassock]*

* Published by Messrs. Harper and Brothers, N. Y.; and also by The University
of Chicago Press, in their collected edition of Charles Rann Kennedy's plays.

Robert [*Getting into it*] Don' know oo you are, ole pal ; but you're a bit of orl right ! . . . Don't I look a corf-drop ? 'Ere, where you teking it to ? . . . [*He watches Manson suspiciously as he places the coat before the fire to dry*] Bit 'andy, ain't yer ? . . . So this is where 'e lives ! A bloomin' palace, as never I did see ! . . . [*Manson prepares a place for him at the table and pours out a cup of tea, etc.*] Right you are, ole comride ! 'E said breakfast, an' breakfast it shall be, I don't fink ! Blimey ! Sossingers ! Ain't 'ad the taste of sossingers in my gizzard for I don't know 'ow long ! [*He sits and devours whilst Manson breaks and hands him bread, waiting upon him*] [*Between bites*] Wouldn't think as I was 'is brother, would yer ? — not to look at me ? But 'strooth, I *am* ; and wot's more, 'e cawn't deny it ! [*He labours with a little joke*] There's a lot of brothers knockin' abaht as people don't know on, eh what ? See wot I mean ? [*Suddenly serious*] Not as I'm one o' them sort, mind yer ; my father married my mother honest, same as I married my little . . . [*After a moment's reflection, he makes fresh onslaught upon the sausages. Presently he looks up*] 'Ere, ain't you goin' ter 'av' none ? . . . Cawn't yer speak ?

Manson Yes.

Robert Well, why cawn't yer arnswer a bloke when 'e arsks yer civil ?

Manson You didn't make it clear that you wanted to eat with me.

Robert Want a bit of 'eart in it, eh ?

Manson Yes, that's all.

Robert [*Largely*] Sit dahn, ole pal ! Mek yourself at 'ome ! [*Manson obeys*]

Robert See, wot was I tawkin' abaht, just afore you turned narsty ?

Manson You were going to say something about your little girl's mother. [*Robert's cutlery bristles up like bayonets*]

Robert Look, 'ere, mate, don't you come tryin' it on with me ! I don't care *oo* you are !

Manson I know that.

Robert Then let me be, I tell yer ! You tek all the taste out of my sossingers.

Manson I should like to hear about her, comrade.

Robert *You* cawn't bring 'er back. She's dead.

Manson What was her name?

Robert Mary — same as the little gel's.

Manson I wonder whether they are anything alike.

Robert That's wot I come to see! . . . She 'ad 'er mother's nose when she was a biby — and *'er* eyes! Gorstrike, she was the very spit — far as a biby could be! . . . Swelp me Moses, if I find 'er anything like Bill's old geezer, I'll cut 'er throat!

Manson And if she's like her mother? What then?

Robert Why, then . . . there's allus my own! I nearly did it once.

Manson [*After a pause*] How did you come to lose her?

Robert [*Roughly*] Never you mind!

Manson How did you come to lose her?

Robert [*Sullenly*] Typhoid fever. [*Manson notes the evasion with a glance. He helps Robert to more tea, and waits for him to speak. Robert wriggles under his gaze, and at last he says, reluctantly*] Oh, it was my own fault, as I lost the *kid*!

Manson That was a sore loss, comrade.

Robert I know it! Needn't rub it in! . . . Look 'ere, Comride, I 'adn't a bad nature to begin with Didn't me an' my brother Joshua pinch an' slave the skin orf our bones to send that spotted swine to school? Didn't we 'elp 'im out with 'is books an' 'is mortar-boards an' 'is bits of clothes to try and mek 'im look respectable? That's wot *we* did, till he got 'is lousy scholyships, an' run away to get spliced with that she-male pup of a blood-hound! Cos why? Cos we was proud of the little perisher! — proud of 'is 'ead-piece! We 'adn't got none ourselves — leastways, I 'adn't; Joshua was different to me; and now . . .

Manson And your brother Joshua: what of him? Where is *he* now?

Robert I don't know — gone to pot, like me! P'r'aps eatin' 'is bleedin' 'eart out, same as I am, at the base ingratitood of the world!

RIP VAN WINKLE*

By Joseph Jefferson

Coming home drunk once too often for the patience of his wife, *Gretchen, Rip Van Winkle* is driven out into the storm with his gun and dog. He wanders up into the Kaatskill Mountains, where he unexpectedly comes upon the ghostly crew of *Henry Hudson,* bowling and drinking.

[*Hudson extends a cup to Rip, as if inviting him to drink*]

Rip [*Doubtfully*] You want me to drink mit you? [*Hudson nods. Rip approaches him cautiously, unable to resist the temptation of a drink*] Well, I swore off drinkin'; but as this is the first time I see you, I won't count this one— [*He takes the cup. Hudson holds up another cup. Rip is reassured, and his old geniality returns*] You drink mit me? We drink mit one another? [*Hudson nods affirmatively. Rip feels at home under these familiar circumstances, and becomes familiar and colloquial again*] What's the matter mit you, old gentleman, anyhow? You go and make so [*Imitating the demon*] mit your head every time; was you deaf? [*Hudson shakes his head*] Oh, nein. [*Laughing at his error*] If you was deaf, you wouldn't hear what I was sayin'. Was you dumb? [*Hudson nods yes*] So? You was dumb? [*Hudson nods again*] Has all of your family the same complaint? [*Hudson nods*] All the boys dumb, hey? All the boys dumb. [*All the demons nod. Then, suddenly, as if struck with an idea*] Have you got any girls? [*Hudson shakes his head*] Don't you? Such a big family, and all boys? [*Hudson nods*]

Rip [*With profound regret*] That's a pity; my, that's a pity. Oh, my, if you had some dumb girls, what wives they would make— [*Brightening up*] Well, old gentleman, here's your good health, and all your family— [*Turning and waving to them*] —may they live long and prosper. [*Rip drinks. As he does, all the demons lean forward, watching the effect of the liquor. Rip puts his hand to his head. The empty cup falls to the ground*]

Rip [*In an awed and ecstatic voice*] What for licker is that! [*As he turns, half reeling, he sees Hudson holding out to him another cup. He snatches it with almost frantic eagerness*]

* Reprinted by the courtesy of Dodd, Mead and Company.

Give me another one! [*He empties it at a draught. A long pause follows during which the effect of the liquor upon Rip becomes apparent; the light in his eyes fades, his exhilaration dies out, and he loses his grasp on the reality of his surroundings. Finally, he clasps his head with both hands, and cries in a muffled, terrified voice*] Oh, my, my head was so light, and now, it's heavy as lead! [*He reels, and falls heavily to the ground. A long pause. The demons begin to disappear. Rip becomes dimly conscious of this, and raises himself on his elbow*] Are you goin' to leave me, boys? Are you goin' to leave me all alone? Don't leave me; don't go away. [*With a last effort*] I will drink your good health, and your family's — [*He falls back heavily, asleep*]

JOINT OWNERS IN SPAIN *

By ALICE BROWN

Miss Dyer, an inmate in the *Home*, is to become *Mrs. Blair's* roommate because "there are just two of you in the Home that are impossible to live with." *Miss Dyer* is a thin, weak, tearful, self-pitying, old woman. *Mrs. Blair* is her opposite — "high spirited, and over-bearing." Not wanting to move in with the "snuffin' and sittin'" *Miss Dyer*, *Mrs. Blair* at once sets about to make her uncomfortable by dominating the situation in her usual blustering, complaining, backbiting manner.

Mrs. Blair [*Explosively*] Humph! [*Puts her arms akimbo and looks about the room. Bitterly*] To think of all the wood I've burnt up in my air-tight an' my kitchen stove an' thought nothin' of it! To think o' all the wood there is now growin' an' rottin' from Dan to Beersheba an' I can't lay my fingers on it!

Miss Dyer I dunno what ye want o' wood. This place's hot enough to fry in.

Mrs. Blair Ye don't know what I want on't? Well, I'll tell ye. I want some two-inch boards to nail up a partition in the middle o' this room. I don't want no more'n my own, but I want it mine.

Miss Dyer [*Drearily*] You wouldn't have no gre't of an outlay for boards. 'Twouldn't have to be knee-high to keep me out.

* Reprinted by the courtesy of Walter H. Baker and Company.

Mrs. Blair [*As if electrified by a sudden thought*] What d'you say?

Miss Dyer [*With no interest*] Ye wouldn't have to build more'n a shingle's thickness to keep me out. I never was no hand to go where I ain't wanted; an' if I ever was, I guess I'm cured on't now.

Mrs. Blair [*With the air of pouncing*] Last week they said you was markin' out a tumbler quilt. You must ha' had a piece o' chalk. Where is it?

Miss Dyer [*Drawing forth a piece of chalk from the workbag hanging on her chair; quavering*] Here 'tis. I hope you won't do nothin' out o' the way with it. I should hate to git into trouble here.

Mrs. Blair [*Seizing it, diving to the bottom of her baggy pocket and, drawing forth a ball of twine, chalking the length of it and forcing one end of it on the bewildered Miss Dyer*] You git up here. Take that end.

Miss Dyer [*Obeying, bewildered*] Don't ye tole me into nothin'. I ain't that kind.

Mrs. Blair You step there to the middle square o' that winder and hold your end o' the string down on the floor. I'll snap it.

Miss Dyer [*Taking the string laxly and sidling to the door, opening it and calling*] Mis' Mitchell!

Mrs. Blair [*Ruthlessly jerking her away and shutting the door*] You step in here an' do as I tell you! There's the spot. You stan' right here.

Miss Dyer [*Wailing*] Oh, Mis' Blair, you're as crazy as a loon, an' here I be shet up in this room with ye, an' Mis' Mitchell ain't within hearin', an' I wisht my troubles was over an' I was under the sod.

Mrs. Blair [*Pushing her into place, snatching the end of string from her, putting it on the floor, lifting Miss Dyer's foot with one hand and setting it emphatically on the string*] Stan' there an' stan' still. Don't you ease up now. [*She twitches a bedstead round and hitches the cord about the leg so that it makes a straight line, dividing the room in two, talking absorbedly while she works*] Wonderful are the ways o' Providence and past findin' out. Here be we yoked up together, an' the yoke is lifted an' we're goin' to lay down in separate stalls. [*Snaps the cord. Triumphantly*] Step off on't, will ye? You gimme the chalk an' I'll go over it an' make it so's't anybody can see it in the dead o' night. [*Miss Dyer gingerly passes her the chalk. Mrs. Blair snatches it, kneels and chalks vigorously along the line, while Miss Dyer, hovering in a corner and softly lamenting, apprehensively watches her*]

Miss Dyer Oh, Mis' Blair, I dunno what you're doin' no more'n the dead, and if I found out mebbe I should be scairter'n I be now. You stop, Mis' Blair. Don't you go markin' up the floor. Seems terrible mis*chiev*ous to go to markin' up floors. [*Mrs. Blair, entangled in her skirt, staggers to her feet*]

Mrs. Blair [*Triumphantly*] There! now here's two rooms. Here's the partition. See?

Miss Dyer [*Struggling with the idea*] 'Tain't nothin' but a mark.

Mrs. Blair That chalk mark's the partition. You can have the mornin' sun, for I'd jest as soon live by a taller candle in a place that's my own. Gimme the chalk. [*Miss Dyer interestedly passes it*] I'll chalk a lane into the cluzzet so's't we can both keep a right o' way. Now I'm to home an' so be you. Don't you dast to speak a word to me unless you come an' knock here on my headboard —

Miss Dyer [*A little bewildered*] What be I goin' to knock for?

Mrs. Blair That headboard's my front door. If I want to run into your house, I'll knock on yourn. Well, if I ain't glad to be alone. I've hung my harp on a willer long enough. [*She pulls out a little table in her "house" and begins to unpack treasures from her ancient carpet-bag and range them there. Meanwhile she sings, either "Coronation" or the Doxology, in a strenuous voice. Miss Dyer, more timidly, glancing at her from time to time to see if she is playing right, takes her knitting and settles quite cozily by the window. She evidently wishes to test the theory, gets up and knocks timidly on the headboard. Mrs. Blair, cordially*] That you, Miss Dyer? Come right in.

Miss Dyer [*Evidently feeling her way*] No, I didn't come to stop.

Mrs. Blair I s'pose you were goin' by and see me at the winder. I'm proper busy. I was jest gittin' round to measurin' off my settin'-room. Seems to me it needs new paper.

Miss Dyer Why, this paper ain't been on — [*Catches herself up, stops and chuckles*] I've had it in mind myself to paper, but I ain't fixed on the pattern yit.

THE SHOW-OFF *

By George Kelly

Mrs. Fisher is the typical plump "advice-giving" mother. She has an answer for every problem, and she finds many of them. She is very critical of anything that doesn't agree with her own ideas. *Mrs. Fisher's* greatest concern at the moment is her daughter *Amy,* and "that fellow," she goes with. "She doesn't know how she stands him." Her older daughter, *Clara,* is also concerned.

Clara Is that fellow still coming here?

Mrs. Fisher Oh, right on the dot — such as he is. Sunday nights too now, as well as Wednesdays. It looks like a steady thing. And you never in your life heard anybody talk so much, Clara, — I don't know how she stands him. Your Pop can hardly stay in the room where he is. I believe in my heart that's the reason he went over to Gillespie's tonight — so he wouldn't be listenin' to him.

Clara Doesn't she take him into the parlor?

Mrs. F. She does, yes; but she might just as well leave him out here; for he's not in there five minutes till he's out here again — talkin' about Socialism. That's all you hear, — Socialism — and capital and labor. You'd think he knew somethin' about it. And the Pennsylvania Railroad. He's always talkin' about that, too. That's where he works, you know. I don't know what he does down there. He sez himself he's head of the freight department; but as I sez to our Joe, I sez, "I don't know how *he* can be head of *anything*, from the talk of him. Joe sez he thinks he's a nut. And your Pop told him right to his face here last Sunday night — that he didn't know the meanin' of the *word* Socialism. [*She checks herself and gets up*] I'd better not be talkin' so loud, — he's apt to walk in on us. [*She moves up toward the hall-door, and glances out*] He's a great joker, you know — That's what he did last Sunday night. [*Coming forward again to a point above the center-table*] I never got such a fright in my life. Your Pop and me was sit-

* From "The Show-Off" by George Kelly. Reprinted by permission of Little, Brown & Company.

219

tin' here talkin', just the way we are now, when, all of a sudden, I glanced up, and there he was,—standin' in the doorway there, doin' this [*She points her forefinger and thumb at Clara and wiggles her thumb. Clara laughs faintly*]   —as though he was a bandit, you know. Well,—I thought the breath'd leave my body. Then he sez, "Haha!—that's the time I fooled you!"   I don't know how long he had been standin' there. But, as luck'd have it, we wasn't talkin' about him at the time : although we *had* been talkin' about him not five minutes before. I don't know whether he heard us or not, for I don't know how long he'd been standing there. I hope he did : it'd just be the price of him, for bein' so smart. [*With a glance toward the hall-door, and speaking very confidentially*]   But, you know, what'd kill you, Clara, you can't say a *word* about him in front of her. [*Clara moves*] Oh, not a word. No matter what he sez, she thinks it's lovely. When Joe told her here the other night he thought he was a nut, she just laughed, and said that Joe was jealous of him—because *he* could express himself, and *he* couldn't. [*Clara smiles*] You never *heard* such talk. And, you know, Clara, *I* think he wears a wig. [*Clara laughs*] I do, honestly. And our Joe sez he thinks he does too. But when I asked *her* about it here one mornin', I thought she'd take the head right off me. You never *seen* anybody get themselves into such a temper. She sez, "It's a lie," she sez, "he don't wear a wig." She sez, "People always say somethin' like that about a fellow that makes a good appearance." But, I think he does, just the same ; and the first chance I get I'm goin' to take a good look. [*She moves around to her chair again, at the right of the table*] He often sits right here, you know, under this light, while he's talkin' ; [*Selecting another piece of candy*]   and I'm goin' to look close the very first chance I get. [*She sits down*] I can tell a wig as good as anybody. [*She rocks and looks straight out, chewing*] She won't make a liar out of me.

Amy [*From the head of the stairs*] Mom, did you see anything of that blue bar-pin of mine ?

Mrs. Fisher [*Calling back to her*] Which blue bar-pin ?

Amy Well now, how many blue bar-pins have I got ?

Mrs. Fisher I don't know how many you've got, and I don't care ! [*Turning back again and speaking rather to herself*] So don't be botherin' me about it. [*Calling up to Amy again*]

If you can't find it, go look for it. [*She resumes her rocking and her chewing*] She thinks all she's got to do is come to the head of them stairs and holler and everybody'll jump.—But she'll get sadly left—I've got somethin' else to do besides waitin' on her. [*She takes another bite of candy, and turns casually to Clara*] Did you *get* your lamp yet?

Clara No, that's what I was in town today about. The girl sez they haven't been able to match the silk till yesterday.

Mrs. Fisher I wish I could get somethin' done to that one of mine there in the parlor; the wire's right out through the silk in two places.

Clara Why doesn't Amy take it in some day [*Mrs. Fisher makes a sound of amusement*] —when she's going to work?

Mrs. Fisher Why don't she! It's all Amy can do to take *her*self in to work these days. I've got to *push* her out the door every morning.

Clara Couldn't she take it over at lunch-time?

Mrs. Fisher She sez she hasn't time at lunch-time.

Clara Oh, she has so time.

Mrs. Fisher Of course she has.

Clara It's only at Ninth and Chestnut, and she's at Eighth.

Mrs. Fisher That's what I told her. I sez, "I bet if it was somethin' for yourself you'd have plenty time." [*Leaning towards Clara*] But, you know,—what *I* think, Clara, I think she's meetin' this fellow at lunch-time. Because in the mornin's here she stands fixin' herself there in front of that glass till it's a wonder to me she don't drop on the floor. And whenever you see them gettin' very particular that way all of a sudden— there's somethin' in the wind. I sez to her the other morning, when she was settlin' herself there till I got tired lookin' at her, I sez, "You must be goin' to see him today, ain't you?" And she sez, "He must be on your mind, isn't he?" "No," I sez, "but by the looks of things, I think he's on yours. And," I sez, "maybe after you get him you won't think he was worth all the bother you went to." Because, you know, Clara, she don't know a *thing* about him; except that he works in the Pennsylvania freight office.—I believe he *did* tell her that much. But *she* don't know whether he works there or not. He could tell her anything; and she'd believe it [*Taking another bite of candy and settling herself in her chair*] —before she'd believe me.

SUN-UP *

By LULA VOLLMER

Mrs. Cagle is a "frail, but wiry, type of woman" — a pipe-smoking, fearless mountaineer, who lives by the law of the gun, treating all outsiders with border hospitality.

The court law means nothing to her, except that it shot her husband in the back while he was protecting his own moonshine. Her revenge is to protect all fugitives of the law by "shooting to kill" any officer who trespasses on her property.

Sheriff Now, Mis' Cagle, if ye air satisfied, I reckon I can take my prisoner.

Mrs. Cagle [*After a moment's hesitation*] No, Sheriff, ye kin wait — outside.

Sheriff All right, as ye say. If ye need me, jest call. [*Satisfied with his triumph he goes out — smiling*]

Emmy [*Coming forward*] Who is he, Mom?

Mrs. Cagle [*Standing erect and making no move except to push Emmy aside. She stares straight at the back room door, and when she speaks it is to herself rather than in answer to Emmy's questions*] I fed him —

Emmy Whut's happened?

Mrs. Cagle And I hid him —

Emmy Tell me whut's up, Mom.

Mrs. Cagle I wuz about to shoot to save him —

Emmy Mom, who is he?

Mrs. Cagle The son of the man who killed Rufe's pap.

Emmy [*Greatly agitated*] Son of the — man who — killed — Rufe's pap!

Mrs. Cagle If his pap had lived Rufe wouldn't a gone to war.

Bud [*Concerned only with his grief*] Rufe's dead.

Mrs. Cagle Yes, Bud, Rufe's dead, and one of his murderers air in thar —

Emmy Ye goin' to give him to the law, Mom?

Mrs. Cagle [*With some hesitation*] No — not to — the law.

* From *Sun-Up*, by Lula Vollmer. Reprinted by Special Permission of Coward-McCann, Inc., Publishers. No performance of any kind may be given of this play without permission first having been obtained in writing from Longmans, Green and Company, 114 Fifth Avenue, N. Y.

Emmy   [*With uneasiness*]   Whut ye goin' to do, Mom?

Mrs. Cagle   [*Suddenly turns and going to door, bars it. Coming back to the table she takes the gun in her hand. She stands for a few seconds staring at the back room door. Bud pays no attention to her. Emmy watches, too confounded for words or action. Mrs. Cagle finally moves toward the door, slowly, but firm in step. She stops for a second at the door, and then in a quiet but commanding voice speaks*]   Come out, Stranger.

Stranger   [*Entering he feels the tenseness of the scene*]   Has the — the sheriff gone?

Mrs. Cagle   Ye air safe from the Sheriff.

Stranger   Thank God.

Mrs. Cagle   Yo' name, Stranger?

Stranger   My name is Zeb Turner.

Mrs. Cagle   And yo' pap's name?   Wuz hit Zeb Turner, too?

Stranger   Yes, Zeb Turner.

Mrs. Cagle.   Wuz he a revenuer?

Stranger   Yes, one of the bravest that ever crossed the mountains.   You don't know him, do you?

Mrs. Cagle   Know him?   Well, Stranger, Zeb Turner killed my son's Pap.

Stranger   Great God!

Mrs. Cagle   Shot him in the back while he wuz protectin' his own property.

Stranger   God Almighty!

Mrs. Cagle   And I've protected ye —

Stranger   I didn't know, Mrs. Cagle, I —

Mrs. Cagle   Hid ye in my own house — ye, the son of my man's murderer.

Stranger   I didn't know.   Besides, you've got to remember, it was law.

Mrs. Cagle   Law! Law! Allus that word, law. Well, Stranger, the feud has a law, and it air a life for a life.

Stranger   I understand how you feel, and I don't blame you. Call the Sheriff and give me up.

Mrs. Cagle   Give ye up!   No, Stranger, ye air mine to deal with.

Emmy   Mom!

Stranger Mrs. Cagle, for your own sake, turn me over to the Sheriff. I'll get what's coming to me.

Mrs. Cagle If ye've got a gun, Stranger, use hit. The feud will give ye a chance the law won't.

Stranger I have no gun.

Mrs. Cagle Thar's Bud's. I'll give ye time to reach hit.

Stranger Why, I can't fight you, Mrs. Cagle.

Mrs. Cagle I'm givin' ye a chance.

Stranger I can't take it.

Mrs. Cagle. Then ye better run.

Stranger They will take your life for this. [*Shows his fear of her*]

Mrs. Cagle My life! Whut does that matter? They've took every life that belonged to me. My pap's — my man's — my son's — my little son's life, they took hit, them that hide behind a thing called law.

Stranger But Mrs. Cagle, you don't understand —

Mrs. Cagle I understand that ye air a son of the law, and that ye air in the power of the feud.

Stranger [*Pleadingly*] Mrs. Cagle. . .

Mrs. Cagle I'm offering ye a chance fer yo' life, but if ye air too much of a coward to take hit, by God I'll— [*Throws gun to her shoulder*]

Emmy [*Throwing herself between Mrs. Cagle and Stranger*] Mom, ye shan't kill him, ye shan't.

Mrs. Cagle Git away, Emmy.

Emmy Mom, he's goin' out thar to shoot the dogs that killed Rufe—

Mrs. Cagle I ain't a believin' him.

Emmy Him and Rufe was a fightin' on the same side —

Mrs. Cagle Out of the way, Emmy —

Emmy Mom, he cain't help whut his pap done.

Mrs. Cagle He's a son of the law. Air ye forgettin' whut the law done to yo pap?

Emmy My pap wuz a-breakin' the law.

Mrs. Cagle Air ye fergettin' that the law killed Rufe?

Emmy No, Mom, I ain't a fergettin' ever. But hit warn't the law, Mom, hit wuz hate — Rufe told me — hate like this thing in yo' heart toward him— [*Pointing to Stranger*] fer somethin' he's got nothin' to do with. It's hate, Mom. Rufe told me the day he went off— [*She breaks into hysterical sobs*] Rufe told me— [*Suddenly Mrs. Cagle seems to be listening intently to something the others do not hear*]

Mrs. Cagle Hush, did ye hear that?

Emmy Whut, Mom?

Mrs. Cagle [*Listening*] Hit's music.

Emmy Hit's the wind on the snow—

Mrs. Cagle Hush, I tell ye. Hit's him— [*Pause*] Cain't ye hear him? [*The Stranger and Emmy exchange glances as much as to say that she has gone mad*]

Emmy Who, Mom?

Mrs. Cagle Wait— [*There is a pause—dead silence*] Yes, son—

Emmy Mom, whut is hit?

Mrs. Cagle Be quiet, I tell ye. Whut is it, son?—yes— yes— [*She turns to the others, listening as she speaks*] Cain't ye hear him speakin'?

Emmy No, Mom.

Mrs. Cagle [*After a pause*]. Say hit again, son, so's I kin tell them. [*There is a moment's pause, and then Mrs. Cagle repeats in a measured voice*] As long as thar air hate—thar will be— feuds. As long as thar air women—thar will be—sons. I ain't no more—to you—than other mothers' sons—air to them. Yes, son—what else? [*Pause*] Take keer of—yo'-self—yes son—and Emmy. Whut else, son?— [*She strains to hear more but it does not come. She turns to the others*] Didn't none of ye hear him speakin'?

Emmy No, Mom. We didn't hear him.

Mrs. Cagle I heared him.

Emmy The dead cain't come back.

Mrs. Cagle No, I reckon my love went on—out yonder and reached him [*The gun slips to the floor*] and he's told me whut to do. I reckon ye better go, Stranger.

Stranger You mean —

Mrs. Cagle I mean the hate of the feud air gone out of me— Go home, boy, if ye kin.

GAMMER GURTON'S NEEDLE *

By STUART WALKER

The puckish *Diccon* has reported that old *Dame Chatte,* who keeps an inn near-by, has taken *Gammer Gurton's* one and only needle. *Gammer,* accompanied by her servant, *Hodge,* promptly goes to fetch it.

Gammer   [*Calling*]

Dame Chatte, I would pray thee fair, let me have what is mine !

I have not this twenty years taken one breath that is thine.

Therefore give me mine own and let me live beside thee !

Chatte   [*Entering*]

Why hast thou crept from home hither to mine own doors to chide me ?

Hence, doting drab, avaunt, or I shall set thee further !

Intendest thou and that knave me in my house to murder ?

Gammer

Tush, gape not so on me, woman !   Shalt not ye eat me !

Nor all the friends thou hast in this shall not entreat me !

Mine own goods, I will have, and ask thee not by leave.

What, woman !   Poor folks must have rights, though the thing you aggrieve.

Chatte

Give thee thy rights and hang thee up with all thy beggar's broods.

What, wilt thou make me a thief and say I stole thy goods ?

Gammer

I'll say nothing, I warrant thee, but that I can prove it well —

Thou tookst my goods e'en from my door, I am able this to tell !

Chatte

Did I, old witch, steal what was thine ?   How should that thing be known ?

Gammer

I cannot tell ; but up thou took it, as though it had been thine own.

* *Gammer Gurton's Needle,* by Stuart Walker, reprinted by courtesy of D. Appleton-Century Company, publishers.

Chatte
Marry, fie on thee, thou old giv, with all my very heart!

Gammer
Nay, fie on thee, thou ramp, thou rig, with all that take thy part!

Chatte
A vengeance on those lips that layeth such things to my charge!

Gammer
A vengeance? A vengeance on those callets' hips whose conscience is so large!

Chatte
Come here, dog!

Gammer
Come out, hog, and let me have a right.

Chatte
Thou arrant witch!

Gammer
Thou bawdy witch, I'll make thee curse this night!

Chatte
You bag, you wallet!

Gammer
A cart for a callet!

Chatte
Why, thinkest thou thus to prevail?
I hold thee a groat I shall patch thy coat!

Gammer
Thou wilt as soon steal my pail!
Thou blab, thou drab, thou rake, thou jade, will not shame make thee hide!

Chatte
Thou scold, thou bold, thou rotten, thou glutton. I will no longer chide!
But I will teach thee to keep home.

Gammer
Wilt thou, drunken beast? [*They clinch*]

Hodge [*Dancing around*]
Stick to her, Gammer, take her by the head,
I'll warrant you this feast!

Smite, I say, Gammer! Bite, I say, Gammer!
  I trow ye will be keen!
Where be your nails? Claw her jaw! Pummel her red face
  green!
'Od's bones, Gammer, hold up your head!

Chatte

I trow, draw, I shall dress thee.
  [*Chases Hodge*]
Tarry, thou knave, I hold thee a groat; I shall make these
  hands bless thee!
  [*Smites Gammer effectively*]
Take thou this, old trot, for amends, and learn thy tongue
  well to tame,
And say thou met at this bickering, not thy fellow, but thy
  dame!

THE PATRIARCH*
By Boyd Smith

Abner Gaunt, the Patriarch of a mountain community, lives by
the Bible, believing justice in all matters can be found in the
readings of the Book. *Abner* is faced with the problem of
judging his own son, *Joe,* who, driven by the taunts of his
deceiving sweetheart, *Leah Tanner,* kills his own brother, *Lem,*
in a fit of passion. *Abner Gaunt* many times in the past has
judged and punished the sins of these simple mountain folk, but
never has his faith in God and Justice been so tried as now, when
he sentences *Joe* to death by Suicide. *Sarah* is *Joe's* mother.

Joe . . . [*Gaunt fills Joe's pipe, takes it to Joe, and holds a
match; fills and lights his own pipe. He draws up a chair close
to Joe. They smoke silently a few moments*]

Gaunt [*Very tenderly and with something of a struggle*] I was
reading not long ago where a man called — it — the great adventure.

Joe [*Musingly*] The great adventure. [*Pause*] Why
course, it is. [*Smiles*]

Gaunt Joe, my boy, you never feared—death before.

Joe Nothin' now to be afraid of. I reckon yuh feel all right when yuh pay your way, when you pay for the things you do. Well, I'm a-payin', Father, an' I feel all right, and I ain't afraid.

Gaunt [*Full of suppressed feeling*] Just what I'd expect my boy to say.

Joe There's only one thing botherin' me now an' that is, who is goin' to mind the sheep.

Gaunt Reckon I'll do it a while. Then if I can't get a good man, I'll sell 'em.

Joe Mother'll fret a lot, too.

Gaunt Yes, Joe. Be careful what you say to her. Talk kinda careless like.

Joe 'Course [*Pause*] S'posin' we go up on th' ridge in th' mornin' an' round up the sheep. There'll be a lot of things to show you about 'em before—I go.

Gaunt [*Brokenly*] Yes, Joe.

Joe Don't you worry, Father, I'm all right. I'm powerful cur'us about all those stars anyway. [*Gaunt nods*] I was talkin' to Lem about 'em last night, and wonderin' how God could pay any attention to us up here on old Allegheny when he has so many millions to look after.

Gaunt The Book says a sparrow can't drop to the ground without his noticin'.

Joe It don't seem possible, somehow.

Gaunt There's no way of knowin'—except by faith.

Joe [*Dreamily*] Faith.

Gaunt Faith. It takes a great faith to live, my boy. Faith in man; faith in God; if you do his biddin', He will bless you; if you do the thing—which you have to do—somehow—sometime, he will bring you peace. [*Pause*]

Joe [*Quietly; with growing exaltation*] I see it, father, I see it. If I have the faith to stand up—an'—pay—He will understand, and bring me peace—

Gaunt Yes.

Joe [*Looking into space*] Good old Lem. Tomorrow night I'll be with you. [*While he is speaking, Sarah enters upper right. She mutely shows that she has come for Joe. Joe sees her, motions Gaunt ; Gaunt turns, sees her, turns back to Joe, and nods for him to go to her ; Joe rises and goes to Sarah, who takes him toward door upper right, and nods him off. Gaunt rises. Sarah turns at the door and comes toward Gaunt*]

Sarah   Abner, he's the last — our baby — an' we are old.

Gaunt   Yes, Sarah.   [*Seeing no sign of Gaunt's relenting, she walks to the window left and stands looking out*]

Sarah   I — I just keep seein' Lem's white face as we covered him — and thinkin' about Joe — an' how we have him yet — an' —   [*Pause. She looks at Gaunt*]   Your head is set ?

Gaunt   [*Sitting, almost collapsing*]   There's nothin' else to do, Sarah.   There's no escapin' it.   [*Sarah looks at him with a mixture of awe and shrinking, then sinks into the chair where she is standing*]

Sarah   [*Dead, monotonous voice*]   I have seen my babies grow to men — and go — from me — I have used up my strength. I am old.   Nothin' have I withheld from you, Abner.   An' now I have nothin' to give.   God has gone from my sight.

Gaunt   [*Looking up slightly*]   God has gone —   [*With each of the following lines his voice gains strength, and he comes up in his chair*]   [*Pause*]   I will lift up mine eyes unto the mountain.   [*Pause*]   My soul, wait thou in silence for God only ;   [*Pause*]   He is our rock and our salvation ; he is our high tower ; — we shall not be moved.   [*Pause. Gaunt rises quietly and goes to Sarah.   He lays his hand on her shoulder.   It is his caress*]   God is very close to us, Sarah.

Sarah   Yes, Abner.   [*She rises with something of a struggle and crosses painfully to the door upper right, where she turns*] What will you be doin' — all night ?

Gaunt   I reckon I'll be stayin' in this room, Sarah, prayin' God to give me strength.

Sarah   Tomorrow evenin' — after you've — what will you be doin' ?

Gaunt   I'll be comin' back — to you — Sarah.

Sarah   An' after that — the next mornin' — when it's light — what will you be doin' ?

Gaunt   I'll have to be tendin' the sheep.   [*Sarah gazes at him a moment in wonder, then slowly departs.   Gaunt falls on his knees by his chair as the curtain falls*]

GREEN GROW THE LILACS *

By Lynn Riggs

The "shivoree" celebrating the marriage of *Curley* and *Laurey* ends tragically when the half-wit *Jeeter*, who was in love with *Laurey* is killed in a fight with *Curley*.

Curley is in jail awaiting trial. *Aunt Eller* tries to console *Laurey*.

Aunt Eller What is it, honey?

Laurey Over and over! The way them men done. The things they said. Oh — why'd it have to be that-a-way!

Aunt Eller Don't let yer mind run on it. Men is always like that at shivorees. Sump'n gits into 'em.

Laurey The one time in a body's life — !

Aunt Eller Sh! I know. It musta been bad.

Laurey Cain't ferget it, I tell you! I've tried and tried!

Aunt Eller [*Gravely, wisely*] Don't try, honey. Don't try. They's things you cain't git rid of — lots of things. Not if you live to be a hundred. You got to learn. You got to look at all the good on one side and all the bad on the other, and say: "Well, all right, then!" to both of them.

Laurey [*Unheeding*] — On top of everything! —

Aunt Eller [*With great compassion*] Yeah, you've had yer troubles. I know, Laurey. But they's been good things, too. Think about that. You ain't had to slave away a-workin' fer others, the way some girls has to do, — things like that. You've had you a good home —

Laurey [*Her mind temporarily diverted to another trouble*] Paw and Maw —

Aunt Eller Yeah, right when you needed 'em most, both gone. But you lived on, didn't you? You been happy since, ain't you? Course. You been strong about it. Why, when yer

Paw died — and you thought the world of him — you was all by yerself here — and you stood it. When they sent for me to Pryor, 'fore I could git here, why he was dead, and in his coffin.

Laurey [*Raising her head, and looking back into the room*] It set right there — on two cheers. The head towards the door.

Aunt Eller Yeah. [*Quietly, without self-pity, stating the fact*] When yore Paw died, and laid there — it was *my brother* in his coffin, too. Oh, and they's lots more, Laurey! I couldn't tell you all. Yer Uncle Jack, the children, both of my sisters, my paw and maw. Troubles thick and fast, you got to put up with. My husband — yer Uncle Jack. When he died. D'you know how? A crazy way to die. No use in it! He'd bought some hogs of Lem Slocum, and they turned out to be full of cholery — and all died. Jack walked over jist acrost the pasture to see Lem about it. Didn't show up and it got night. I tuck a lantern and went out to see. When I come to the worm fence, I found him, in a corner, all huddled down, all bloody from a gun-shot. Laid there all doubled up — dead — in a patch of yeller daisies. Lem Slocum musta shot him. I didn't know who done it. All I knowed was — *my husband was dead*. Oh, lots of things happens to a womern. Sickness, bein' pore and hungry even, bein' left alone in yer old age, bein' afraid to die — it all adds up. That's the way life is — cradle to grave. And you c'n stand it. They's one way. You got to be hearty. You got to be.

Laurey [*Moved*] Oh, Aunt Eller, I'm sich a a baby — !

Aunt Eller There, there!

Laurey Ashamed of myself! I want to be the way you air.

Aunt Eller [*Breaking off*] Fiddlesticks! *Fat* — and *old*? You couldn't *h'ar* me to be the way *I* am! Why, in a year's time, you'll git so tard even of lookin' at me, you and Curly'll run me off the place, 'th a tin can tied on my tail — [*Laurey half-smiles at the spectacle, and leaning over, gives Aunt Eller an affectionate hug*]

Laurey [*Through tears*] Oh, what ud I do 'thout you, you're sich a crazy! —

Aunt Eller Shore's you're borned! —

Laurey I never could live. I never could. [*Rising, happier*] I'll get to bed now.

Aunt Eller And sleep, huh?

Laurey [*Smiling*] Tight.

Aunt Eller And eat hearty from now on, huh? Fried chicken and everythin'?

Laurey Tomorrow.

Aunt Eller Tomorrow, yer foot! [*She gets an apple out of a basket on the organ*] Here, eat that.

Laurey I don't want it.

Aunt Eller Eat it, I said.

CHILDREN OF THE MOON *

By MARTIN FLAVIN

For generations the *Athertons* have been Moon-mad. The full moon has lured them to their deaths, one after the other. *Jane*, however, the last of the *Athertons*, is perfectly normal and has just become engaged to *Major Bannister*. Her neurotic mother, infuriated by the fact that she had not been consulted, is determined to destroy the engagement by implanting the fear of hereditary madness in *Jane's* mind.

Jane My final answer, mother.

Laura [*Cornered, desperate, furious*] Oh! Well, then, you shall know the truth.— You cannot marry this man.— You cannot marry any man.— You have no right to marry.

Jane What — what do you mean?

Laura You are an Atherton.

Jane An Atherton?

Laura Yes, an Atherton — an Atherton — one of the Children of the Moon! [*Jane, bewildered by her words and frightened by the crazy glitter in her eyes, shrinks away from her. She continues in a frenzied torrent*] You shrink from that, and well you may, but you cannot change it. You were born with the curse around your neck and you will wear it to your grave.

You are a Moon child — one of the Moon-mad Athertons.— Your father and his father — the crazy Athertons! Why do you think we live here in this God-forsaken place? Has that never crossed your mind? — To cover up our shame — to hide it from the world — a safe retreat for children of the Moon! — I hate it — hate it — I've always hated it — the endless sea — the dreary sound of it, the barren rocks, the fog, the loneliness, the shame — Ugh! — God, how I hate it! [*She shudders. Jane shrinks further and further away, horror growing in her eyes*] Your father brought me here, a bride. [*She laughs hysterically and bitterly*] It was an evil day for me, and an evil day, the day I met him, too. Oh, yes, I knew the history of his tribe! He told me all there was to tell. He was a man, your father. I had fair warning, but I was headstrong and I loved him. They did not think the curse would fall on him. They thought he would be spared. They thought — they thought — well, they thought wrong — [*She sobs*] Do you know how he died? — how your father died?

Jane [*Leaning weakly against the stairpost*] No.

Laura It was the night that you were born, a brilliant moonlight night. The pain of you was dragging at me. The doctor must be reached. The man who drove our horses was away. Your father hitched the team himself. I begged him not to go. It seemed to me that I would rather die than to endure the agony of waiting — waiting for him to come back. He laughed at my fears, but his hands were trembling, and he had that — that look in his eyes. [*Brokenly*] And he did not come back.— He never came back.

Jane Oh!

Laura They found him in the morning crushed and dying under the wreckage of the buggy in the bottom of a canyon.

Jane [*Faintly*] I never knew.

Laura [*Passionately*] No, no, you never knew. You have been spared and guarded all your life. You could not even dream what I have suffered. And then, my son, my joy, my hope, my pride! You know how Philip died.— I knew before he went. I saw the look beginning in his eyes. I begged him not to go; but he had the Atherton will. He laughed at me, and I knew — I knew then he would not come back. — My life has been a bitter, bitter tragedy.— I would have spared you this but you forced it on yourself.

Jane [*The hideous significance is dawning on her*] Go on.

Laura [*Brutally*] What more is there to say? You see the chasm open at your feet. You know you have no right to a man's life — no right to bear a child.

Jane [*Trembling*] I am not mad.

Laura You are an Atherton.

Jane I am not mad.

Laura You are a Moon child — one of the children of the Moon.

Jane I don't believe you.

Laura You do, you do, you do! — You must! — You shall. [*Suddenly she runs to the terrace door, flings the draperies aside and throws the doors wide open. Judge Atherton is standing close to the wall, gazing through his telescope at the Moon which has but shortly risen and is invisible to the left. He is completely absorbed; his lips are mumbling, and his hands are shaking*] See! Look! There is the future that awaits you, — you and your children. [*She laughs hysterically*]

Jane [*Crouching against the post*] I don't believe you.

Laura You do — you do. Come here! — Come here to me!

Jane No — no. [*She turns as if to run up the stairs*]

Laura [*Contemptuously*] Are you afraid?

Jane [*Stopping and straightening up against the wall*] No, I am not afraid.

Laura You are afraid.

Jane I am not afraid.

Laura Well, then, why don't you come? [*Slowly, deliberately, with a great effort of will, Jane walks to the door. As she reaches it, Laura seizes her arm and half pulls, half pushes her on to the terrace*] Look, now, child of the Moon, and tell me what you see. [*Jane turns bravely to look, when she shouts triumphantly*] Your hands — your hands — look at your hands! [*Jane looks down at her hands. They are shaking. With an exclamation of terror, she holds them over her eyes*]

Jane No — no —

Laura [*Trying to tear her hands away*] Look! Look! I tell you you shall! You shall!

Jane [*Struggling and pulling back into the room*] No — no. — It is a lie — a lie — I am not mad!

Laura　You are afraid — you dare not look.

Jane　No, no, no! [*She breaks from Laura's grasp and runs blindly to the stairs, screaming*]　I am not mad.　It is a lie — I am not mad.

Laura　[*Suddenly coming to her senses. Terrified*]　Jane!

Jane　[*Dashing up the stairs*]　No — no.　[*She pauses on the landing, wild, disheveled, hysterical and motions to her mother to go back*]　It is a lie — a lie — I am not mad — I am not mad.

Laura　[*Falling to her knees at the foot of the stairs. In a tone of heart-broken grief and despair*]　Jane!

Jane　No, no, no, no, no!　[*She runs up the stairs and out of sight*]

THE ROYAL FAMILY*

By EDNA FERBER AND GEORGE KAUFMAN

Julie Cavendish, the famous actress, is determined that her daughter, *Gwen*, shall not sacrifice her happiness for a stage career, as she, herself, has done.

Julie is demanding that *Gwen* leave the stage and marry *Perry*, the man she loves.

Perry　What's the matter?　What's going on?

Julie　Well — what else?　What else?　Come on!　What else?　Perry! for God's sake take her out of this!　Take her away before it's too late.　Take her where she'll never hear stage again!　Take her away!

Fanny　Julie!　Julie!

Gwen　No!　I'm not going to marry him!　[*A warning*]

Julie　[*Pushes her hair back from her forehead with her open palm — a gesture of desperation*]　Not going to marry him!

Not going — [*A finger pointing to the spot where Julie, Gwen and Fanny have talked earlier*]

Gwen I'm not going to marry him and spoil his life!

Perry Gwen!

Gwen No, no!

Julie Oh, no, you won't! If you think I'm going to let you throw away your whole life! . . . And for what? . . . *This!* . . . So that nineteen years from now you can be standing here as I am, a mad woman in a family of maniacs! Money for this one, jobs for that one, rehearsals and readings and tickets for God knows where. I'm damned if you're going to! You're going to marry Perry Stewart —

Gwen No, no!

Julie Oh, yes, you are! You're going to do what I didn't do. They told me I had to be a Cavendish. [*A movement from her mother*] Oh, yes, you did! [*Wheeling to Gwen again*] Well, you're not going to be one. You're going to marry him now — tonight — tomorrow. And I'm going to be there with you and stand up beside you, and cry for happiness, and wish to God it was me! [*Her voice suddenly low, thoughtful*] And why not? I'm not dead yet! I've got some of my life left. And I'm going to live it to suit *me!* You've all had your turn. Who's crazy *now!* I can walk out and nobody can stop me.

Fanny What nonsense!

Dean You're mad!

Julie You don't believe it, h'm? I'll show you. I'm going to marry Gil Marshall and go to Egypt and Venice and Constantinople — and what do you know about that? As far as the stage is concerned — I'm through with it. Cavendish! To hell with Cavendish! I'm never going to act again. I'm never going to set foot on another stage as long as I live. I'm never going inside a theatre! I'm ne —

Jo [*Aghast at finding Julie still at home, has heard her voice, high-pitched. In a voice of alarm*] Miss Julie! It's eight o'clock!

Julie [*Grabs her coat from Jo. Rushes in a panic toward the outer door*] Oh, my God!

PANIC *

By Archibald MacLeish

Factories closed . . . business houses dark. . . Riots. . . Strikes.
. . Failing banks. . . Frozen assets. . . Foreclosures. . .
  Bankers — Ruined men — even the great *Banker, McGafferty* —
panic !
  Out of the fog of Chaos the voice of a blind man —

McGafferty
  There's the thing to scare you — boys like those ! —
  Feeble : underfed : tubercular : crippled :
  Crazy with hatred as a dog with ticks !
  There's the thing to scare you !   Better drop it !
  Better give in to them now while you can !
    [*McGafferty swings his head toward the boys in the door :
     they retreat a step*]
  There's your nightmare !   All your nightmares !   All of them !
  Things you see and don't see !

The Bankers   [*Rapidly*]
  Scolded like schoolboys. . .
    Can't be talked to like . . .
  Serious conference. . .
              . . . crisis !

The Blind Man
  He's right.   He's always right.   You need not fear us !
  And there are millions more you need not fear —
  Feeble as we are : sick as we are : hungry :
  Torpid with hunger : tiring to be dead —
  The torpor of death : the horrible dying of apathy !
  Men who dread to sleep lest dreams deceive them !
  The hopeless — having lost the wish to hope !
  The men with folded hands !   You need not fear them !
  Tongues harangue them but you need not fear !
  Mouths incite them to fight and they will not answer !
  Women hold them their wilted tits in contempt and they
  Look down : they are dumb !   You need not fear them !
  Greatness they have forgotten and pride and the envy of
  Nobler lives than their own and the service of honor.
  To suffer for no gain : to invite death in the
  Hope only of good is a fool's fate to them.

* Used by permission of, and by arrangement with Houghton Mifflin Company.

The man they praise is the man who has gotten away with it —
The slave with the wise slave's tricks — the cleverest victim.
Virtue and nobleness : honor and love they laugh at ! . . .
Their speech is irony : they whipped man's speech ;
They've lived a long life in the world you made them.
They've learned well in your world.   You need not fear.
    [*The Bankers move forward a step*]

The Bankers   [*Rapidly*]
    Haven't we anything better to do than listen to
    Wild talk with the. . .
              Soap box speeches. . .
                        Radicals. . .
       Billions in balance and . . .
              . . . Better to do than listen to. . .

The Blind Man
    It is not we you have the need to fear —
    Our eyes are blind : our broken fingers crippled.
    It is not we should break your sleep at night.
    We are your body — sick that you may perish !
    We are your anguish — paid that you may perish !
    We are your Christ — your million Christs — who writhe : but
    Not that you may live — that you may perish !

A Guard
    Quiet I tell you !   Quiet !   Somebody handle him !

The Blind Man
    It is not we you have the need to fear !
    No !   But when the day comes — when the day is
    Come — when that day comes to you — on that day —
    Needless and nameless though the fear may be — you'll
    Learn the taste of it.   You'll see our hunger —
    Yes !   And that day you will fear our hunger !
    Cold you'll see us and you'll fear our cold !
    Sick — sick till the blood turns — and you'll fear us !
    That day you will see us and the sight will
    Frighten you !   It is not we who kill. . .

The Bankers
    For God's sake McGafferty !
                 Call him off !

The Blind Man
    . . . It is not we who threaten you !   Your ill is
    Time and there's no cure for time but dying !

The Bankers
    That's enough McGafferty!

                        Choke him can't you?

The Blind Man
    Time's the hurt your hearts have : not our hands.
    Your fate is yours but written in our hatred —
    Read in our anguish — shrieking from our graves.
    Your destiny is yours but our arms' burden.

The Bankers
    I'm going : who else?
                    I am!
                    I am!
                        I am!
    That's enough of it for one day!
                            I am!
    [*The Bankers wheel toward the door : face the Blind Man :
        stop*]

McGafferty
    Ask him when the world ends gentlemen.
    Ask him for the date of doom.   He'll tell you.
    [*The Blind Man turns sharply toward McGafferty's voice :
        groping : his hands out.   Speaking he moves toward him*]

The Blind Man
    Yes. . .
            He'll tell you. . .
                    And you'll hear him. . .
                                Listen!
    Listen, McGafferty!   The day will come!
    This time or the next time — now or after —
    One crash or the certain crash beyond!
    You'll sleep between them and forget — but we won't.
    Once the need has left you you'll forget.
    Men forget in good years with the grass green.
    Men will say 'That's done now'— but it's not done :
    Say 'That's over'— It will not be over :
    Say 'What fools we were to fear it.'   Fools! —
    But not to fear it : to forget to fear!

McGafferty   [*Rising from his chair*]
    That's it, gentlemen!   That turns your cheeks white!
    Schoolboys writing bloody words on fences!
    Children with chalk!

The Blind Man [*Moving always toward McGafferty—his hands out*]
                              The prophecies come true
Not of themselves but of the ears that hear them.
The violence works in the blood.   The living inherit the
Hard speech of the dead like the seed of a pestilence.
They carry it close in their mouths and their breath feeds it.
You yourselves will feed it and will die.
You yourselves in your own minds will make the
Fate that murders you.   The bursting seed of
Death is rotting ripe beneath your tongues !

THE QUEEN'S HUSBAND *

By ROBERT E. SHERWOOD

"His Majesty, *King Eric the 8th,* a gentle, ineffectual, and rather weary monarch . . . has learned that he may not use the divine power with which he has been endowed, even to control his own life."
    His only apparent enjoyment in life is an occasional secret game of checkers with the immaculate and formidable elderly footman, *Phipps.*

King   Where the devil have they put that checkerboard ?

Phipps   Begging Your Majesty's pardon, I placed it in here for safe-keeping. [*He goes to the corner cabinet at the right, opens it, and takes out a checker-board and box containing the checker-men*]   Here it is, Your Majesty.

King   [*As he lays out the men*]   I wish you'd all get together and think up some permanent hiding-place for this board.   It's always, invariably, just where I can't find it.

Phipps   Perhaps I should explain, sir, this is a new board.   Her Majesty found the old one and had it thrown out.

King   Well, Phipps — there's one consolation.   There are always more checker-boards. . . Come on, now — sit down — [*Phipps draws up a chair*]   I'm going to beat the hide off you.

Phipps   [*Sitting down*]   It's Your Majesty's first move this time.

King   Very well.   [*He makes a move*]   There !

Phipps   [*Making his move*]   Thank you, sir.

* Reprinted by courtesy of Charles Scribner's Sons.

King　[*As the game progresses*]　You know, Phipps, you have an unfair advantage over me.

Phipps　An unfair advantage, sir?　Does Your Majesty imagine that I'd be guilty of any petty cheating in checkers?

King　Don't be a damn fool, Phipps.　What I meant was — you get a chance to practise.　I'm certain that when you're off duty you train with the finest checker players in the city.　Now, I never get any practice.　You're the only one in the palace who will ever play checkers with me. . . I once had the idea that I might persuade the Queen to take up the game — but, somehow or other, she couldn't seem to appreciate its charms.　Her Majesty is a very remarkable woman, Phipps — a very remarkable woman.　But she just won't play checkers.　[*The King makes a move, but Phipps extends a restraining hand*]

Phipps　Begging your pardon, sir — but you've got to jump.

King　Oh, I have, have I?　I hadn't noticed that.　Well. . . [*He jumps.　Phipps jumps him back twice*]　Damn it, Phipps. You do *practise*.

Phipps　Thank you, sir.

King　[*Going on with the game*]　Have you any children, Phipps?

Phipps　Six, sir.

King　How very commendable.　All sons, I suppose.

Phipps　No, sir.　There is one daughter.

King　Is she married?

Phipps　She is, sir.

King　To a young man of her own choice?

Phipps　Yes, sir — unfortunately.　She chose an agriculturist, and I may say that it has been a source of some regret to her mother and me.

King　Oh — you wanted her to marry some one else?

Phipps　Yes, sir.　We did not consider the agriculturist quite — ah — shall I say eligible?　We hoped that the girl would marry in her own class.

King　Is she happy, Phipps?

Phipps　Yes, sir — I suppose she's happy — in a rather rustic sort of way.　[*He jumps up*]　Beg pardon, sir — the buzzer's ringing.　[*He goes out ; the King hastily arranges his handker-*

chief over the checker-board and starts scattering papers above it to hide it. Phipps re-enters]

Phipps [*In his formal manner*] The Duke of Langart is here for the second time today to see His Majesty the King.

King Kindly tell the Duke of Langart that His Majesty the King is at present confined to his bed with an acute attack of cholera.

Phipps Very good, Your Majesty.

King Excellent, if you ask me.

THEY KNEW WHAT THEY WANTED *
By SIDNEY HOWARD

Tony, a sixty-year-old jovial, excitable Italian, asks nothing of his young twenty-three-year-old bride, *Amy*, except the privilege of loving her and the hope of children. During the three months that she has nursed him, following an accident, *Amy* has learned to love *Tony*.

Now she is forced to tell him that she is to have a child by his foreman, *Joe*. She has never cared for *Joe*, but, because of her respect for *Tony*, decides she must leave. *Tony* tries to kill *Joe*, but is overpowered and subsides into a "slobbering, half-intelligible rage."

[*Amy goes quickly into the bedroom. Tony's sobs keep up wretchedly and terribly*]

Tony Amy! Amy! Amy! Amy!

Amy [*She comes back, with her hat on and her coat over her arm. She has her yellow grip half open with clothes sticking out. Joe takes it from her*] Here I am, Tony. Here I am.

Tony W'ere you goin' Amy? W'ere you goin' away from here?

Amy I dunno. . . Frisco, I guess. . .

Tony [*Bitter sobs*]   You goin' be livin' with Joe?

Amy [*Vague misery*]   I dunno. . . No, I ain't going to live with Joe. . . No matter what happens, I ain't.

Tony   Who is goin' be lookin' after you, Amy?

Joe   I am, Tony.   I'll do the right thing if it kills me.

Tony   You? . . . You? . . . Oh, Dio   mio!   Dio   mio! No!   No!

Joe   Come on, Amy, for the love of Pete!

Amy   I'm coming.

Tony [*A hand out to stop her*]   You ain' got no money, Amy.

Amy   It don't matter.

Tony   Yes!

Joe   I got plenty.

Tony   No! . . . No! . . . No!   Joe is no good for lookin' after womans an' baby!

Amy   Don't take on, Tony. . . Please don't take on!   Let me go, and forget all about me.   There ain't no use in talking any more.

Tony   You goin' have baby!

Amy   God, I know I am!

Tony   How you goin' mak' money for keep him?   Before you go, tell me dat!

Amy   God knows. . . I don't.

Tony   Pretty quick Joe is leavin' you desert, and den w'at is goin' happen?

Joe   I swear I'll stick, Tony!

Tony   No!   *No!   NO!!*   Ees no good!   My Amy havin' baby in da street.   Ees no good.

Amy   Don't say that!   For God's sake, Tony, don't say that. . .

Tony   W'at is goin' happen, Amy?   W'at's goin' happen with you?

Amy   Joe. . . I can't stand no more of this.

Tony [*Frenzied*]   No!   *No!   NO!!   NO!!!*

Amy   Let go, Tony!   Let go of my skirt!

Tony   You ain' goin', Amy!   I don't let you go!   You stayin' here with Tony!

Amy   Don't talk that way, Tony!   It ain't no good.

Tony   No!   No!   You goin' listen to w'at Tony say now. You goin' listen, Amy.   You don' love Joe.   You love Tony. You been good wife, Amy. . .

Amy   Good wife!

Tony   W'at is Tony goin' do without you?

Joe   Come on!

Tony   Amy, I get excit' just now, Amy.   Excuse!   Excuse! I think verra good once more.   You ain' goin' with Joe.   You stayin' here with Tony just like nothin' is happen', an' by and by da little fella is come. . .

Amy   Don't talk that way, Tony!

Tony   W'y not?

Amy   Because it ain't no way to talk!

Tony   Yes . . . yes . . . ees good sense!   Ees w'at is evrabody wantin' here!   You an' Joe an' me! . . . Looka Joe. Joe is wantin' go with Wobblies, eh?   With goddam Wobblies. All right. . . Looka Amy. . . Amy is wantin' stay here nice an' safe in dees fine house with Tony.   Is not true, eh?   [*Amy nods through her tears*]   Sure is true.   Look Tony, Dio mio, an' ask him w'at he want?   Don' he want baby?

OVERTONES *

By ALICE GERSTENBERG

Harriet gave up *John,* whom she loved, in order to marry for money.   This fact she will not admit to *John's* wife, *Margaret,* but *Hetty, Harriet's* inner self, and *Maggie, Margaret's* counterpart, tell us of the inner strife between the two, when *Margaret* comes to visit *Harriet,* in the hope that she will commission *John* for a portrait.

Margaret   [*In superficial voice throughout*]   It's enchanting to see you, Harriet.

Maggie   [*In an emotional voice throughout*]   I'd bite you, if I dared.

Harriet   [*To Margaret*]   Wasn't our meeting a stroke of luck?

Margaret   [*Coming down left of table*]   I've thought of you

* Reprinted by courtesy of Longmans, Green and Company.

so often, Harriet ; and to come back and find you living in New York.

Harriet [*Coming down right of table*] Mr. Goodrich has many interests here.

Maggie [*To Margaret*] Flatter her.

Margaret I know, Mr. Goodrich is so successful.

Hetty [*To Harriet*] Tell her we're rich.

Harriet [*To Margaret*] Won't you sit down ?

Margaret [*Takes a chair*] What a beautiful cabinet !

Harriet Do you like it ? I'm afraid Charles paid an extravagant price.

Maggie [*To Hetty*] I don't believe it.

Margaret [*Sitting down. To Harriet*] I am sure he must have.

Harriet [*Sitting down*] How well you are looking, Margaret.

Hetty Yes you are not. There are circles under your eyes.

Maggie [*To Hetty*] I haven't eaten since breakfast and I'm hungry.

Margaret [*To Harriet*] How well you are looking too.

Maggie [*To Hetty*] You have hard lines about your lips, are you happy ?

Hetty [*To Harriet*] Don't let her know I'm unhappy.

Harriet [*To Margaret*] Why shouldn't I look well ? My life is full, happy, complete —

Maggie I wonder.

Hetty [*In Harriet's ear*] Tell her we have an automobile.

Margaret [*To Harriet*] My life is complete, too.

Maggie My heart is torn with sorrow ; my husband cannot make a living. He will kill himself if he does not get an order for a painting.

Margaret [*Laughs*] You must come and see us in our studio. John has been doing some excellent portraits. He cannot begin to fill his orders.

Hetty [*To Harriet*] Tell her we have an automobile.

Harriet [*To Margaret*] Do you take lemon in your tea ?

Maggie Take cream. It's more filling.

Margaret [*Looking nonchalantly at tea things*] No, cream, if you please. How cozy !

Maggie [*Glaring at tea things*] Only cakes! I could eat them all!

Harriet [*To Margaret*] How many lumps?

Maggie [*To Margaret*] Sugar is nourishing.

Margaret [*To Harriet*] Three, please. I used to drink very sweet coffee in Turkey and ever since I've —

Hetty I don't believe you were ever in Turkey.

Maggie I wasn't, but it is none of your business.

Harriet [*Pouring tea*] Have you been in Turkey? Do tell me about it.

Maggie [*To Margaret*] Change the subject.

Margaret [*To Harriet*] You must go there. You have so much taste in dress you would enjoy seeing their costumes.

Maggie Isn't she going to pass the cake?

Margaret [*To Harriet*] John painted several portraits there.

Hetty [*To Harriet*] Why don't you stop her bragging and tell her we have an automobile?

Harriet Cake? [*Offers cake across the table to Margaret*]

Maggie [*Stands back of Margaret, shadowing her as Hetty shadows Harriet. Maggie reaches claws out for the cake and groans with joy*] At last! [*But her claws do not touch the cake*]

Margaret [*With a graceful, nonchalant hand places the cake upon her plate and bites at it slowly and delicately*] Thank you.

Hetty [*To Harriet*] Automobile!

Maggie [*To Margaret*] Follow up the costumes with the suggestion that she would make a good model for John. It isn't too early to begin getting what you came for.

Margaret [*Ignoring Maggie*] What delicious cake.

Hetty [*Excitedly to Harriet*] There's your chance for the auto.

Harriet [*Nonchalantly to Margaret*] Yes, it is good cake, isn't it? There are always a great many people buying it at Harper's and I sat in my automobile fifteen minutes this morning waiting for my chauffeur to get it.

THE ENEMY*

By CHANNING POLLOCK

Fritz, back from the war which has wrecked him physically and mentally, has just lost his job and comes home to find that *Behrend*, capitalistic father of his best friend, has been *decorated for services during the war.*

Professor   Really. . . [*He is interrupted by a shrill, sustained, maniacal laugh. Fritz from whom the laugh comes . . . is standing in the doorway*]

Behrend   [*Startled*]   Who's that?

Mizzi   Fritz!

Bruce   [*To Fritz*]   See here, old man. . .

Fritz   I see!   [*And he comes down to Behrend, staring at the decoration*]

Behrend   What's wrong?

Fritz   Nothing's wrong.   I've lost my job.   Will you give me another?

Mizzi   [*To Fritz*]   Mr. Behrend doesn't . . .

Behrend   I don't employ people.

Fritz   You spoke of your workmen!

Behrend   You're not fit. . .

Fritz   I was fit to pull your chestnuts out of the fire!

Behrend   You're crazy!

Fritz   And you're rich! . . . Do I get a job?

Behrend   No!

Fritz   I'm fired, and you're decorated!   [*His right hand in his pocket suddenly is pointed at Behrend*]   Not much!

Behrend   He's got a pistol!

Bruce   Steady!

Mizzi   No!   Fritz!

Fritz   [*To all of them squaring himself*]   Keep off!

Behrend   You'd . . . murder me?

Fritz   Why not?   You taught me the trade!   Every day I killed men!   Every night I kill them again!   You got the profit, and I want to be paid!   [*He starts toward Behrend*]

* Reprinted by courtesy of Coward-McCann, Inc.

Behrend Grab him! [*Bruce seizes his arm, and pulls out his hand . . . clutched upon a crust of bread*]

Fritz [*Beginning to laugh*] Nothing but a crust! I've given you one moment—of what we faced for years, and you've given me the laugh of my life! [*Laughs*] "Watch and see!" I see . . . you and your decoration! If I could tell the hungry women!

Mizzi Come, Fritz!

Fritz The homeless people in the ruined villages!

Mizzi [*Getting him nearer the door*] Come, my dear!

Fritz People who don't know yet what it was all about!

Mizzi Come!

Fritz If I could tell the dead! [*Shrieks with laughter*]

Bruce I'll go with you!

Mizzi It's all right. Come Fritz! He's been like this before! It'll wear off out-doors! [*Fritz' laughter begins to die out*]

Professor I'll go!

Mizzi It's all right! Keep an eye on Kurt! Come, Fritz! We've got each other! Nothing else matters! [*He begins to sob*] Come, my dear one! [*They exeunt*]

ELIZABETH THE QUEEN *

By MAXWELL ANDERSON

Elizabeth, Queen of England, who has sentenced her ambitious young lover, *Lord Essex*, to be beheaded for treason against the throne, sends for him an hour before his execution.

Essex . . . I played for power and lost, but if I had
Another chance I think I'd play and win.

Eliz. Why do you say this?

Essex I say it because it's true.
I have loved you, love you now, but I know myself.
If I were to win you over and take my place
As it used to be, it would gall me. I have a weakness
For being first wherever I am. I refuse
To take pardon from you without warning you.
Of this. And when you know it, pardon becomes
Impossible

* Reprinted by courtesy of Longmans, Green and Company.

Eliz.   You do this for me?

Essex   Why, yes,
But not altogether.   Partly for England, too.
I've lost conceit of myself a little.   A life
In prison's very quiet.   It leads to thinking.
You govern England better than I should.
I'd lead her into wars, make a great name,
Perhaps like Henry Fifth and leave a legacy
Of debts and bloodshed after me.   You will leave
Peace, happiness, something secure.   A woman governs
Better than a man, being a natural coward.
A coward rules best.

Eliz.   Still bitter.

Essex   Perhaps a little.
It's a bitter belief to swallow, but I believe
You were right all the time.
        [*The chimes ring three-quarters*]
And now, if you'll pardon me,
I have an appointment near-by with a headsman.
He comes sharp on the hour.

Eliz.   You have an hour yet.
It's but struck five.

Essex   It struck five some time since.

Eliz.   It cannot go this way!

Essex   Aye, but it has.
It has and will.   There's no way out.   I've thought of it
Every way.   Speak frankly.   Could you forgive me
And keep your throne?

Eliz.   No.

Essex   Are you ready to give
Your crown up to me?

Eliz.   No.   It's all I have.
        [*She rises*]
Why, who am I
To stand here paltering with a rebel noble!
I am Elizabeth, daughter of a king,
The queen of England, you are my subject!
What does this mean, you standing here eye to eye
With me, your liege?   You whom I made and gave
All that you have, you, an upstart, defying

Me to grant pardon, lest you should sweep me from power
And take my place from me ?   I tell you if Christ his blood
Ran streaming from the heavens for a sign
That I should hold my hand you'd die for this,
You pretender to a throne upon which you have
No claim, you pretender to a heart, who have been
Hollow and heartless and faithless to the end !

Essex   If we'd met some other how we might have been happy. . .
But there's an empire between us !   I am to die. . .
Let us say that . . . let us begin with that. . .
For then I can tell you that if there'd been no empire
We could have been great lovers.   If even now
You were not queen and I were not pretender,
That God who searches heaven and earth and hell
For two who are perfect lovers, could end his search
With you and me.   Remember . . . I am to die. . .
And so I can tell you truly, out of all the earth
That I'm to leave, there's nothing I'm very loath
To leave save you.   Yet if I live I'll be
Your death or you'll be mine.

Eliz.   Give me the ring.

Essex   No.

Eliz.   Give me the ring.   I'd rather you killed me
Than I killed you.

Essex   It's better for me as it is
Than that I should live and batten my fame and fortune
On the woman I love.   I've thought of it all.   It's better
To die young and unblemished than to live long and rule,
And rule not well.

Eliz.   Aye, I should know that.

Essex   Is it not ?

Eliz.   Yes.

Essex   Goodbye, then.

OF THEE I SING *

By George Kaufman and Morrie Ryskind

"A room in a hotel, and a pretty shabby room it is. It is, however, the temporary headquarters of those mysterious politicians who make up the National Campaign Committee."

"The room is thick with cigar smoke," and the game of solitaire is being constantly interrupted by the telephone bell, and finally, by a faint, yet persistent knocking at the door. At their "Come in," the door is slowly opened, and "Enter a timid little man — hopefully smiling."

Throttlebottom Hi, gentlemen!

Fulton Yes, sir. What can we do for you?

Throttlebottom [*All smiles*] Hello, Mr. Fulton.

Fulton I'm afraid I don't quite place you. Your face is familiar, but —

Throttlebottom I'm Throttlebottom.

Fulton What?

Throttlebottom Alexander Throttlebottom.

Jones [*Pushing him right out*] We're very busy, my good man. If you'll just —

Throttlebottom But I'm Throttlebottom.

Fulton I understand, Mr. Teitelbaum, but just at present —

Gilhooley You come back later on.

Lippman After we're gone.

Throttlebottom [*Insistent about it*] But I'm Throttlebottom. I'm the candidate for vice-president.

Fulton That's the fellow!

Gilhooley Of course!

Lippman Sure!

Fulton What's your name again?

Throttlebottom Alexander —

Fulton Of course! I nominated you! Alexander! Boys, this is — What's your first name, Mr. Alexander?

Throttlebottom That's my first name. Alexander.

Fulton Well, well, Alexander Alexander.

* Reprinted from "Of Thee I Sing" by George S. Kaufman, by permission of and special arrangement with Alfred A. Knopf, Inc., authorized publishers.

Gilhooley Well, that certainly is a coincidence. [*A Waiter has arrived with the accessories. Check in hand, he looks uncertainly around for the victim*]

Throttlebottom But that isn't my last name. It's Throttlebottom.

Lippman Throttle what?

Throttlebottom Bottom.

Lippman How do you spell it?

Throttlebottom [*As he starts to spell Lippman takes the check from the Waiter and writes*] "T-h-r-o-t-t-l-e-b-o-t-t-o-m."

Lippman Right! And thank you very much. [*The waiter goes, and with him the signed check*]

Fulton Well, sir, we're very glad indeed to see you, and very proud to have you on our ticket. Sit down. [*They all sit, leaving no place for Throttlebottom*]

Throttlebottom Thanks. I won't sit. I'm only going to stay a minute. There's something I came up to see you about.

Fulton What's that?

Throttlebottom Being vice-president. I want to know if you won't let me off.

Fulton What!

Gilhooey What do you mean?

Throttlebottom I don't want to be vice-president. I want to resign.

Fulton Why, you can't do that!

Jones That's treason!

Lyons Absurd, suh!

Lippman Why don't you want to be vice-president? That's a good job.

Throttlebottom It's — it's on account of my mother. Suppose she found out?

Fulton You've got a mother?

Gilhooley He's got a mother?

Lippman This is a fine time to tell us!

Fulton Yes, why didn't you tell us? You can't back out now. Everything's printed.

Gilhooley Listen — she'll never hear about it.

Jones Of course not.

Throttlebottom But maybe she will. Somebody may tell her.
Lippman Who'll tell her?
Fulton Nobody'll know!
Gilhooley You'll forget it yourself in three months.
Fulton Of course!
Lippman [*Ever the salesman*] Besides, suppose something should happen to the president?
Throttlebottom What?
Lippman Suppose something should happen to the president? Then you become president.
Throttlebottom Me?
Lippman Sure.
Throttlebottom President! Say!
Lippman Let's drink to that! To our next President!

MARY THE THIRD *

By RACHEL CROTHERS

There has been a "row," and this morning at breakfast "*Father* sits holding the newspaper so that it completely hides him from *Mother,* who sits opposite, trying to drink her coffee, and making a pretense of reading a few letters." *Granny,* seventy-five, "enters from the hall, cheerful and chipper."

Granny Good morning.
Mother Good morning, Mother.
Granny I said good morning, Robert.
Father [*From behind the paper*] Oh — good morning.
Granny [*Opening her napkin with cheerful fussiness*] The paper must be even more entertaining than usual. Didn't I get any letters, Mary?
Mother No — nothing.
Granny Who are yours from?
Mother Oh, nobody in particular.
Granny They must be from *somebody.* Pass me the sugar, Robert, please. Isn't there anything you want me to read, Mary?

* Copyright, 1923, by Rachel Crothers. Reprinted by courtesy of Walter H. Baker Company, publishers.

Mother Oh — here's one from Cousin Maria.

Granny Funny she didn't write it to me. She owes me one. Sugar — sugar, Robert. [*Poking Robert's arm, then opening the letter*] I don't see why Maria *will* use this paper. I've told her twice I don't like it. [*Robert passes the sugar to Granny*] Thank you, Robert. [*Patting his hand and smiling at him in her most irresistible way*] Feel a little grumpy this morning? Didn't sleep well, I expect. Mary, are you going to give me any coffee or not? Is your coffee all right, Robert? Nobody's paying any attention to you. I believe in petting a man a little in the morning till he gets the creaks out, and sort of warmed up. I'm always sorry for a man when he has to leave his comfortable home and start off for the day. Goodness! Maria's writing gets worse and worse. I can't read a word she says. Read it to me, Mary.

Mother I will after breakfast, Mother.

Granny You aren't eating a thing. At least you do come down to the table. I'm glad you're not like the lazy women who lie in bed and have their *own* breakfasts and let their husbands come down to the table. I think breakfast is the nicest meal of the day and the time people ought to be the cheeriest. Where are the children? You certainly do let them lag behind, Mary.

Mother They were up late. I'm letting them sleep.

Granny It wouldn't hurt them to come and see their father. I know a man likes to see his family 'round him before he starts off for the day. Does Maria say anything about coming?

Mother Um — sort of a hint.

Granny Well, just don't you take it. I love Maria dearly, but I can't stand her in the same house. There's nothing she hasn't got her nose in — [*Nora enters*] just boss, boss, boss. Maria's got money. Let her stay home and spend it. Don't you say so, Robert? Do put down that old paper, Robbie, and eat your breakfast. What's the news?

Father Oh — nothing.

Granny I never saw a man in my life who found any news in the paper after having his head stuck in it for a week. [*Nora serves the eggs to Granny*] Oh! Scrambled eggs again! I wonder if she stirred cream in these? Did you tell Lizzie what I said, Nora?

Nora   Yes m'am.

Granny   What did she say?

Nora   Well—

Granny   Lizzie's a mule.   It's the only way they're fit to eat. [*Nora goes out*]   See how tough these are?   [*She takes a bite of egg complacently and looks from Mother to Father*]   What is the matter?   What's the matter, Mary?

Mother   Why nothing, Mother.

Granny   You two had a tiff?   What if you have?   This is another day.   You have to begin all over again.

Father   It looks like rain.

Granny   Does it?   [*A pause*]

Father   We need rain.   The country needs it badly.

Granny   Yes, I s'pose it does.

Father   [*After another pause*]   It's been the driest spell we've had for some time.

Granny   [*With a chuckle*]   Robert's doing pretty well, Mary. You might say *something*.

Mother   I have a headache, Mother.   I can't talk.   [*Nora enters, with more eggs and toast*]

Granny   If I'd stopped talking to your father every time I had a headache many a thing would have happened that didn't.

HOLIDAY *

By PHILIP BARRY

Linda Seton hates the greed and smug conventionalities of her "influential" family.   *Linda's* sister arrives home with her fiancé, unpretentious *Johnny Case*, in whom *Linda* finds a kindred spirit. They exchange views when left alone upstairs to dance.

Linda   I'm afraid I don't know how to entertain you.   I've done all my stuff.

Johnny I don't need entertaining. [*Another pause, a very long one. Linda looks uncertainly toward the music-box. Finally*]

Linda You wouldn't care to step into a waltz, Mr. Case?

Johnny I'd love it. [*She extends her arms, he takes her in his, they begin to waltz slowly to the music-box*] —There's a conspiracy against you and me, child.

Linda What's that?

Johnny The Vested Interests—

Linda I know.

Johnny —They won't let you have any fun, and they won't give me time to think.

Linda I suppose, like the great fathead you are, you told them all your little hopes and dreams.

Johnny Um.

Linda —Pretty disappointing?

Johnny Bad enough.

Linda Poor boy.

Johnny How about your own evening?

Linda Not so good, either.

Johnny Poor girl.

Linda But we won't mind, will we?

Johnny Hell, no, we won't mind.

Linda We'll get there—

Johnny We'll get there! [*She stops in the dance and looks up at him for a moment, curiously. Then he smiles at her and she smiles back*]

Johnny —Place head, A, against cheek, B, and proceed as before— [*They begin to dance again*] —Of course they may be right.

Linda Don't you believe it!

Johnny They seem—awfully sure.

Linda It's your ride still, isn't it? You know where you want to go, don't you?

Johnny Well, I thought I did

Linda So did I.—Pathetic, wasn't it—all my fuss and fury over anything so unimportant as this party.

Johnny Maybe it was important.

Linda Well, if it was, I'm not. And I guess that's the answer.

Johnny Not quite.

Linda Me and my little what-do-you-call-it — defense mechanism — so pathetic. Yes, I'm just chock-full of pathos, I am.

Johnny You're a brick, Linda.

Linda Oh, shut your silly face — [*Then*] You're right, you know — there *is* nothing up the fun-alley.

Johnny Fun-alley?

Linda I had a nice little seven-word motto for my life, but I guess she doesn't work —

Johnny What was it?

Linda "Not very important — but pretty good entertainment."

Johnny H'm —

Linda For "pretty good" read "rotten." [*They dance for a few moments, silently. Then Linda stops*] There. That's enough. I'm getting excited.

ALISON'S HOUSE *

By SUSAN GLASPELL

Miss Agatha is a sister of *Alison Stanhope,* a famous American poet, who has been dead for eighteen years. Now she is aged and infirm. "She retains the manner of strength, though obviously feeble." She has guarded well the precious belongings of her famous sister. Now the old home, so dear to her, is about to be sold. Members of the family gather to get their share of the belongings. *Agatha* protects above all else a manuscript of poems which reveals the secret of the poet's inner life. This manuscript she finally gives to the beautiful and sensitive *Elsa.*

Agatha [*As they come in*] I'm no prisoner, am I? Why should I stay up in my room if I don't want to? [*Her brother*

*is steadying her arm; on her other arm swings a silk bag, closed
by a draw-string. Both Eben and Stanhope help in seating her,
more feeble than in the morning. As soon as she is seated she
clutches for the bag, holding it. Elsa brings a footstool, which
her aunt disregards.*]

Eben [*Cheerfully*] All right now?

Agatha If it's the last day I'll ever be here, then I want to be here.

Eben That's right, Aunt Agatha, and here we all are.

Agatha But tomorrow. We won't be here tomorrow.

Elsa Then let's think about our being here today. [*She sits on
the footstool. Eben throws more papers on the fire from the
heap on the floor.*]

Agatha Yes. Make it burn. [*Turning a little to see*] Burn
them. Burn them all. [*She clutches the bag*] What are
they?

Eben Old things we don't need any more.

Agatha Old things we don't need any more. [*Stanhope, who
has been watching her, can bear it no longer, goes out*]

Elsa You'll have your tea now, won't you, Aunt Agatha?

Agatha [*After a moment of not coming from her own
thought*] What? No. No, I don't want it. [*She turns her
head to the fire, taking the bag from her arm, holding it in her
hands*] Put on — old things we don't need any more. [*After
an anxious look at her, Eben puts more papers on the fire*]

Eben [*Briskly*] It's going to be fine for you up at Father's.
That's going to be the most comfortable room you ever had.

Agatha If Elsa hadn't run away and left her father I wouldn't
be turned out.

Elsa I'm sorry, Aunt Agatha.

Agatha [*Quite differently*] Little Elsa. [*With a low sob
Elsa leans against her aunt. Eben goes softly out. So they sit
a moment, Agatha's hand on Elsa's hair. But from this she goes
into a curious, fixed state*] Where is Alison?

Elsa She isn't here. Though she seemed here, just a moment ago.

Agatha I have to take care of Alison.

Elsa Yes. You always did.

Agatha I always did.

Elsa Always.

Agatha But she—went away. How could I tell—what she wanted me to do? [*Pause*] Who is looking at us?

Elsa No one is looking at us. You and I are here alone.

Agatha You are Elsa?

Elsa I am Elsa. [*With trembling fingers Agatha undoes the string of her bag and takes out a small leather portfolio. Looks fearfully around, looks at the fire. She tries to rise.*]

Elsa What is it, Aunt Agatha? I will do anything you want done.

Agatha You will—do anything I want done?

Elsa Why yes, Aunt Agatha. I will do anything in the world for you.

Agatha Elsa will do it. Elsa.

Elsa Yes. Elsa will do it.

Agatha Then— [*She holds out the leather case, but withdraws it. Then suddenly gives it*] Take it! For—Elsa. [*She falls forward.*]

Elsa [*Frightened*] Aunt Agatha! [*She leans her back in the chair, though not letting go the small portfolio Agatha has given her. Becomes more frightened as she looks*] Aunt Agatha! What is it? Speak to me! [*After another moment of growing fear she runs to the door*] Father! Eben! [*Eben hurries in.*]

Eben What is it? [*Stanhope enters.*]

Elsa She—has she fainted?

Stanhope [*Bending over her*] Agatha! Agatha! [*On her other side Eben takes one of her hands, he is feeling for her pulse.*] [*Eben lays his head against her heart.*]

Eben [*Looking up*] Why, Father, I don't— [*Her eyes are closed. Stanhope lifts one of the lids, looking at the eye.*]

Elsa Has she—fainted?

Stanhope She has died. [*Elsa, who has not let go the leather case, presses it against her breast.*]

Eben It is better.

Stanhope [*Who is kneeling by her*] My sister! Agatha! Forgive me. [*Lifting his head, taking her two hands, looking into her face. Softly, as if putting her to sleep*] Yes, yes. Find Alison, dear. Find Alison.

SHAKESPEARE SELECTIONS

AS YOU LIKE IT

Rosalind has been banished for political reasons from the court of her uncle, *Duke Frederick*. Disguised as *Ganymede*, and *Ganymede's* sister, *Celia*, *Rosalind* and her cousin take refuge in the forest of Arden.

There they meet *Orlando*, *Rosalind's* lover, who does not recognize her. *Rosalind* tells him she will cure him of this love if he will but pretend that *Ganymede* is *Rosalind* and come every day to her cottage and woo her, which he does.

Rosalind . . . But come, now I will be your Rosalind in a more coming-on disposition ; and ask me what you will, I will grant it.

Orlando Then love me, Rosalind.

Rosalind Yes, faith will I, Fridays and Saturdays and all.

Orlando And wilt thou have me?

Rosalind Ay, and twenty such.

Orlando What sayest thou?

Rosalind Are you not good?

Orlando I hope so.

Rosalind Why then, can one desire too much of a good thing? Come, sister, you shall be the priest and marry us. Give me your hand, Orlando. What do you say, sister?

Orlando Pray thee, marry us.

Celia I cannot say the words.

Rosalind You must begin, 'Will you, Orland —'

Celia Go to. Will you, Orlando, have to wife this Rosalind?

Orlando I will.

Rosalind Ay, but when?

Orlando Why now ; as fast as she can marry us.

Rosalind Then you must say 'I take thee, Rosalind, for wife.'

Orlando I take thee, Rosalind, for wife.

Rosalind I might ask you for your commission ; but I do take thee, Orlando, for my husband ; there's a girl goes before the priest ; and certainly a woman's thought runs before her actions.

Orlando So do all thoughts ; they are winged.

Rosalind Now, tell me how long you would have her after you have possessed her.

Orlando For ever and a day.

Rosalind Say 'a day' without the 'ever.' No, no Orlando ; men are April when they woo, December when they wed ; maids are May when they are maids, but the sky changes when they are wives. I will be more jealous of thee than a Barbary cock-pigeon over his hen, more clamorous than a parrot against rain, more new-fangled than an ape, more giddy in my desires than a monkey ; I will weep for nothing, like Diana in the fountain, and I will do that when you are disposed to be merry ; I will laugh like a hyena, and that when thou art inclined to sleep.

Orlando But will my Rosalind do so ?

Rosalind By my life, she will do as I do.

Orlando O, but she is wise.

Rosalind Or else she could not have the wit to do this ; the wiser, the waywarder ; make the doors upon a woman's wit and it will out at the casement ; shut that and 'twill out at the keyhole ; stop that, 'twill fly with the smoke out at the chimney.

Orlando A man that had a wife with such a wit, he might say, 'Wit, whither wilt ?'

Rosalind Nay, you might keep that check for it till you met your wife's wit going to your neighbour's bed.

Orlando And what wit could wit have to excuse that ?

Rosalind Marry, to say she came to seek you there. You shall never take her without her answer, unless you take her without her tongue. O, that woman that cannot make her fault her husband's occasion, let her never nurse her child herself, for she will breed it like a fool !

Orlando For these two hours, Rosalind, I will leave thee.

Rosalind Alas ! dear love, I cannot lack thee two hours.

Orlando I must attend the duke at dinner ; by two o'clock I will be with thee again.

Rosalind Ay, go your ways, go your ways; I knew what you would prove; my friends told me as much and I thought no less; that flattering tongue of yours won me; 'tis but one cast away, and so, come, death! Two o'clock is your hour?

Orlando Ay, sweet Rosalind.

Rosalind By my troth, and in good earnest, and so God mend me, and by all pretty oaths that are not dangerous, if you break one jot of your promise or come one minute behind your hour, I will think you the most pathetical break-promise, and the most hollow lover, and the most unworthy of her you call Rosalind, that may be chosen out of the gross band of the unfaithful; therefore beware my censure and keep your promise.

Orlando With no less religion than if thou wert indeed my Rosalind; so adieu.

Rosalind Well, Time is the old Justice that examines all such offenders, and let Time try adieu.

HAMLET

Polonius, an old Courtier, advises his son *Laertes,* who is about to leave his native Denmark for France.

Polonius Yet here, Laertes! aboard, aboard, for shame!
The wind sits in the shoulder of your sail,
And you are stay'd for. There; my blessing with
    thee!
And these few precepts in thy memory
See thou character. Give thy thoughts no tongue,
Nor any unproportion'd thought his act.
Be thou familiar, but by no means vulgar.
Those friends thou hast, and their adoption tried,
Grapple them to thy soul with hoops of steel;
But do not dull thy palm with entertainment
Of each new-hatch'd, unfledged comrade. Beware
Of entrance to a quarrel, but being in,
Bear't that the opposed may beware of thee.
Give every man thy ear, but few thy voice;
Take each man's censure, but reserve thy judgement.
Costly thy habit as thy purse can buy,
But not express'd in fancy; rich, not gaudy;
For the apparel oft proclaims the man,

And they in France of the best rank and station
Are of a most select and generous chief in that.
Neither a borrower nor a lender be;
For oft loan loses both itself and friend,
And borrowing dulls the edge of husbandry.
This above all; To thine own self be true,
And it must follow, as the night the day,
Thou canst not then be false to any man.
Farewell; my blessing season this in thee!

JULIUS CAESAR

Brutus and his political conspirators have plotted against and killed
Julius Caesar.

Antony, another official-of-state, is delivering an oration at the
bier of *Caesar.*

Antony   Friends, Romans, countrymen, lend me your ears;
I come to bury Caesar, not to praise him.
The evil that men do lives after them;
The good is oft interred with their bones;
So let it be with Caesar. The noble Brutus
Hath told you Caesar was ambitious;
If it were so, it was a grievous fault,
And grievously hath Caesar answer'd it.
Here, under leave of Brutus and the rest —
For Brutus is an honourable man;
So are they all, all honourable men —
Come I to speak in Caesar's funeral.
He was my friend, faithful and just to me;
But Brutus says he was ambitious;
And Brutus is an honourable man.
He hath brought many captives home to Rome
Whose ransoms did the general coffers fill;
Did this in Caesar seem ambitious?
When that the poor have cried, Caesar hath wept;
Ambition should be made of sterner stuff;
Yet Brutus says he was ambitious;
And Brutus is an honourable man.
You all did see that on the Lupercal
I thrice presented him a kingly crown.
Which he did thrice refuse; was this ambition?

Yet Brutus says he was ambitious ;
And, sure, he is an honourable man.
I speak not to disprove what Brutus spoke,
But here I am to speak what I do know.
You all did love him once, not without cause ;
What cause withholds you then, to mourn for him ?
O judgment ! thou art fled to brutish beasts,
And men have lost their reasons.   Bear with me ;
My heart is in the coffin there with Caesar,
And I must pause till it come back to me.

KING HENRY V

The small army of *King Henry V* has just captured the larger forces of the French army — and *Henry* is established as king.

In order to make his position more secure, *Henry* demands the hand of the French princess, *Katharine,* whom he finds difficult to woo because he cannot speak the French language.

King Henry   Marry, if you would put me to verses or to dance for your sake, Kate, why you undid me ; for the one, I have neither words nor measure, and for the other, I have no strength in measure, yet a reasonable measure in strength.   If I could win a lady at leap-frog, or by vaulting into my saddle with my armour on my back, under the correction of bragging be it spoken, I should quickly leap into a wife.   Or if I might buffet for my love, or bound my horse for her favours, I could lay on like a butcher and sit like a jackanapes, never off.   But, before God, Kate, I cannot look greenly nor gasp out my eloquence, nor I have no cunning in protestation ; only downright oaths, which I never use till urged, nor never break for urging.   If thou canst love a fellow of this temper, Kate, whose face is not worth sunburning, that never looks in his glass for love of anything he sees there, let thine eye be thy cook.   I speak to thee plain soldier ; if thou canst love me for this, take me ; if not, so say to thee that I shall die, is true ; but for thy love, by the Lord, no ; yet I love thee too.   And while thou livest, dear Kate, take a fellow of plain and uncoined constancy ; for he perforce must do thee right, because he hath not the gift to woo in other places ; for these fellows of infinite tongue, that can rhyme themselves into ladies' favours, they do always reason themselves out again.   What !   A speaker is but a prater ; a rhyme is but a ballad. A good leg will fall ; a straight back will stoop ; a black beard will turn white ; a curled pate will grow bald ; a fair face will wither ; a full eye will wax hollow ; but a good heart, Kate, is the sun and the moon ; or rather the sun and not the moon ; for it shines bright and never changes, but keeps his course truly. If thou would have such a one, take me ; and take me ; take a soldier ; take a soldier, take a king. And what sayest thou then to my love ? Speak, my fair, and fairly, I pray thee.

KING LEAR

After dividing his kingdom between his two elder daughters, *Regan* and *Goneril, King Lear* is disowned by them. Driven to madness by their abuses, he wanders about "fantastically dressed with wild flowers." The *Earl of Gloucester,* betrayed by his bastard son, *Edmund,* falls prey to the political jealousies of *Regan,* and *Cornwall,* her husband, who put out his eyes and "thrust him out at gates." Later his son, *Edgar,* finds him, and together they come upon *King Lear.*

Lear

Ha ! Goneril, with a white beard ! They flattered me like a dog and told me I had the white hairs in my beard ere the black ones were there. To say "ay" and "no" to everything that I said ! — "Ay" and "no" too was no good divinity. When the rain came to wet me once, and the wind to make me chatter ; when the thunder would not peace at my bidding ; there I found 'em, there I smelt 'em out. Go to, they are not men o' their words ; they told me I was everything ; 't is a lie, I am not ague-proof.

Glou.

The trick of that voice I do well remember. Is't not the king ?

Lear

Ay, every inch a king ! When I do stare, see how the subject quakes. I pardon that man's life. What was the cause ? Adultery ?
Thou shalt not die. Die for adultery ! No ;
The wren goes to 't, and the small gilded fly
Does lecher in my sight.
Let copulation thrive ; for Gloucester's bastard son

Was kinder to his father than my daughters
Got 'tween the lawful sheets.
To 't, luxury, pell-mell! for I lack soldiers.
Behold yond simp'ring dame,
Whose face between her forks presages snow;
That minces virtue, and does shake the head
To hear of pleasure's name;
The fitchew, nor the soiled horse, goes to 't
With a more riotous appetite.
Down from the waist they are Centaurs,
Though women all above;
But to the girdle do the gods inherit,
Beneath is all the fiends';
There's hell, there's darkness, there's the sulphurous pit,
Burning, scalding, stench, consumption; fie, fie, fie! pah, pah!
  Give me an ounce of civit; good apothecary, to sweeten
  my imagination.
There's money for thee.

Glou.
O, let me kiss that hand!

Lear
  Let me wipe it first; it smells of mortality.

Glou.
  O ruin'd piece of nature! This great world
  Shall so wear out to nought. Dost thou know me?

Lear
  I remember thine eyes well enough.
  Dost thou squint at me? No, do thy worst, blind cupid;
  I'll not love. Read thou this challenge; mark but the pen-
  ning of it.

Glou.
  Were all the letters suns, I could not see one.

Edg. [*Aside*]
  I would not take this from report; It is;
  And my heart breaks at it.

Lear
  Read.

Glou.
  What, with the case of eyes?

Lear

Oh, ho, are you there with me ?   No eyes in your head, nor
no money in your purse ?   Your eyes are in a heavy case,
your purse in a light ; yet you see how this world goes.

Glou.

I see it feelingly.

Lear

What, art mad ?   A man may see how this world goes with
no eyes.   Look with thine ears ; see how yond justice rails
upon yond simple thief.   Hark, in thine ear ; change
places, and, handy-dandy, which is the justice, which is the
thief ?   Thou hast seen a farmer's dog bark at a beggar ?

Glou.

Ay, sir.

Lear

And the creature run from the cur ?
There thou mightst behold the great image of authority ; a
dog's obey'd in office.
Thou rascal beadle, hold thy bloody hand !
Why dost thou lash that whore ?   Strip thy own back ;
Thou hotly lusts to use her in that kind
For which thou whip'st her.   The usurer hangs the cozener.
Through tatter'd clothes small vices do appear ;
Robes and furr'd gowns hide all.   Plate sin with gold,
And the strong lance of justice hurtless breaks ;
Arm it in rags, a pigmy's straw does pierce it,
None does offend, none, I say, none ; I'll able 'em.
Take that of me, my friend, who have the power
To seal the accuser's lips.   Get thee glass eyes,
And, like a scurvy politician, seem
To see the things thou dost not.   Now, now, now, now ;
Pull off my boots ; harder, harder ; so.

Edg.

O, matter and impertinency mix'd !
Reason in madness !

Lear

If thou wilt weep my fortunes, take my eyes.
I know thee well enough ; thy name is Gloucester.
Thou must be patient ; we came crying hither.
Thou know'st, the first time that we smell the air,
We wawl and cry.   I will preach to thee ; mark.

Glou.
  Alack, alack the day !
Lear
  When we are born, we cry that we are come
  To this great stage of fools ; This' a good block.
  It were a delicate stratagem ; to shoe
  A troop of horses with felt ; I'll put 't in proof ;
  And when I have stol'n upon these sons-in-law
  Then, kill, kill, kill, kill, kill, kill !

MACBETH

Swayed by prophecies of his great future and by the ambitions of
Lady Macbeth, Macbeth plans to murder the kindly *King Duncan.*
As the time approaches for the sounding of the bell which is to
summon him to the chamber of the sleeping *Duncan,* he becomes
reluctant to commit the ghastly deed.

Macbeth   Is this a dagger which I see before me,
            The handle toward my hand ?   Come, let me clutch
              thee.
            I have thee not, and yet I see thee still !
            Art thou not, fatal vision, sensible
            To feeling as to sight ?   Or art thou but
            A dagger of the mind, a false creation,
            Proceeding from the heat-oppressed brain ?
            I see thee yet, in form as palpable
            As this which now I draw.
            Thou marshall'st me the way that I was going ;
            And such an instrument I was to use.
            Mine eyes are made the fools o' the other senses,
            Or else worth all the rest ; I see thee still,
            And on thy blade and dudgeon gouts of blood,
            Which was not so before.   There's no such thing ;
            It is the bloody business which informs
            Thus to mine eyes.   Now o'er the one half-world
            Nature seems dead, and wicked dreams abuse
            The curtain'd sleep ; now witchcraft celebrates
            Pale Hecate's offerings, and wither'd murder,
            Alarum'd by his sentinel, the wolf,
            Whose howl's his watch, thus with his stealthy pace,
            With Tarquin's ravishing strides, towards his design

Moves like a ghost.   Thou sure and firm-set earth,
Hear not my steps, which way they walk, for fear
The very stones prate of my whereabout,
And take the present horror from the time,
Which now suits with it.   Whiles I threat, he lives ;
Words to the heat of deeds too cold breath gives.
                              [*A bell rings*]
I go, and it is done ; the bell invites me.
Hear it not, Duncan ; for it is a knell
That summons thee to heaven or to hell.

MACBETH

After a night of carousing, the drunken porter appears to answer
the knocking at the castle gates.

Porter   Here's a knocking indeed !   If a man were porter of
hell-gate, he should have old turning the key. [*Knocking
within*]   Knock, knock, knock !   Who's there, i' the name of
Beelzebub ?   Here's a farmer, that hanged himself on the ex-
pectation of plenty ; come in time ; have napkins enow about
you ; here you'll sweat for't. [*Knocking within*]   Knock,
knock !   Who's there, in the other devil's name ?   Faith, here's
an equivocator, that could swear in both the scales against either
scale ; who committed treason enough for God's sake, yet could
not equivocate to heaven ; O, come in, equivocator.   [*Knocking
within*]   Knock, knock, knock !   Who's there ?   Faith, here's
an English tailor come hither, for stealing out of a French hose ;
come in, tailor ; here you may roast your goose.   [*Knocking
within*]   Knock, knock ; never at quiet.   What are you ?   But
this place is too cold for hell.   I'll devil-porter it no further ; I
had thought to have let in some of all professions that go the
primrose way to the everlasting bonfire.   [*Knocking within*]
Anon, anon !   I pray you, remember the porter.

MACBETH

Confident of keeping secret the murders of *Duncan* and *Banquo*
during her waking hours, *Lady Macbeth*, during her sleep-walking,
reveals the crimes to the *Doctor* and a *Gentle-woman*.

Doctor   Hark ! she speaks ; I will set down what comes from
her, to satisfy my remembrance the more strongly.
Lady M.   Out, damned spot ! out, I say ! — One ; two ; why,

me to do 't.—Hell is murky!—Fie, my lord, fie!
afeard? What need we fear who knows it, when
our power to account?—Yet who would have
old man to have had so much blood in him?

you mark that?

he thane of Fife had a wife; where is she now?—
these hands ne'er be clean?—No more o' that, my
re o' that; you mar all with this starting.

o to, go to; you have known what you should not.

e has spoke what she should not, I am sure of that;
Heaven knows what she has known.

Lady M. Here's the smell of the blood still; and the perfumes
of Arabia will not sweeten this little hand. Oh, oh, oh!

Doctor What a sigh is there! The heart is sorely charged.

Gent. I would not have such a heart in my bosom for the
dignity of the whole body.

Doct. Well, well, well,—

Gent. Pray God it be, sir.

Doct. This disease is beyond my practice; yet I have known
those which have walk'd in their sleep who have died holily in
their beds.

Lady M. Wash your hands, put on your nightgown; look not
so pale.—I tell you yet again, Banquo's buried, he cannot come
out on 's grave.

Doct. Even so?

Lady M. To bed, to bed! there's knocking at the gate; come,
come, come, come, give me your hand. What's done cannot
be undone.—To bed, to bed, to bed!

THE MERCHANT OF VENICE

Shylock, a revengeful, merciless Jewish money lender, comes before
the *Duke* to exact the forfeit of a pound of *Antonio's* flesh,
pledged for a loan.

Shylock I have possess'd your Grace of what I purpose;
And by our holy Sabbath have I sworn
To have the due and forfeit of my bond;
If you deny it, let the danger light
Upon your charter and your city's freedom.

You'll ask me, why I rather choose to have
A weight of carrion flesh than to receive
Three thousand ducats; I'll not answer that;
But, say, it is my humour; is it answer'd?
What if my house be troubled with a rat
And I be pleased to give ten thousand ducats
To have it baned? What, are you answer'd yet?
Some men there are love not a gaping pig;
Some, that are mad if they behold a cat;
And others, when the bagpipe sings i' the nose,
Cannot contain their urine; for affection,
Master of passion, sways it to the mood
Of what it likes or loathes. Now, for your answer;
As there is no firm reason to be render'd,
Why he, cannot abide a gaping pig;
Why he, a harmless necessary cat;
Why he, a swollen bagpipe; but of force
Must yield to such inevitable shame
As to offend himself being offended;
So can I give no reason, nor I will not,
More than a lodged hate and a certain loathing
I bear Antonio, that I follow thus
A losing suit against him. Are you answer'd?

THE MERCHANT OF VENICE

Jessica, Shylock's daughter, meets her Christian lover, *Lorenzo,* in
the garden.

Lorenzo   The moon shines bright; in such a night as this,
When the sweet wind did gently kiss the trees
And they did make no noise, in such a night
Troilus methinks mounted the Troyan walls
And sigh'd his soul toward the Grecian tents,
Where Cressid lay that night.

Jessica   In such a night
Did Thisbe fearfully o'er trip the dew
And saw the lion's shadow ere himself
And ran dismay'd away.

Lorenzo   In such a night
Stood Dido with a willow in her hand
Upon the wild sea banks and waft her love
To come again to Carthage.

Jessica   In such a night
Medea gather'd the enchanted herbs
That did renew old Aeson.

Lorenzo   In such a night
Did Jessica steal from the wealthy Jew
And with an unthrift love did run from Venice
As far as Belmont.

Jessica   In such a night
Did young Lorenzo swear he loved her well,
Stealing her soul with many vows of faith
And ne'er a true one.

Lorenzo   In such a night
Did pretty Jessica, like a little shrew,
Slander her love, and he forgave it her.

Jessica   I would out-night you, did no body come ;
But hark, I hear the footing of men.

*   *   *

Lorenzo   How sweet the moonlight sleeps upon this bank !
Here will we sit and let the sounds of music
Creep in our ears ; soft stillness and the night
Become the touches of sweet harmony.
Sit, Jessica.   Look how the floor of heaven
Is thick inlaid with patines of bright gold ;
There's not the smallest orb which thou behold'st
But in his motion like an angel sings,
Still quiring to the young-eyed cherubins ;
Such harmony is in immortal souls ;
But whilst this muddy vesture of decay
Doth grossly close it in, we cannot hear it.
   [*Enter Musicians*]
Come, ho ! and wake Diana with a hymn ;
With sweetest touches pierce your mistress' ear
And draw her home with music.   [*Music*]

Jessica   I am never merry when I hear sweet music.

Lorenzo   The reason is, your spirits are attentive ;
For do but note a wild and wanton herd,
Or race of youthful and unhandled colts,
Fetching mad bounds, bellowing and neighing loud,
Which is the hot condition of their blood ;
If they but hear perchance a trumpet sounds,

Or any air of music touch their ears,
You shall perceive them make a mutual stand,
Their savage eyes turn'd to a modest gaze
By the sweet power of music ; therefore the poet
Did feign that Orpheus drew trees, stones and floods ;
Since nought so stockish, hard and full of rage,
But music for the time doth change his nature.
The man that hath no music in himself,
Nor is not moved with concord of sweet sounds,
Is fit for treasons, stratagems and spoils ;
The motions of his spirit are dull as night
And his affections dark as Erebus ;
Let no such man be trusted.   Mark the music.

THE MERCHANT OF VENICE

According to the will of *Portia's* father, the man who wins her
hand must choose correctly among three caskets. *Portia* is
anxious that *Bassanio,* whom she loves, be successful.

Bassanio   So may the outward shows be least themselves ;
The world is still deceived with ornament.
In law, what plea so tainted and corrupt
But, being season'd with a gracious voice,
Obscures the show of evil ?   In religion,
What damned error, but some sober brow
Will bless it and approve it with a text,
Hiding the grossness with fair ornament ?
There is no vice so simple but assumes
Some mark of virtue on his outward parts ;
How many cowards, whose hearts are all as false
As stairs of sand, wear yet upon their chins
The beards of Hercules and frowning Mars,
Who, inward search'd, have livers white as milk ;
And these assume but valour's excrement
To render them redoubted !

* * *

Bassanio   Therefore, thou gaudy gold,
Hard food for Midas, I will none of thee,
Nor one of thee, thou pale and common drudge
'Tween man and man ; but thou, thou meagre lead,
Which rather threatenest than dost promise aught,

Thy plainness moves me more than eloquence ;
And here choose I ; joy be the consequence !

Portia [*Aside*] How all the other passions fleet to air,
As doubtful thoughts, and rash-embraced despair,
And shuddering fear, and green-eyed jealousy !
O love !
Be moderate ; allay thy ecstasy ;
In measure rein thy joy ; scant this excess.
I feel too much thy blessing ; make it less,
For fear I surfeit.

Bassanio What find I here ?
     [*Opening the leaden casket*]
Fair Portia's counterfeit !   What demi-god
Hath come so near creation ?   Move these eyes ?
Or whether, riding on the balls of mine,
Seem they in motion ?   Here are sever'd lips,
Parted with sugar breath ; so sweet a bar
Should sunder such sweet friends.   Here in her hairs
The painter plays the spider and hath woven
A golden mesh to entrap the hearts of men
Faster than gnats in cobwebs ; but her eyes,
How could he see to do them ?   Having made one,
Methinks it should have power to steal both his
And leave itself unfurnish'd.   Yet look, how far
The substance of my praise doth wrong this shadow
In underprizing it, so far this shadow
Doth limp behind the substance.   Here's the scroll,
The continent and summary of my fortune.
[*Reads*]   You that choose not by view,
          Chance as fair and choose as true !
          Since this fortune falls to you,
          Be content and seek no new.
          If you be well pleased with this
          And hold your fortune for your bliss,
          Turn you where your lady is
          And claim her with a loving kiss.
A gentle scroll.   Fair lady, by your leave ;
I come by note, to give and to receive.

Portia You see me, Lord Bassanio, where I stand,
Such as I am ; though for myself alone
I would not be ambitious in my wish,

To wish myself much better ; yet, for you
I would be trebled twenty times myself ;
A thousand times more fair, ten thousand times
More rich ;
That only to stand high in your account,
I might in virtues, beauties, livings, friends,
Exceed account ; but the full sum of me
Is sum of something, which, to term in gross,
Is an unlesson'd girl, unschool'd, unpractised ;
Happy in this, she is not yet so old
But she may learn ; happier than this,
She is not bred so dull but she can learn ;
Happiest of all is that her gentle spirit
Commits itself to yours to be directed,
As from her lord, her governor, her king.
Myself and what is mine to you and yours
Is now converted ; but now I was the lord
Of this fair mansion, master of my servants,
Queen o'er myself ; and even now, but now,
This house, these servants and this same myself
Are yours, my lord ; I give them with this ring ;
Which when you part from, lose, or give away
Let it presage the ruin of your love
And be my vantage to exclaim on you.

Bassanio Madam, you have bereft me of all words,
Only my blood speaks to you in my veins ;
And there is such confusion in my powers ;
As, after some oration fairly spoke
By a beloved prince, there doth appear
Among the buzzing pleased multitude ;
Where every something, being blent together,
Turns to a wild of nothing, save of joy.
Express'd and not express'd.   But when this ring
Parts from this finger, then parts life from hence ;
O, then be bold to say Bassanio's dead !

THE MERCHANT OF VENICE

Launcelot, a guileless joker, a light-hearted amiable jester who likes words and invents occasions to prattle, is the dissatisfied servant of *Shylock.*

Launcelot Certainly my conscience will serve me to run from this Jew, my master. The fiend is at mine elbow and tempts me saying to me 'Gobbo, Launcelot Gobbo, good Launcelot,' or 'good Gobbo,' or 'good Launcelot Gobbo, use your legs, take the start, run away.' My conscience says 'No; take heed, honest Launcelot; take heed, honest Gobbo,' or, as aforesaid, 'honest Launcelot Gobbo; do not run; scorn running with thy heels.' Well, the most courageous fiend bids me pack; 'Via!' says the fiend; 'away!' says the fiend; 'for the heavens, rouse up a brave mind,' says the fiend, 'and run.' Well, my conscience, hanging about the neck of my heart, says very wisely to me 'My honest friend Launcelot, being an honest man's son,' or rather an honest woman's son; for, indeed, my father did something smack, something grow to, he had a kind of taste; well my conscience says, 'Launcelot, budge not.' 'Budge,' says the fiend. 'Budge not,' says my conscience. 'Conscience,' says I, 'you counsel well;' 'Fiend,' says I, 'you counsel well;' to be ruled by my conscience, I should stay with the Jew my master, who, God bless the mark, is a kind of devil; and, to run away from the Jew, I should be ruled by the fiend, who, saving your reverence, is the devil himself. Certainly the Jew is the very devil incarnate; and, in my conscience, my conscience is but a kind of hard conscience, to offer to counsel me to stay with the Jew. The fiend gives the more friendly counsel; I will run, fiend; my heels are at your command; I will run. [*Enter Old Gobbo, with a basket*]

Gobbo Master young man, you, I pray you, which is the way to Master Jew's?

Launcelot [*Aside*] O heavens, this is my true-begotten father! who, being more than sand-blind, high-gravel blind, knows me not; I will try confusions with him.

Gobbo By God's sonties, 'twill be a hard way to hit. Can you tell me whether one Launcelot that dwells with him, dwell with him or no?

Launcelot Talk you of young Master Launcelot? [*Aside*]

277

Mark me now ; now will I raise the waters.   Talk you of young Master Launcelot ?

Gobbo   No master, sir, but a poor man's son ; his father, though I say it, is an honest exceeding poor man, and, God be thanked, well to live.

Launcelot   Well, let his father be what a' will, we talk of young Master Launcelot.

Gobbo   Your worship's friend and Launcelot, sir.

Launcelot   But I pray you, ergo, old man, ergo, I beseech you, talk you of young Master Launcelot ?

Gobbo   Of Launcelot, an't please your mastership.

Launcelot   Ergo, Master Launcelot.   Talk not of Master Launcelot, father ; for the young gentleman, according to Fates and Destinies and such odd sayings, the Sisters Three and such branches of learning, is indeed deceased, or, as you would say in plain terms, gone to heaven.

Gobbo   Marry, God forbid ! the boy was the very staff of my age, my very prop.

Launcelot   Do I look like a cudgel or a hovelpost, a staff or a prop ?   Do you know me, father ?

Gobbo   Alack the day, I know you not, young gentleman ; but, I pray you, tell me, is my boy, God rest his soul, alive or dead ?

Launcelot   Do you not know me, father ?

Gobbo   Alack, sir, I am sand-blind ; I know you not.

Launcelot   Nay, indeed, if you had your eyes, you might fail of the knowing me ; it is a wise father that knows his own child.   Well, old man, I will tell you news of your son ; give me your blessing ; truth will come to light ; murder cannot be hid long ; a man's son may, but at the length truth will out.

Gobbo   Pray you, sir, stand up ; I am sure you are not Launcelot, my boy.

Launcelot   Pray you, let's have no more fooling about it, but give me your blessing ; I am Launcelot, your boy that was, your son that is, your child that shall be.

Gobbo   I cannot think you are my son.

Launcelot   I know not what I shall think of that ; but I am Launcelot, the Jew's man, and I am sure Margery your wife is my mother.

Gobbo   Her name is Margery, indeed ; I'll be sworn, if thou be Launcelot, thou art mine own flesh and blood.   Lord worshipped might he be ! what a beard hast thou got ! thou hast got more hair on thy chin than Dobbin my fill-horse has on his tail.

Launcelot   It should seem, then, that Dobbin's tail grows backward ; I am sure he had more hair of his tail than I have of my face when I last saw him.

Gobbo   Lord, how art thou changed !   How dost thou and thy master agree ?   I have brought him a present.   How 'gree you now ?

Launcelot   Well, well ; but, for mine own part, as I have set up my rest to run away, so I will not rest till I have run some ground.   My master's a very Jew ; give him a present ! give him a halter ; I am famished in his service ; you may tell every finger I have with my ribs.   Father, I am glad you are come ; give me your present to one Master Bassanio, who, indeed, gives rare new liveries ; if I serve not him, I will run as far as God has any ground.   O rare fortune ! here comes the man ; to him, father ; for I am a Jew, if I serve the Jew any longer.

A MIDSUMMER-NIGHT'S DREAM

The impish *Puck*, alias "Robin Goodfellow," is the faithful servant of *Oberon*, King of fairies, who is in love with *Titania*.

Oberon sends *Puck* into the forest to anoint the eyes of *Titania*, queen of fairies — a knavish trick that will cause her to fall in love with *Oberon*, whom she will see when she awakes.

In the dense woods near Athens, *Puck* is delayed when he meets a fairy servant of *Titania*.

Puck   The King doth keep his revels here tonight ;
Take heed the queen come not within his sight ;
For Oberon is passing fell and wrath,
Because that she as her attendant hath
A lovely boy, stolen from an Indian king.
She never had so sweet a changeling ;
And jealous Oberon would have the child
Knight of his train, to trace the forests wild ;
But she perforce withholds the loved boy,
Crowns him with flowers and makes him all her joy ;
And now they never meet in grove or green,

By fountain clear, or spangled starlight sheen,
But they do square, that all their elves for fear
Creep into acorn-cups and hide them there.

Fairy Either I mistake your shape and making quite,
Or else you are that shrewd and knavish sprite
Called Robin Goodfellow ; are not you he
That frights the maidens of the villagery ;
Skim milk, and sometimes labour in the quern
And bootless make the breathless housewife churn ;
And sometime make the drink to bear no barm ;
Mislead night-wanderers, laughing at their harm ?
Those that Hobgoblin call you and sweet Puck
You do their work, and they shall have good luck ;
Are not you he ?

Puck Thou speak'st aright ;
I am that merry wanderer of the night.
I jest to Oberon and make him smile
When I a fat and bean-fed horse beguile,
Neighing in likeness of a filly foal ;
And sometimes lurk in a gossip's bowl,
In very likeness of a roasted crab,
And when she drinks, against her lips I bob
And on her wither'd dewlap pour the ale,
The wisest aunt, telling the saddest tale,
Sometime for three foot stool mistaketh me ;
Then slip I from her bum, down topples she ;
And 'tailor' cries, and falls into a cough ;
And then the whole quire hold their hips and laugh,
And waxen in their mirth and neeze and swear
A merrier hour was never wasted there.
But room, fairy !   Here comes Oberon.

A MIDSUMMER-NIGHT'S DREAM

Several good gentlemen of the village have produced a play for the pleasure of *Theseus*, Duke of Athens, *Hippolyta*, queen of the Amazons, his betrothed, and their guests.

The characters in the play : —

Lovers: *Pyramus* and *Thisbe*, played by *Nick Bottom*, the weaver, and *Francis Flute*, the bellows-mender.

Thisbe's Mother : Played by Tom Snout, the tinner.

Pyramus' Father : Played by *Robert Starveling*, the tailor.

The Lion : Unwillingly taken by *Snug*, the joiner.

Amid the flourish of trumpets, the curtain rises on the first prologue.

Prologue   Gentles, perchance you wonder at this show ;
But wonder on, till truth make all things plain.
This man is Pyramus, if you would know ;
This beauteous lady Thisby is certain.
This man, with lime and rough-cast, doth present
Wall, that vile Wall which did these lovers sunder ;
And through Wall's chink, poor souls, they are
    content,
To whisper.   At the which let no man wonder.
This man, with lanthorn, dog, and bush of thorn,
Presenteth Moonshine ; for, if you will know,
By Moonshine did these lovers think no scorn
To meet at Ninus' tomb, there, there to woo.
This grisly beast, which Lion hight by name,
The trusty Thisby, coming first by night,
Did scare away, or rather did affright ;
And, as she fled, her mantle she did fall,
Which lion vile with bloody mouth did stain.
Anon comes Pyramus, sweet youth and tall,
And finds his trusty Thisby's mantle slain ;
Whereat, with blade, with bloody blameful blade,
He bravely broach'd his boiling bloody breast ;
And Thisby, tarrying in mulberry shade,
His dagger drew, and died.   For all the rest,
Let Lion, Moonshine, Wall, and lovers twain
At large discourse, while here they do remain.
    [*Exeunt Prologue, Pyramus, Thisbe, Lion and
    Moonshine*]

Theseus	I wonder if the lion be to speak.
Demetrius	No wonder, my lord ; one lion may, when many asses do.
Wall	In this same interlude it doth befall That I, one Snout by name, present a wall ; And such a wall, as I would have you think, That had in it a crannied hole or chink, Through which the lovers, Pyramus and Thisby, Did whisper often very secretly. This loam, this rough-cast and this stone doth show That I am the same wall ; the truth is so ; And this the cranny is, right and sinister. Through which the fearful lovers are to whisper.
Theseus	Would you desire lime and hair to speak better ?
Demetrius	It is the wittiest partition that ever I heard discourse, my lord. [*Re-enter Pyramus*]
Theseus	Pyramus draws near the wall ; silence !
Pyramus	O grim-look'd night ! O night with hue so black ! O night, O night ! Alack, alack, alack, I fear my Thisby's promise is forgot ! And thou, O wall, O sweet, O lovely wall, That stand'st between her father's ground and mine ! Thou wall, O wall, O sweet and lovely wall, Show me thy chink, to blink through with mine eyne ! [*Wall holds up his fingers*] Thanks courteous wall ; Jove shield thee well for this ! But what see I ? No Thisby do I see. O wicked wall, through whom I see no bliss ! Curst be thy stones for thus deceiving me !
Theseus	The wall, methinks, being sensible, should curse again.
Pyramus	No, in truth, sir, he should not. 'Deceiving me' is Thisby's cue ; she is to enter now, and I am to spy her through the wall. You shall see, it will fall pat as I told you. Yonder she comes. [*Re-enter Thisbe*]
Thisbe	O wall, full often hast thou heard my moans, For parting my fair Pyramus and me !

	My cherry lips have often kiss'd thy stones, Thy stones with lime and hair knit up in thee.
Pyramus	I see a voice; now will I to the chink, To spy an' I can hear my Thisby's face. Thisby!
Thisbe	My love thou art, my love I think.
Pyramus	Think what thou wilt, I am thy lover's grace; And, like Limander, am I trust still.
Thisbe	And I like Helen, till the Fates me kill.
Pyramus	Not Shafalus to Procrus was so true.
Thisbe	As Shafalus to Procrus, I to you.
Pyramus	O, kiss me through the hole of this vile wall!
Thisbe	I kiss the wall's hole, not your lips at all.
Pyramus	Wilt thou at Ninny's tomb meet me straightway?
Thisbe	'Tide life, 'tide death, I come without delay.

[Exeunt Pyramus and Thisbe]

Wall	Thus have I, Wall, my part discharged so; And, being done, thus Wall away doth go. [Exit]
Theseus	Now is the mural down between the two neighbors.
Demetrius	No remedy, my lord, when walls are so willful to hear without warning.
Hippolyta	This is the silliest stuff that ever I heard.
Theseus	The best in this kind are but shadows; and the worst are no worse, if imagination amend them.
Hippolyta	It must be your imagination then, and not theirs.
Theseus	If we imagine no worse of them than they of themselves, we may pass for excellent men. Here come two noble beasts in, a man and a lion.

[Re-enter Lion and Moonshine]

| Lion | You, ladies, you, whose gentle hearts do fear The smallest monstrous mouse that creeps on floor, May now perchance both quake and tremble here, When lion rough in wildest rage doth roar. Then know that I, one Snug the joiner, am A lion-fell, nor else no lion's dam; For, if I should as lion come in strife Into this place, 'twere pity on my life. |

*   *   *

Pyramus   Sweet moon, I thank thee for thy sunny beams;
I thank thee, Moon, for shining now so bright;
For, by thy gracious, golden, glittering gleams,
I trust to take of truest Thisby's sight.
> But stay, O spite!
> But mark, poor knight,
What dreadful dole is here!
> Eyes, do you see?
> How can it be?
O, dainty duck! O dear!
> Thy mantle good,
> What, stain'd with blood!
Approach, ye Furies fell —
> O Fates, come, come,
> Cut thread and thrum;
Quail, crush, conclude, and quell!

Theseus   This passion, and the death of a dear friend, would
go near to make a man look sad.

Hippolyta   Beshrew my heart, but I pity the man.

Pyramus   O wherefore, Nature, didst thou lions frame?
Since lion vile hath here deflower'd my dear;
Which is — no, no — which was the fairest dame
That lived, that loved, that liked, that look'd with
  cheer.
> Come tears, confound;
> Out, sword, and wound
The pap of Pyramus;
> Ay, that left pap.
> Where heart doth hop; [*Stabs himself*]
Thus die I, thus, thus, thus.
> Now am I dead,
> Now am I fled;
> My soul is in the sky;
Tongue, loose thy light;
> Moon, take thy flight; [*Exit Moonshine*]
> Now die, die, die, die, die. [*Dies*]

        * * *

Thisbe   Asleep, my love?
What, dead, my dove?
O, Pyramus, arise!

Speak, speak.   Quite dumb?
Dead, dead?   A tomb
Must cover thy sweet eyes.
These lily lips.
This cherry nose.
These yellow cowslip cheeks,
Are gone, are gone;
Lovers, make moan;
His eyes were green as leeks.
O Sisters Three,
Come, come to me,
With hands as pale as milk;
Lay them in gore,
Since you have shore
With shears his thread of silk.
Tongue, not a word;
Come, trusty sword;
Come, blade, my breast imbrue; [*Stabs herself*]
And, farewell, friends;
Thus Thisby ends;
Adieu, adieu, adieu.

MUCH ADO ABOUT NOTHING

The witty young *Beatrice* scoffs at love and is only too ready to give her opinion on the uselessness of man.   This attitude disturbs her uncles, *Antonio* and *Leonata,* and her cousin, *Hero.*

Leonato   By my troth, niece, thou wilt never get thee a husband, if thou be so shrewd of thy tongue.

Antonio   In faith, she's too curst.

Beatrice   Too curst is more than curst; I shall lessen God's sending that way; for it is said, "God sends a curst cow short horns;" but to a cow too curst he sends none.

Leonato   So, by being too curst, God will send you no horns.

Beatrice   Just, if he send me no husband; for the which blessing I am at him upon my knees every morning and evening.   Lord, I could not endure a husband with a beard on his face; I had rather lie in the woollen.

Leonato   You may light on a husband that hath no beard.

Beatrice What should I do with him? Dress him in my apparel and make him my waiting-gentle woman? He that hath a beard is more than a youth, and he that hath no beard is less than a man; and he that is more than a youth is not for me, and he that is less than a man, I am not for him; therefore I will even take sixpence in earnest of the bear-ward and lead his apes into hell.

Leonato Well, then, go you into hell?

Beatrice No, but to the gate; and there will the devil meet me, like an old cuckold, with horns on his head, and say, "Get you to heaven, Beatrice, get you to heaven; here's no place for you maids;" so deliver I up my apes, and away to Saint Peter for the heavens. He shows me where the bachelors sit, and there live we as merry as the day is long.

Antonio [*To Hero*] Well, niece, I trust you will be rul'd by your father.

Beatrice Yes, faith; it is my cousin's duty to make curtsy and say, "Father, as it please you." But yet for all that, cousin, let him be a handsome fellow, or else make another curtsy and say, "Father, as it please me."

Leonato Well, niece, I hope to see you one day fitted with a husband.

Beatrice Not until God make men of some other metal than earth. Would it not grieve a woman to be overmaster'd with a piece of valiant dust? to make an account of her life to a clod of wayward marl? No, uncle, I'll none; Adam's sons are my brethren; and, truly, I hold it a sin to match in my kindred.

Leonato Daughter, remember what I told you. If the Prince do solicit you in that kind, you know your answer.

Beatrice The fault will be in the music, cousin, if you be not wooed in good time. If the Prince be too important, tell him there is measure in everything and so dance out the answer. For, hear me, Hero; wooing, wedding, and repenting, is as a Scotch jig, a measure, and a cinque pace; the first suit is hot and hasty, like a Scotch jig, and full as fantastical; the wedding, mannerly-modest, as a measure, full of state and ancientry; and then comes repentance and, with his bad legs, falls into the cinque pace faster and faster, till he sink into his grave.

ROMEO AND JULIET

The old *Nurse* is sent to awaken *Juliet*, that she may make ready for her bridegroom, the *Count Paris*.

Nurse   Mistress! what, mistress! Juliet!
       Fast, I warrant her, she:
       Why, lamb! why, lady! fie, you slug-a-bed!
       Why, love, I say, madam! sweetheart! why bride!
       What, not a word? You take your pennyworths now;
       Sleep for a week; for the next night, I warrant,
       The Count Paris hath set up his rest,
       That you shall rest but little. God forgive me,
       Marry, and amen, how sound is she asleep!
       I needs must wake her. Madam, madam, madam!
       Ay, let the County take you in your bed;
       He'll fright you up, i' faith. Will it not be?
         [Draws back the curtains]
       What, dress'd, and in your clothes! and down again!
       I must needs wake you. Lady! lady! lady!
       Alas, alas! Help, help! my lady's dead!
       O, well-a-day, that ever I was born;
       Some *aqua vitae*, ho! My lord! my lady!

ROMEO AND JULIET

Romeo and *Juliet*, a young couple whose parents are warring with each other, are secretly married by a Friar. Shortly afterward, *Romeo* slays *Juliet's* cousin, *Tybalt*, in a duel, and is exiled from the country. Meanwhile, *Juliet's* father, knowing nothing of the secret marriage, commands *Juliet* to marry *Paris*. *Juliet* seeks the Friar for help and advice. He gives her a vial filled with a potent drug which will make her appear dead; the plan being that she shall be brought to the family vault from where *Romeo* will escape with her into another country.

Juliet retires to her chamber and prepares to take the draught.

Juliet   Farewell! God knows when we shall meet again.
       I have a faint cold fear thrills through my veins,
       That almost freezes up the heat of life;
       I'll call them back again to comfort me;
       Nurse! What should she do here?
       My dismal scene I needs must act alone.
       Come, vial.

What if this mixture do not work at all ?
Shall I be married then tomorrow morning ?
No, no ; this shall forbid it ; lie thou there.
   [*Laying down her dagger*]
What if there be a poison, which the friar
Subtly hath minister'd to have me dead,
Lest in this marriage he should be dishonour'd,
Because he married me before to Romeo ?
I fear it is ; and yet, methinks, I should not,
For he hath still been tried a holy man.
How if, when I am laid into the tomb,
I wake before the time that Romeo
Come to redeem me ? there's fearful point !
Shall I not, then, be stifled in the vault,
To whose foul mouth no healthsome air breathes in,
And there die strangled ere my Romeo comes ?
Or, if I live, is it not very like,
The horrible conceit of death and night,
Together with the terror of the place, —
As in a vault, an ancient receptacle,
Where, for these many hundred years, the bones
Of all my buried ancestors are pack'd ;
Where bloody Tybalt, yet but green in earth,
Lies festering in his shroud ; where, as they say,
At some hours in the night spirits resort ; —
Alack, alack, is it not like that I,
So early waking, what with loathsome smells,
And shrieks like mandrakes' torn out of the earth,
That living mortals, hearing them, run mad ; —
O, if I wake, shall I not be distraught,
Environed with all these hideous fears ?
And madly play with my forefathers' joints ?
And pluck the mangled Tybalt from his shroud ?
And, in this rage, with some great kinsman's bone,
As with a club, dash out my desperate brains ?
O, look ! methinks I see my cousin's ghost
Seeking out Romeo, that did spit his body
Upon a rapier's point ; stay, Tybalt, stay !
Romeo, I come !   This do I drink to thee.
   [*She falls upon her bed, within the curtains*]

ROMEO AND JULIET

Romeo and *Juliet* have been unable to declare their love for each other because of the enmity existing between their families. *Juliet's* father entertains the townspeople with a feast, which *Romeo* attends, and there meets and falls in love with *Juliet*. Later he returns, scales a wall, enters *Juliet's* garden, and hides himself beneath her window. *Juliet* enters the balcony, and, thinking herself alone, confesses her love for *Romeo*, who overhears her.

Romeo	Lady, by yonder blessed moon swear That tips with silver all these fruit-tree tops —
Juliet	O, swear not by the moon, the inconstant moon, That monthly changes in her circled orb, Lest that thy love prove likewise variable.
Romeo	What shall I swear by ?
Juliet	Do not swear at all ; Or, if thou wilt, swear by thy gracious self, Which is the god of my idolatry, And I'll believe thee.
Romeo	If my heart's dear love —
Juliet	Well, do not swear ; although I joy in thee, I have no joy of this contract tonight ; It is too rash, to unadvised, too sudden ; Too like the lightning, which doth cease to be Ere one can say 'It lightens.' Sweet, good night ! This bud of love, by summer's ripening breath, May prove a beauteous flower when next we meet. Good night, good night ! as sweet repose and rest Come to thy heart as that within my breast !
Romeo	O, wilt thou leave me so unsatisfied ?
Juliet	What satisfaction canst thou have tonight ?
Romeo	The exchange of thy love's faithful vow for mine.
Juliet	I gave thee mine before thou didst request it ; And yet I would it were to give again.
Romeo	Wouldst thou withdraw it ? for what purpose, love ?
Juliet	But to be frank, and give it thee again. And yet I wish but for the thing I have ; My bounty is as boundless as the sea, My love as deep ; the more I give thee,

The more I have, for both are infinite.
　　[*Nurse calls within*]
I hear some noise within ; dear love, adieu !
Anon, good nurse !   Sweet Montague, be true.
Stay but a little, I will come again.
　　[*Exit, above*]

Romeo　　O blessed, blessed night !   I am afeard,
Being in night, all this is but a dream,
Too flattering-sweet to be substantial.
　　[*Re-enter Juliet, above*]

Juliet　　Three words, dear Romeo, and good night indeed.
If that thy bent of love be honourable,
Thy purpose marriage, send me word tomorrow,
By one that I'll procure to come to thee,
Where and what time thou wilt perform the rite ;
And all my fortunes at thy foot I'll lay,
And follow thee my lord throughout the world.

Nurse　　[*Within*]   Madam !

Juliet　　I come, anon.— But if thou mean'st not well,
I do beseech thee —

Nurse　　[*Within*]   Madam !

Juliet　　By and by, I come : —
To cease thy suit, and leave me to my grief ;
Tomorrow will I send.

Romeo　　So thrive my soul —

Juliet　　A thousand times good night !
　　[*Exit above*]

Romeo　　A thousand times the worse, to want thy light.
Love goes toward love, as school boys from their books,
But love from love, toward school with heavy looks.
　　[*Retiring*]
　　[*Re-enter Juliet, above*]

Juliet　　Hist ! Romeo, hist ! O, for a falconer's voice,
To lure this tassel-gentle back again !
Bondage is hoarse, and may not speak aloud ;
Else would I tear the cave where Echo lies,
And make her airy tongue more harsh than mine,
With repetition of my Romeo's name.

Romeo　　It is my soul that calls upon my name ;
How silver-sweet sound lovers' tongues by night,
Like softest music to attending ears !

Juliet   Romeo!
Romeo   My dear?
Juliet   At what o'clock tomorrow
          Shall I send to thee?
Romeo   At the hour of nine.
Juliet   I will not fail; 'tis twenty years till then.
          I have forgot why I did call thee back.
Romeo   Let me stand here till thou remember it.
Juliet   I shall forget, to have thee still stand there,
          Remembering how I love thy company.
Romeo   Then I'll still stay, to have thee still forget,
          Forgetting any other home but this.
Juliet   'Tis almost morning; I would have thee gone;
          And yet no further than a wanton's bird;
          Who lets it hop a little from her hand,
          Like a poor prisoner in his tristed gyves,
          And with a silk thread plucks it back again,
          So jealous-loving of his liberty.
Romeo   I would I were thy bird.
Juliet   Sweet, so would I;
          Yet I should kill thee with much cherishing.
          Good night, good night! parting is such sweet sorrow,
          That I shall say good night till it be morrow.
                                   [*Exit, above*]
Romeo   Sleep dwell upon thine eyes, peace in thy breast!
          Would I were sleep and peace, so sweet to rest!
          Hence will I to my ghostly father's cell.
          His help to crave, and my dear hap to tell.
                                   [*Exit*]

ROMEO AND JULIET

Romeo and *Mercutio*, accompanied by a crowd of merry-makers, are on their way to a feast at the Capulet house. *Romeo*, a Montague, therefore eternal foe of the Capulets, has been invited by mistake. He is morose and sad, for he considers himself in love with a maiden who is indifferent to him. *Mercutio* is trying to pull him "from the mire of this sir-reverence love wherein thou sticks't up to thine ears." *Romeo* makes a remark about a dream he has had, which he is sure is true.

Mercutio replies —

Mercutio   O, then, I see Queen Mab hath been with you.
She is the fairies' midwife, and she comes
In shape no bigger than agate-stone
On the fore-finger of an alderman,
Drawn with a team of little atomies
Athwart men's noses as they lie asleep ;
Her waggon-spokes made of long spinners' legs,
The cover of the wings of grasshoppers,
The traces of the smallest spider's web,
The collars of the moonshine's watery beams,
Her whip of cricket's bone, the lash of film,
Her waggoner a small grey-coated gnat,
Not half so big as a round little worm
Prick'd from the lazy finger of a maid ;
Her chariot is an empty hazel-nut
Made by the joiner squirrel or old grub,
Time out o' mind the fairies' coachmakers.
And in this state she gallops night by night
Through lovers' brains, and then they dream of love ;
O'er courtiers' knees, that dream on court'sies straight,
O'er lawyers' fingers, who straight dream on fees,
O'er ladies' lips, who straight dream on kisses,
Which oft the angry Mab with blisters plagues,
Because of their breaths with sweetmeats tainted are ;
Sometimes she gallops o'er a courtier's nose,
And then dreams he of smelling out a suit ;
And sometimes comes she with a tithe-pig's tail
Tickling a parson's nose as a' lies asleep,
Then dreams he of another benefice ;
Sometimes she driveth o'er a soldier's neck,
And then dreams he of cutting foreign throats,
Of breaches, ambuscadoes, Spanish blades.

Of healths five-fathom deep ; and then anon
Drums in his ear, at which he starts and wakes,
And being thus frighted, swears a prayer or two
And sleeps again.   This is that very Mab
That plats the manes of horses in the night,
And bakes the elf-locks in foul sluttish hairs,
Which once untangled much misfortune bodes ;
This is the hag, when maids lie on their backs,
That presses them and learns them first to bear,
Making them women of good carriage ;
This is she —

ROMEO AND JULIET

The old *Nurse* falls into reminiscence with *Lady Capulet.*

Juliet
How now !   Who calls ?

Nurse
Your mother.

Juliet
                    Madam, I am here.
What is your will ?

Lady Capulet
This is the matter.— Nurse, give leave awhile,
We must talk in secret.— Nurse, come back again ;
I have rememb'red me, thou's hear our counsel.
Thou know'st my daughter's of a pretty age.

Nurse
Faith, I can tell her age unto an hour.

Lady Capulet
She's not fourteen.

Nurse
                    I'll lay fourteen of my teeth,—
And yet, to my teeth be it spoken, I have but four,—
She is not fourteen.   How long is it now
To Lammas-tide ?

Lady Capulet
A fortnight and odd days.

Nurse
Even or odd, of all days in the year,
Come Lammas-eve at night shall she be fourteen.

Susan and she — God rest all Christian souls ! —
Were of an age.   Well, Susan is with God ;
She was too good for me.   But, as I said,
On Lammas-eve at night shall she be fourteen ;
That shall she, marry ; I remember it well.
'Tis since the earthquake now eleven years ;
And she was wean'd, — I never shall forget it, —
Of all the days of the year, upon that day.
For I had then laid wormwood to my dug,
Sitting in the sun under the dove-house wall ;
My lord and you were then at Mantua ; —
Nay, I do bear a brain ; — but, as I said,
When it did taste the wormwood on the nipple
Of my dug and felt it bitter, pretty fool,
To see it tetchy and fall out wi' the dug !
'Shake' quoth the dove-house ; 't was no need, I trow,
To bid me trudge.
And since that time it is eleven years ;
For then she could stand high-lone ; nay, by the rood,
She could have run and waddled all about ;
For even the day before, she broke her brow ;
And then my husband — God be with his soul !
'A was a merry man — took up the child.
"Yea," quoth he, "dost thou fall upon thy face ?
Thou wilt fall backward when thou hast more wit ;
Wilt thou not, Jule ?" and, by my holidame,
The pretty wretch left crying and said, "Ay."
To see, now, how a jest shall come about !
I warrant, an I should live a thousand years,
I never should forget it !   "Wilt thou not, Jule ?" quoth he ;
And, pretty fool, it stinted and said, "Ay."

Lady Capulet
Enough of this ; I pray thee, hold thy peace.

Nurse
Yes, madam ; yet I cannot choose but laugh,
To think it should leave crying and say, "Ay."
And yet, I warrant, it had upon its brow
A bump as big as a young cockerel's stone ;
A perilous knock ; and it cried bitterly ;
"Yea," quoth my husband, "fall'st upon thy face ?
Thou wilt fall backward when thou comest to age ;
Wilt thou not, Jule ?"   It stinted and said, "Ay."

Juliet
    And stint thou, too, I pray thee, nurse, say I.

Nurse
    Peace, I have done.   God mark thee to his grace!
    Thou wast the prettiest babe that e'er I nurs'd.
    An I might live to see thee married once,
    I have my wish.

THE SECOND PART OF HENRY THE
FOURTH

The fat, sensual, cowardly soldier, *Sir John Falstaff*, is being pursued by the *Lord Chief Justice*, who wants to have a word with him.   Knowing that he is to be reprimanded for some escapade, *Sir John* employs several means of avoiding the *Chief Justice*.

Page   Sir, here comes the nobleman that committed the prince for striking him about Bardolph.

Falstaff   Wait close; I will not see him.

Ch. Just.   What's he that goes there?

Servant   Falstaff, an't please your Lordship.

Ch. Just.   He that was in question for the robbery?

Servant   He, my lord; but he hath since done good service at Shrewsbury; and, as I hear, is now going with some charge to the Lord John of Lancaster.

Ch. Just.   What, to York?   Call him back again.

Servant   Sir John Falstaff!

Falstaff   Boy, tell him I am deaf.

Page   You must speak louder; my master is deaf.

Ch. Just.   I am sure he is, to the hearing of anything good. Go, pluck him by the elbow; I must speak with him.

Servant   Sir John!

Falstaff   What! a young knave, and begging!   Is there not wars?   Is there not employment?   Doth not the King lack subjects?   do not the rebels need soldiers?   Though it be a shame to be on any side but one, it is worse shame to beg than to be on the worst side, were it worse than the name of rebellion can tell how to make it.

Servant   You mistake me, sir.

Falstaff Why, sir, did I say you were an honest man? Setting my knighthood and my soldiership aside, I had lied in my throat, if I had said so.

Servant I pray you, sir, then set your knighthood and your soldiership aside; and give me leave to tell you, you lie in your throat, if you say I am any other than an honest man.

Falstaff I give thee leave to tell me so! I lay aside that which grows to me! If thou get'st any leave of me, hang me; if thou tak'st leave, thou wert better be hanged. You must counter; hence! avaunt!

Servant Sir, my lord would speak with you.

Ch. Just. Sir John Falstaff, a word with you.

Falstaff My good lord! God give your lordship good time of day. I am glad to see your lordship abroad; I heard say your lordship was sick; I hope your lordship goes abroad by advice. Your lordship, though not clean past your youth, hath yet some smack of age in you, some relish of the saltness of time; and I most humbly beseech your lordship to have a reverent care of your health.

Ch. Just. Sir John, I sent for you before your expedition to Shrewsbury.

Falstaff An 't please your lordship, I hear his Majesty is returned with some discomfort from Wales.

Ch. Just. I talk not of his Majesty; you would not come when I sent for you.

Falstaff And I hear, moreover, his highness is fallen into this same whoreson apoplexy.

Ch. Just. Well, God mend him! I pray you, let me speak with you.

Falstaff This apoplexy, as I take it, a kind of lethargy, an't please your lordship; a kind of sleeping in the blood, a whoreson tingling.

Ch. Just. What tell you me of it? Be it as it is.

Falstaff It hath its original from much grief, from study and perturbation of the brain; I have read the cause of his effects in Galen; it is kind of deafness.

Ch. Just. I think you are fallen into the disease; for you hear not what I say to you.

Falstaff Very well, my lord, very well; rather, an 't please you, it is the disease of not listening, the malady of not marking, that I am troubled withal.

Ch. Just.   To punish you by the heels would amend the attention of your ears ; and I care not if I do become your physician.

Falstaff   I am as poor as Job, my lord, but not so patient ; your lordship may minister the potion of imprisonment to me in respect of poverty ; but how I should be your patient to follow your prescriptions, the wise may make some dram of a scruple, or indeed a scruple itself.

Ch. Just.   I sent for you, when there were matters against you for your life, to come speak with me.

Falstaff   As I was then advised by my learned counsel in the laws of this land-service, I did not come.

Ch. Just.   Well, the truth is, Sir John, you live in great infamy.

Falstaff   He that buckles himself in my belt cannot live in less.

Ch. Just.   Your means is very slender, and your waste is great.

Falstaff   I would it were otherwise ; I would my means were greater, and my waist slenderer.

Ch. Just.   You have misled the youthful prince.

Falstaff   The young prince hath misled me. I am the fellow with the great belly, and he my dog.

Ch. Just.   Well, I am loath to gall a new-healed wound ; your day's service at Shrewsbury hath a little gilded over your night's exploit on Gads-hill. You may thank the unquiet time for your quiet o'er-posting that action.

Falstaff   My lord ?

Ch. Just.   But since all is well, keep it so, wake not a sleeping wolf.

Falstaff   To wake a wolf is as bad as to smell a fox.

Ch. Just.   What ! you are as a candle, the better part burnt out.

Falstaff   A wassail candle, my lord, all tallow. If I did say of wax, my growth would approve the truth.

Ch. Just.   There is not a white hair on your face but should have his effect of gravity.

Falstaff   His effect of gravy, gravy, gravy.

Ch. Just.   You follow the young prince up and down, like his ill angel.

Falstaff Not so, my lord : Your ill angel is light ; but I hope he that looks upon me will take me without weighing ; and yet, in some respects, I grant, I cannot go ; I cannot tell. Virtue is of so little regard in these costermonger times that true Valour is turned bear-herd ; Pregnancy is made a tapster, and hare-quick wit wasted in giving reckonings ; all the other gifts appertinent to man, as the malice of this age shapes them, are not worth a gooseberry. You that are old consider not the capacities of us that are young ; you do measure the heat of our livers with the bitterness of your galls ; and we that are in the vaward of our youth, I must confess, are wags too.

THE TAMING OF THE SHREW

Arriving to prepare for the homecoming of his master, *Petruchio,* and *Petruchio's* bride, *Grumio* relates to the housekeeper, *Curtis,* the rebukes he has suffered at the hands of his "mad master," who has taken it upon himself to "tame" his bride, *Katharine,* the *Shrew.*

Grumio Fie, fie on all tired jades, on all mad masters, and all foul ways ! Was ever man so beaten ? Was ever man so ray'd ? Was ever man so weary ? I am sent before to make a fire, and they are coming after to warm them. Now, were not I a little pot and soon hot, my very lips might freeze to my teeth, my tongue to the roof of my mouth, my heart in my belly, ere I should come by a fire to thaw me ; but I, with blowing the fire, shall warm myself ; for, considering the weather, a taller man than I will take cold. Holla, ho ! Curtis.
[*Enter Curtis*]

Curtis Who is that calls so coldly ?

Grumio A piece of ice ; If thou doubt it, thou mayst slide from my shoulder to my heel with no greater a run but my head and my neck. A fire, good Curtis.

Curtis Is my master and his wife coming, Grumio ?

Grumio O, ay, Curtis, ay ; and therefore fire, fire ; cast on no water.

Curtis Is she so hot a shrew as she's reported ?

Grumio She was, good Curtis, before this frost ; but, thou know'st, winter tames man, woman and beast ; for it hath tamed my old master and my new mistress and myself, fellow Curtis.

Curtis Away, you three-inch fool! I am no beast.

Grumio Am I but three inches? Why, thy horn is a foot; and so long am I at the least. But wilt thou make a fire, or shall I complain on thee to our mistress, whose hand, she being now at hand, thou shalt soon feel to thy cold comfort, for being slow in thy hot office?

Curtis I prithee, good Grumio, tell me, how goes the world?

Grumio A cold world, Curtis, in every office but thine; and therefore fire. Do thy duty and have thy duty; for my master and mistress are almost frozen to death.

Curtis There's fire ready; and therefore, good Grumio, the news.

Grumio Why, "Jack, boy! ho! boy!" and as much news as thou wilt thaw.

Curtis Come, you are so full of cony-catching!

Grumio Why, therefore fire; for I have caught extreme cold. Where's the cook? Is supper ready, the house trimm'd, rushes strew'd, cobwebs swept; the serving-men in their new fustian, the white stockings, and every officer his wedding-garment on? Be the jacks fair within, the jills fair without, the carpets laid, and every thing in order?

Curtis All ready; and therefore, I pray thee, news.

Grumio First, know, my horse is tired; my master and mistress fallen out.

Curtis How?

Grumio Out of their saddles into the dirt; and thereby hangs a tale.

Curtis Let's ha't, good Grumio.

Grumio Lend thine ear.

Curtis Here.

Grumio There. [*Strikes him*]

Curtis This is to feel a tale, not to hear a tale.

Grumio And therefore 't is called a sensible tale; and this cuff was but to knock at your ear, and beseech listening. Now I begin: *Imprimis*, we came down a foul hill, my master riding behind my mistress,—

Curtis Both of one horse?

Grumio What's that to thee?

Curtis Why, a horse.

Grumio Tell thou the tale; but hadst thou not crossed me, thou shouldst have heard how her horse fell and she under her horse; thou shouldst have heard in how miry a place, how she was bemoiled, how he left her with the horse upon her, how he beat me because her horse stumbled, how she waded through the dirt to pluck him off me, how he swore, how she prayed, that never prayed before.   How I crossed me, thou shouldst have heard how her bridle was burst, how I lost my crupper, with many things of worthy memory, which now shall die in oblivion and thou return unexperienc'd to thy grave.

Curtis By this reckoning he is more shrew than she.

Grumio Ay; and that thou and the proudest of you all shall find when he comes home.   But what talk I of this?   Call forth Nathaniel, Joseph, Nicholas, Philip, Walter, Sugarsop and the rest; let their heads be slickly com'b, their blue coats brush'd and their garters of an indifferent knit; let them curtsy with their left legs and not presume to touch a hair of my master's horse-tail till they kiss their hands.   Are they all ready?

Curtis They are.

Grumio Call them forth.

Curtis Do you hear, ho?   You must meet my master to countenance my mistress.

Grumio Why, she hath a face of her own.

Curtis Who knows not that?

Grumio Thou, it seems, that calls for company to countenance her.

Curtis I call them forth to credit her.

THE TEMPEST

Trinculo, a witty jester, who is wandering about the strange island, comes upon *Caliban*, a misshapen monster, who is gathering wood.

[*Enter Trinculo*]

Caliban
     Lo, now, lo!
     Here comes a spirit of his, and to torment me
     For bringing wood in slowly.   I'll fall flat;
     Perchance he will not mind me.

Trinculo
Here's neither bush nor shrub, to bear off any weather at all, and another storm brewing; I hear it sing i' the wind; yond same black cloud, yond huge one, looks like a foul bombard that would shed his liquor. If it should thunder as it did before, I know not where to hide my head; yond same cloud cannot choose but fall by pailsfuls. What have we here? a man or a fish? dead or alive? A fish: he smells like a fish; a very ancient and fish-like smell; a kind of not of the newest Poor-John. A strange fish! Were I in England now, as once I was, and had but this fish painted, not a holiday fool there would give me a piece of silver; there would this monster make a man; any strange beast there makes a man; when they will not give a doit to relieve a lame beggar, they will lay out ten to see a dead Indian. Legged like a man! and his fins like arms! Warm o' my troth! I do now loose my opinions; hold it no longer; this is no fish, but an islander, that hath lately suffered by a thunderbolt. [*Thunder*] Alas, the storm is come again! My best way is to creep under his gaberdine; there is no other shelter hereabout; misery acquaints a man with strange bed-fellows. I will here shroud till the dregs of the storm be past.

THE TEMPEST

For twelve years *Prospero*, the Duke of Milan, an old man now, and *Miranda*, his fifteen-year-old daughter, have been living in a cave on an island. ·

Prospero is explaining to *Miranda* that they were exiled here because of foul play.

Prospero   My brother and thy uncle, call'd Antonio —
I pray thee, mark me — that a brother should
Be so perfidious! — He whom next thyself
Of all the world I loved and to him put
The manage of my state; as at that time
Through all the signories it was the first
And Prospero the prime duke, being so reputed
In dignity, and for the liberal arts
Without a parallel; those being all my study,
The government I cast upon my brother
And to my state grew stranger, being transported

     And rapt in secret studies. Thy false uncle —
     Dost thou attend me ?

Miranda Sir, most heedfully.

Prospero Being once perfected how to grant suits,
     How to deny them, who to advance and who
     To trash for over-topping, new created
     The creatures that were mine, I say, or changed them,
     Or else form'd 'em ; having both the key
     Of officer and office, set all hearts i' the state
     To what tune pleased his ear ; that now he was
     The ivy which had hid my princely trunk,
     And suck'd my verdure on 't. Thou attends't not.

Miranda O, good sir, I do.

Prospero I pray thee, mark me,
     I, thus neglecting worldly ends, and dedicated
     To closeness and the bettering of my mind
     With that which, but by being so retired
     O'er prized all popular rate, in my false brother
     Awaked an evil nature ; and my trust,
     Like a good parent, did beget of him
     A falsehood in its contrary as great
     As my trust was ; which had indeed no limit,
     A confidence sans bound. He being thus lorded,
     Not only with what my revenue yielded,
     But what my power might else exact, like one
     Who having into truth, by telling of it,
     Made such a sinner of his memory,
     To credit his own lie, he did believe
     He was indeed the duke ; out o' the substitution
     And executing the outward face of royalty,
     With all prerogative ; hence his ambition growing —
     Dost thou hear ?

Miranda Your tale, sir, would cure deafness.

Prospero To have no screen between this part he play'd
     And him he play'd it for, he needs will be
     Absolute Milan. Me, poor man, my library
     Was dukedom large enough ; of temporal royalties
     He thinks me now incapable ; confederates —
     So dry was he for sway — wi' the King of Naples
     To give him annual tribute, do him homage,
     Subject his coronet to his crown and bend

	The dukedom yet unbow'd — alas, poor Milan ! —
	To most ignoble stooping.
Miranda	O the heavens !
Prospero	Mark his condition and the event ; then tell me
	If this might be a brother.
Miranda	I should sin
	To think but nobly of my grandmother ;
	Good wombs have borne bad sons.
Prospero	Now the condition.
	This King of Naples, being an enemy
	To me inveterage, hearkens my brother's suit ;
	Which was, that he, in lieu o' the premises
	Of homage and I know not how much tribute,
	Should presently extirpate me and mine
	Out of the dukedom and confer fair Milan
	With all the honours on my brother ; whereon,
	A treacherous army levied, one midnight
	Fated to the purpose did Antonio open
	The gates of Milan, and, i' the dead of darkness,
	The ministers for the purpose hurried thence
	Me and thy crying self.
Miranda	Alack, for pity !
	I, not remembering how I cried out then,
	Will cry it o'er again ; it is a hint
	That wrings my eyes to 't.
Prospero	Here a little further
	And then I'll bring thee to the present business
	Which now's upon 's ; without the which this story
	Were most impertinent.
Miranda	Wherefore did they not
	That hour destroy us ?
Prospero	Well demanded, wench ;
	My tale provokes that question. Dear, they durst not,
	So dear the love my people bore me, nor set
	A mark so bloody on the business, but
	With colours fairer painted their foul ends.
	In few, they hurried us aboard a bark,
	Bore us some leagues to sea ; where they prepared
	A rotten carcass of a boat, not rigg'd,
	Nor tackle, sail, nor mast ; the very rats
	Instinctively have quit it ; there they hoist us.

To cry to the sea that roar'd to us, to sigh
To the winds whose pity, sighing back again,
Did us but loving wrong.

TWELFTH NIGHT

Olivia has withdrawn to the seclusion of her chamber, grieving over the death of her brother. She wanders about her room, weeping. Her uncle, *Sir Toby Belch*, a carefree, reckless individual, has no patience with his niece in her grief, and is discovered discussing his niece's state of mind with *Marie*, her maid.

Sir Toby What a plague means my niece, to take the death of her brother, thus? I am sure care's an enemy to life.

Maria By my troth, Sir Toby, you must come in earlier o' nights; your cousin, my lady, takes great exceptions to your ill hours.

Sir Toby Why, let her except, before excepted.

Maria Ay, but you must confine yourself within the modest limits of order.

Sir Toby Confine! I'll not confine myself no finer than I am; these clothes are good enough to drink in; and so be these boots too; an they be not, let them hang themselves, in their own straps.

Maria That quaffing and drinking will undo you; I heard my lady talk of it yesterday; and of a foolish knight that you brought in one night here to be her wooer.

Sir Toby Who, Sir Andrew Aguecheek?

Maria Ay, he.

Sir Toby He's as tall a man as any's in Illyria.

Maria What's that to the purpose?

Sir Toby Why, he has three thousand ducats a year.

Maria Ay, but he'll have but a year in all these ducats; he's a very fool and a prodigal.

Sir Toby Fie, that you'll say so! he plays o' the viol-de-gamboys, and speaks three or four languages word for word without book, and hath all the good gifts of nature.

Maria He hath indeed, almost natural; for besides that he's a fool, he's a great quarreller; and but that he hath the gift of a coward to allay the gust he hath in quarrelling, 'tis thought among the prudent he would quickly have the gift of a grave.

Sir Toby By this hand, they are scoundrels and substractors that say so of him.   Who are they?

Maria They that add, moreover, he's drunk nightly in your company.

Sir Toby With drinking healths to my niece; I'll drink to her as long as there is a passage in my throat and drink in Illyria; he's a coward and a coystrill that will not drink to my niece till his brains turn o' the toe like a parish-top.   What, wench! Castiliano vulgo! for here comes Sir Andrew Agueface.

INDEX OF TITLES

INDEX OF AUTHORS